The Princess
at the Window
A dissident feminist view of men,
women and sexual politics

Donna Laframboise

ISBN: 978-1-894984-10-2

Ivy Avenue Press
Port Dover, Canada
IvyAvenue.com

for Alan, my husband and my best friend

The sudden assertion of human criteria within a dehumanizing framework of political manipulation can be like a flash of lightning illuminating a dark landscape. And truth is suddenly truth again, reason is reason, and honour honour.[1]

Vaclav Havel

Foreword to the 20th Anniversary Edition   1

Introduction   19

Part 1 - Whither the Women's Movement?

1 - Ann Landers and the Lunatic Fringe   33

2 - He Says, She Says   59

3 - Double Standards, '90s Style   92

4 - Office Politics   124

Part 2 - Flinging Open New Windows

5 - Enter: The Men's Movement   159

6 - Men and Power   188

7 - Our Secret Garden   211

8 - Sex, Lies and Court Transcripts   240

Epilogue: Approaching Tomorrow   268

Notes   277

About the Author   273

2016 Acknowledgments   275

1996 Acknowledgments   276

Foreword to the 20th Anniversary Edition

I.

During the dark days of Communism, there was a women's movement in the Soviet Union. But it was fake. Government controlled and approved, it was just another expression of the establishment.

The feminists who spoke truth to power were those who wrote clandestinely about forbidden topics—alcoholism, appalling maternity care, lack of access to birth control. These women paid a high price for their independent thought. Harassed and interrogated by the KGB, they were urged to think of their families. Some were exiled, reduced to the status of undocumented refugees the moment their citizenship papers were shredded.[2]

People who challenged the Soviet establishment were known as 'dissidents.' Their minds were brave and free.

Twenty years ago I was part of a wave of North American dissidents who raised our heads above the parapet to challenge mainstream feminism. The women's movement has its own Party line. Rock stars such as Gloria Steinem, Susan Faludi, Naomi Wolf, Marilyn French, Robin Morgan, Catherine MacKinnon, and Andrea Dworkin were the establishment. From the pages of *Ms.* magazine, between the covers of bestsellers, and from the podiums of lucrative speaking gigs, they declared what was good—and bad—for women. Those of us who begged to differ were disparaged. Who were we to be commenting on such matters?

I have an undergraduate degree in women's studies from Canada's premier university, but thinking for myself was forbidden. As a journalist, I acknowledged that females are sometimes violent. I discussed how schools are failing boys. I championed free speech rather than censorship. I argued that unjust laws could not be supported, even if their intent was to help women. I took feminism to the next level by participating in grownup, nuanced conversations about the real world.

For this, I was dismissed as a 'backlash babe,' a 'feminist basher,' and an 'anti-woman writer.' Feminist icon Michele Landsberg compared me to a stripper in the pages of Canada's largest circulation newspaper, *The Toronto Star*.[3] From behind the bulletproof glass of her impressive salary and union seniority, she ridiculed young, fledgling, dissident *moi* whose freelance earnings rarely rose above the poverty line—and who was advised, while on promotional tour for the book you are now reading, that *The Toronto Star* no longer required my once-weekly column.

In 1995, I pointed out that an upcoming conference had received $15,000 in government funding to talk about Satanic cults sexually abusing children, even though investigators on two continents had found no evidence that such a phenomenon existed.[4] Fellow journalist Judy Steed retorted that "Ritual abuse deniers, like Holocaust deniers, are trapped in an untenable position."[5] That was the first occasion in which I was compared to a Holocaust denier. It would not be the last.

A few years after the first edition of this book appeared, I wrote an exposé of taxpayer-funded battered women's shelters and rape crisis centers. In a series of articles, I described profound problems in numerous facilities across Canada, including "financial disarray, weak accountability, criminal charges, lawsuits, mass resignations, and vicious infighting." One article revealed that outstanding fraud charges had not prevented a woman named Anne Marie Aikins from serving two terms as president of the Ontario Coalition of Rape Crisis Centres. My overarching point was that facilities that were supposed to be providing safe harbour were instead causing harm.[6]

In response, Sally Armstrong, the feminist editor of a Canadian women's magazine, devoted an entire editorial to asking, in essence, how dare I? According to her, I was a member of an imaginary media cabal that regularly behaves "like scavengers, scratching the earth for garbage that may, if they get their tiresome tirades printed, bring the sisters down."

In Armstrong's opinion, I wasn't doing my job as an investigative reporter. I wasn't judging women-run facilities by the same standards that apply to everyone else. Nor was I helping to ensure that vulnerable women receive high-quality social services. Instead, I had penned a "thinly disguised assault on women's work."[7]

Woman power sounds great. But diverge from the Party line and your feminist sisters will turn on you like a pack of wolves. You will be demeaned in overtly sexual terms. You moral compass will be compared to those who deny the historical annihilation of millions. You will be accused of writing sordid filth.

II.
A few years ago I received the kind of fan letter every writer dreams of. It was from a student at a prominent US college. He said he was halfway through the first edition of this book, which had been published around the time he was born:

> wow, learning about feminist orthodoxy has helped me understand my campus climate even more, especially how certain individuals become powerful or belligerent by emphasizing their group status while denigrating perfectly respectable and progressive individuals... Thanks again for being a role model and a progressive thinker.

This student shall remain nameless because, incredibly, we are living through a period in which voicing unpopular opinions leads to serious grief. Bullying people into silence is now mistaken for bold feminist action. A distressing example took place in October 2016, attracting media attention around the globe.

Newspaper letters-to-the-editor sections have traditionally been a forum in which ideas are vigorously debated. Readers are exposed to a variety of viewpoints. Sarcasm and light-hearted banter appear in abundance. But after a tiny weekly (circulation 5,000), in a small Rhode Island community (population 16,000),[8] published a satirical letter under the headline "Please, women, put away the yoga pants," its male author was targeted in an alarming manner.

This was a simple case of a private citizen expressing his personal opinion that yoga pants are unflattering when worn by those over the age of 20. The letter included the following: "What's next? Wearing a 'Speedo' to the supermarket? Imagine if men did that. Yuck!"[9]

Alan Sorrentino, the author of the letter, is not a public figure. His opinion in no way interferes with anyone who wishes to wear yoga pants 24/7. Yet those who took exception to his rant didn't respond by merely writing their own letter to the editor, as generations of Americans have done before them.

Instead, via social media and the mainstream press, they announced their intention to protest outside his private residence on the following Sunday afternoon. In the process, they visited every one of his neighbours "to explain our event."[10] Some individuals telephoned his home and left expletive-laden voice messages, a few of which took the form of death threats.[11] Police were on hand when the march occurred.[12]

A woman identified both as Jamie Patrice and Jamie Burke organized the march.[13] According to her, the newspaper shouldn't have printed a letter expressing views with which she disagrees. "Shame on you Barrington Times and fvck you Alan Sorrentino," she wrote on Facebook.[14] The BBC quoted her further: "When I saw this about yoga pants, it was like a punch in the gut. I was so upset by the entire letter and the fact that it was even published."[15]

Elsewhere, she characterized the march as a public affirmation that female "clothing choices should not matter to anyone." She called it a joyful celebration of "a woman's right to wear what she wants."[16] How a private citizen's belief that yoga pants are a fashion disaster threatens that right was never addressed.

Patrice Burke's public statements are, in fact, a knot of contradictions. A few days after the event, in a written opinion piece, she described the march as "Four hundred people [who] gathered with love in their heart and pride in their bodies." That makes it sound all puppy-dog innocent. But in this same piece, she's militantly political. She says the marchers were standing up to sexism, "to the long history of men policing our bodies." She talks about those who "reached out from across the country to personally tell me their stories of catcalling, groping, and body shaming." She mentions that the march collected donations for a domestic violence shelter. She also insists: "This was never about yoga pants. I hope everyone understands that. This was about women and empowerment."[17]

In 21st century North America, women's empowerment involves browbeating and frightening those who express opinions you don't like. Sorrentino has previously written other humorous letters to the editor.[18] In this instance, he says he was attempting a comedic, Joan Rivers-style commentary.[19]

Describing himself as a "short little gay Italian," at age 64 he's old enough to have experienced decades of fear of physical attack by gay bashers. For him, there's nothing joyous about hundreds of people with megaphones, signs, and banners marching past your house.[20] 'We know where you live,' has long been colloquially understood as a threat. In his words, targeting an individual's home is about "fear and intimidation."[21]

These protesters could have confined their event to a public space—a park, or the vicinity of a government building. Prior to the march, Sorrentino pleaded with them to hold it elsewhere.[22] Rattled by the death threats and with an ailing person staying with him and his partner, he found himself reacting to "Every little bump, every little noise."[23] He said he felt "very fearful."[24] He characterized this disproportionate response to a mere letter to the editor as "vicious," "scary," and "designed to hurt me."[25]

His pleas fell on deaf ears. To some observers, it seemed obvious the march was really about revenge. Sorrentino's neighbours have, no doubt, learned a grim lesson. The letters section of their community newspaper isn't a place to be tongue-in-cheek. Nor is it a place to be honest. Say something off-colour or controversial and you may be the next person to experience the feminist vigilante version of love and joy.

Differences of opinion about women's fashion should never lead to a march on someone's private residence. In a civilized society, there are some lines you do not cross. Yet the wildly popular website, *UpWorthy.com*, jubilantly presented this story as just desserts. The protesters, it said, were there "to make something abundantly clear: [Sorrentino] doesn't get to decide what women can and can't wear."[26]

What nonsense. Not for one moment did anyone believe that a private citizen wields such power. An opinion is just that. If pro-lifers started parading outside the homes of those who write pro-choice letters to the editor, websites such as *UpWorthy* would correctly identify such behaviour as vile. Or here's another hypothetical: it's shocking that Amnesty International hasn't been allowed into Cuba since 1990. But holding human rights marches outside the homes of people who choose to vacation there would be despicable.[27]

The importance of boundaries has been a big theme in feminist thought. Targeting ordinary citizens to make a political point crosses a decisive boundary. In the 1960s, during China's Cultural Revolution, hordes of fanatical young people verbally abused and physically assaulted those they deemed politically incorrect. Hundreds of thousands were beaten to death in an atmosphere of frenzied denunciation—by their fellow citizens.[28] Many others were publicly humiliated, professionally ruined, and driven to suicide before the authorities, who had encouraged such behaviour, reined it in.[29]

Citizens targeting fellow citizens takes us to horrific places. We should never go there. Not in the name of women or any other cause.

III.

This book focuses on events and documents from the early 1990s. By then, ample evidence indicated that mainstream feminism had become extreme, arrogant, and intolerant. Back then, I thought it important to connect the dots, to meticulously document—via nearly 500 footnotes—how crazy things had become. I thought that if I could just show people what a monster feminism had turned into we could all take a deep breath and start thinking more carefully and clearly. I was part of a battle over the soul and destiny of the women's movement and, for a brief moment, I fancied I had a chance of influencing things for the better.

But I'm all grown up now. An additional 20 years of observing how people and political movements behave leads me to harsher conclusions. In my eagerness to be impeccably reasonable and unimpeachably fair, I think I gave too many people the benefit of the doubt.

Back then, I believed sweet reason had a chance of prevailing. But some things require time. Some seedlings need to unfurl into fully grown, noxious weeds before sufficient numbers of people notice their existence. During the intervening years the dogmatism described within these pages has gathered momentum, mushrooming into the aggressive intolerance now rampant on college campuses and beyond.

Students who learned two decades ago that it was acceptable to use sexual harassment arguments to ban a reproduction of Francisco Goya's *Nude Maja* from the campus of Pennsylvania State University, are today's professors and college administrators.[30] (Incidentally, that same painting, which features an unabashedly naked reclining woman, was con-

7

fiscated by the Spanish Inquisition and kept out of sight for decades on the grounds that it was obscene. The feminist response to female nudity in the late 20th century, in other words, was in accord with one of history's most repressive religious institutions.)

When the sensible professors I discuss in Chapter 4 abandoned the politicized hellholes known as women's studies departments 20 years ago, who do we suppose filled the vacuum? Within the walls of hundreds of taxpayer funded colleges, poisonous politics and odious analyses have been swelling, multiplying, and oozing over ever larger swaths of the wider world. The warning bells have been ringing for a long time.[31]

IV.

Has progress been made? During the intervening decades, have the disturbing statistics cited in this book improved? A quick peek yields mixed results.

4,600 people died from workplace accidents in America in 2013. Ninety-three percent were male.[32] It therefore remains true that men are wildly over-represented in the most dangerous jobs. The good news is that, when this book first appeared, it was normal for more than 6,000 people to lose their lives in such a manner each year. Since 2009, less than 5,000 do.[33]

In the early 1990s, six times more American males than females aged 15 to 24 were committing suicide. Few members of the public were aware of that startling ratio. Decades later, many parents still don't appreciate that their sons are at markedly higher risk of succumbing to despair than are their daughters.

The six to one ratio held steady until 1999.[34] By 2014, it had decreased to four male suicides for every female suicide in that age category. But that's not because matters have improved. The suicide rate per hundred thousand people has actually risen—from 16.8 to 18.2 for males, and from 3 to 4.6 for females.[35] In every age group and in every country, males commit suicide more frequently. The World Health Organization estimates that 782,014 people died that way in 2008. Two-thirds (more than half a million souls) were male.[36]

In recent decades, the US murder rate has plummeted to about half of what it used to be. What hasn't changed is that males account for 78% of homicide victims.[37]

Big picture: 20 years ago males were at astonishingly higher risk of being fatally injured on the job. They were significantly more likely to be murdered, and they took their own lives dramatically more often. These stark realities remain true today.

But talking about the downside of being male remains controversial, as the director of a 2016 documentary film, *The Red Pill,* has discovered. In 2010, Cassie Jaye, now aged 30, released *Daddy I Do.*[38] It examines sex education in America by, among other things, shining a spotlight on those who advocate abstinence to the point of organizing father-daughter Purity Balls at which daughters pledge to eschew premarital sex.[39] Jaye's 2012 documentary, *The Right to Love: An American Family,* sympathetically tells the story of a married gay couple, their adopted children, and the heated political debate over how marriage should be legally defined. In both films, diverse points of view are given screen time and treated respectfully.

Before turning to Jaye's latest film, some background is helpful. The Red Pill cultural metaphor began with *The Matrix,* a 1999 Hollywood blockbuster in which the main character is offered a momentous choice. If he swallows a blue pill, he will remain in a world in which humans are enslaved but, due to virtual reality computer simulations, aren't even aware that this is the case. Conversely, swallowing the red pill will liberate him and permit him to see what's actually going on.

Reddit.com is one of the world's most popular websites. In late 2012, a subsection called The Red Pill was founded, as a result of experiences some men had had elsewhere on Reddit. In the words of a 2014 Red Pill policy statement:

Most of us had nowhere to go. We knew the popular so-cial narrative regarding dating was horseshit, but eve-ry time we said anything about it we were met with vitriol and shaming tactics trying to keep us in line like good little drones. A few of us got ourselves banned from every major gender based sub and decided enough was enough.[40]

Similar to many online forums, Reddit's Red Pill is often a negative and abrasive place. It's frequently openly hostile to feminism, women in general, and certain kinds of female behaviour. Its *Rules* page, for example, instructs women to avoid using phrases such as "as a female" when participat-ing in discussions there. "Having a vagina does not afford your words special weight or wisdom," it declares. "Your comments and posts should be able to stand on the merit of your ideas alone."[41]

According to the aforementioned policy statement, "Wom-en worth giving your commitment to are **rare**. So rare in fact we call them Unicorns..." (bold in the original). This state-ment also acknowledges that the behaviour of some Red Pill members is "dumb" and "stupid." It further says the com-munity is "small."[42]

By March 2015, a follow-up policy statement reported that The Red Pill had grown to **100,000** users. It's clear this community provides a sense of belonging to people who've been unable to find it elsewhere. Some were evidently in crisis and felt they had nowhere else to turn.[43]

A late 2015 post titled "NEWBIES READ THIS: A Com-prehensive Guide to The Red Pill," begins by offering dating advice similar to what appears in mainstream magazines such as *Men's Health*. Readers are encouraged to "hit the gym," "eat right," "dress your best," and "Get into the habit of talking to everyone!"[44]

Now back to Cassie Jaye, whose latest film shares its name with this controversial online community. An extended trailer for *The Red Pill* includes a clip in which she declares:

"I've been a feminist my entire life."[45] A synopsis on the film's website reads:

> When a feminist filmmaker sets out to document the mysterious and polarizing world of the Men's Rights Movement, she begins to question her own beliefs. The Red Pill chronicles Cassie Jaye's journey exploring an alternate perspective on gender equality, power and privilege.[46]

Jaye is an exceptional young woman. First: She's genuinely curious about the world. Second: She actually listens to those with whom she disagrees. She gives them a chance to explain.

After visiting *A VoiceforMen.com*, a website devoted to men's rights, Jaye didn't merely recoil at what she read there, she made an honest effort to understand it. Men's rights activists (MRAs) appear in her film. So do feminists. Because screen time is limited, a film such as this can never be the last word. It's about beginning a dialogue.

But some people are opposed to dialogue. In late 2015, after Jaye had invested more than two years of labour and had accumulated 100 hours of interview footage, her film was in jeopardy. Media contacts were declining to give her project any ink.[47] A male animator felt the need to distance himself from it.[48] Grant applications were rejected. Executive producers were happy to be associated with a feminist film, she discovered, but not one that talks about male pain. In her words, "Films that support one side and act as propaganda do better than those that try to have an honest look. I won't be getting support from feminists. They want a hit piece and I won't do that."[49]

As a last resort, Jaye launched a 30-day Kickstarter campaign, with the goal of raising $97,000 from sympathetic members of the public. Donors were invited to support free speech, multiple points-of-view, and critical thinking. Between them, 2,732 individuals from around the world contributed $211,260.[50] During those 30 days, Jaye felt the need to issue a statement responding to what she called "a full-on smear campaign" against her "character and reputation." She passionately rejected accusations that the direction of her film would be unduly influenced due to donations by men's rights activists.[51] (There's no way of knowing the motives of these thousands of people—or the ratio of free speech supporters compared to those who gave for other reasons.) It was a bizarre situation. Male bloggers were attacking a feminist filmmaker whose only sin was trying to make a documentary in which male activists would receive a fair hearing.

The money raised allowed *The Red Pill* to be completed to a high technical standard. It also enabled Jaye to jump through a series of hoops in order to qualify for Oscar consideration. But a new set of hurdles loomed. To be eligible for an Oscar, a documentary must be shown at least four times daily for at least seven days in a New York City movie theatre, as well as in a Los Angeles venue. These screenings must be advertised in one of three New York newspapers, and in one of two LA newspapers. The ads must be a minimum size, include specific information, and must appear in print on the first day of the theatrical release.[52]

The *Village Voice* is one of these designated newspapers. Its focus is on NYC news, food, culture, and events. You'd think a film by a young, award-winning, feminist director would fit comfortably in more than one of those categories. But in a decision that might have had dire consequences for the timing of events as required by the Academy Awards, the *Village Voice* rejected Jaye's advertisement. Her publicist was advised that Alan Scherstuhl, the *Voice's* film editor, had expressed hostility to the film and that his colleagues were loathe to trigger him by accepting it. So in an era in which newspaper advertising revenues are in freefall, they turned down her money.

Because a second newspaper's deadline had already passed, Jaye was compelled to spend an additional $1,500 more than she'd budgeted in order to run the ad in the *New York Times*. On Facebook, her team posted a photograph of the ad along with the comment: "We're extremely thankful that the NYTimes did not censor us."[53]

To qualify for Oscar consideration, a documentary must also receive "a movie critic review in either *The New York Times* and/or *Los Angeles Times*."[54] *The Red Pill* cleared this hurdle when the latter newspaper published a seven-paragraph review under the headline "'The Red Pill' only makes worse the divide between men's and women's rights activists."

According to Katie Walsh, "the film is built on a fundamental misunderstanding" of terms such as feminism and patriarchy. Everyone involved, she wrote, should have watched a *Mad Max* film "to comprehend the ways in which patriarchal systems control resources to exploit both women and men."[55]

Spend more than three years working on a project, battling prejudice and disapproval. Then thank your lucky stars that a movie critic has deigned to take notice. No matter how much scorn has been heaped upon you, you can now check off another box.

In late 2016, *The Red Pill* was shown in 20 US cities. Screenings also took place in Canada, Germany, Mexico, New Zealand, Norway, and the UK. However, a screening scheduled for early November in Melbourne, Australia was cancelled after an online petition generated what Palace Cinemas describes as "overwhelming negative response... from our valued customers."[56]

The theatre chain hadn't seen the documentary. Nor had any of the more than 2,300 people who signed a petition describing it as a "misogynistic propaganda film."[57] The petition falsely claims that the documentary "follows members of online hate-group 'The Red Pill,' known to most as the sexist cesspit of the internet." This is a reference to the Reddit community discussed above. In fact, none of the 27 individuals whose interview footage appears in *The Red Pill* are associated with that community.

The petition further alleges that one of these 27 individuals made inflammatory statements six years ago.[58] After examining his words in context, we might agree with that assessment or not. What's beyond dispute is that this petition is itself full of inflammatory language.

It accuses Jaye's film of spreading a "disgusting, violent message" and of promoting "misogynistic hate." It tells Palace Cinemas that permitting the film to be screened will "associate your cinema with the kind of people who teach men how to violate women physically and emotionally." Indeed, the petition is an example of *actual* propaganda: emotionally manipulative, defamatory, and almost totally disconnected from reality.

Nevertheless, Palace Cinemas caved. Free speech lost. On the upside, these events attracted media attention that brought the film to the notice of people who might not have heard about it otherwise. But that's not the end of the story. Someone named Rachel Woods launched yet another petition demanding that the Minister of Immigration "ensure Cassie Jaye is banned from ever entering Australia."[59] It reads, in part:

> Unfortunately, the supporters of this film have found another venue, allowing them to spout their hateful propaganda. In a country where 1 in 3 women will experience violence from a man and 2 women a week are murdered by their significant partner we MUST stand against this kind of misogyny. We must make it clear to the world that this kind of disgusting rhetoric spouted by this film and its film-maker Cassie Jaye will not be tolerated in Australia.
>
> As a way to fight back we must go to the source and make sure the MRA film-maker Cassie Jaye is banned from Australia. Don't be fooled by her appearance and demeanour, she's a wolf in sheep's clothing...

After one encounters a few of these situations, the pattern becomes obvious. Anything a feminist doesn't agree with is sexist. It's misogynist. It's hate speech. It's propaganda. It

14

promotes violence. No distinction is made between listening to a men's rights activist and actually being one. Those willing to entertain an alternative point-of-view are enemies of women. Their crime is so severe they should be banned from entering the country. Forever.

This is what feminism has come to: Close minded. Punitive. Tyrannical.

Jaye has been on a journey. She says that, in the process of making her film, she became aware that "maybe feminism isn't the entire picture of gender."[60] That idea is at the center of this book.

She also reports that her relationship with her live-in boyfriend "is so much better" now. Listening to men talk about their struggles has changed her. In place of the "anger and rage" that used to flare up within her, forming a barrier between them during times of conflict, she now feels "more respect and compassion" for the man with whom she shares her life.[61] By metaphorically walking in the shoes of the other half of the population, she has grown as a human being. How marvelous. Would the world not be a saner place if more of us understood each other better?

Cassie Jaye is a shining example of how feminists ought to behave. Her heart is brave and her mind is free.

V.

I owe feminist pioneers an immense debt of gratitude. Working class girls from Canadian mining towns didn't attend university a generation before me. But I managed to do so, partly because the women's movement flung open windows and declared it possible.

When I wrote this book I was firmly left-of-center politically. One of the ways establishment feminists tried to shut down alternative viewpoints was by linking the names of dissident feminists to conservative public figures and organizations. In the universe these women inhabit, that's how you discredit someone. Michele Landsberg did this. So did Susan Faludi. So did Gloria Steinem.[62]

In my own case, no such link existed, and not a shred of evidence was ever proffered. I once considered these accusations too absurd to be taken seriously, but I now understand that activists of all stripes behave this way. While you are trying to have an intelligent conversation, their primary concern is signalling to third parties that your ideas are forbidden. They do this by name calling and insulting and smearing. Their response is almost wholly emotional.

That's where the kids learned it from. The college students who today insist that perspectives with which they disagree are, by definition, intolerable hate speech are merely following the example of earlier feminists, anti-racists, and environmentalists. Opinions aren't exchanged calmly and respectfully. Instead, opponents are demonized. They're stamped with the 'morally deficient' label and banished from the debate stage.

Those of us who are primarily interested in ideas are sometimes slow to figure out that others are playing an entirely different game. There's a personality type out there that feels no affinity for the live-and-let-live, *vive la différence* approach to the universe. Rather than being intellectual explorers, they spend their energy trying to impose their narrow worldview on the rest of us.

This book argues that diverse perspectives have much to teach us, but in hindsight I see that my younger self was less than charitable toward an entire swath of the political spectrum. By default, I believed myself to be at odds with right wing thinkers. But the truth is that I had spent no time listening to conservative arguments firsthand. I hadn't read a single book written by an articulate conservative. Almost everything I, a well-educated and informed journalist, believed about conservatives had come from obviously hostile sources. There were multiple windows in my castle, but political prejudice prevented me from recognizing several others.

VI.

The American Library Association defines intellectual freedom as "the right of every individual to both seek and receive information from all points of view without restriction."[63]

It has been a long time since feminism had any connection to that kind of freedom.

1 - Introduction

Once upon a time there was a princess with silken hair and bright, flashing eyes. She lived in a beautiful castle, surrounded by luxury. But an evil spell had been cast on her when she was a child. One day, while she stood looking out her bedroom window, thick vines grew up from the floor and spread over her feet, rooting her to that one spot. From that day forward, the princess had to sleep sitting upright in a velvet-lined chair. She had to have her shimmering gowns and breakfasts of fruit and honey brought to her each morning.

The princess spent much of her time staring down at the bluebells and hollyhocks that grew beneath her window. Through silver opera glasses she watched the songbirds flit from tree branch to tree branch, and the squirrels chase each other through the royal hedges. By the time she was a young woman, the princess knew a great deal about the garden — and had come to believe the entire world was just like it.

When her brother told her that, to the south of the castle, a gurgling stream flowed down from the mountains and passed under a lavender bridge, the princess laughed. "We all know water comes in ponds," she said, pointing to the one below her window. "There's no such thing as a stream, so don't try to confuse me."

When her father told her that, to the west, the trees grew tall and dark and that only a few white flowers bloomed in the shade near the cool earth, the princess scoffed. "Flowers appear in abundance," she said impatiently. "They're many-hued and lush. Just look out my window."

When her mother told her that, near the eastern entrance to the castle, the frogs were bluish-green with voices as beautiful as nightingales, the princess grew angry. "I've spent years studying frogs. I understand them better than you ever will," she declared haughtily. "Frogs are greyish-green and have rasping, loathsome voices."

The king and queen consulted far and wide about how to break the spell, but nothing helped free their daughter. Then, one afternoon, the sky darkened. The ground shook and the castle trembled as a whirling tornado swept through the kingdom. Arriving at the princess' room, the king and queen gasped. The vines that had imprisoned their child for so long were now withered and limp, but the room was empty.

From down another hallway, they heard the princess shrieking. "Oh dear, oh dear!" she shouted. "This isn't right. It isn't right, I say."

The whirling winds had set the princess down in front of a different window. But just as the king and queen arrived, a new set of vines pushed up through the floor and wound around their daughter's feet once again.

Later, having become used to her new view, the princess hugged her parents for the first time in many months. "How silly I've been," she said, looking out at the stream that gurgled beneath the lavender bridge, "to believe in ponds. Water comes from the mountains. It flows and flows, going right by us without stopping."

The princess put her opera glasses to her eyes. "Never speak to me of ponds again."

Like the princess, when our society embraces one idea it often repudiates another. Like the princess, we aren't good at remembering the complexity of the world around us—at acknowledging that ponds and streams can exist at the same time. The pendulum of public opinion swings from one extreme to the next.

Not long ago, the traditional family was considered the foundation of a healthy, stable society. Today, it's frequently portrayed as the root of all evil, as a place where violence and abuse flourish. Not long ago, sexual harassment wasn't even recognized as a problem in the workplace. Today, being accused of a minor offence can destroy a man's career. Not long ago, qualities traditionally considered male were exalted over female ones. Today, males and masculinity are routinely demonized.

I think of humanity as inhabiting an enormous castle with hundreds of windows, each of which reveals something important about our world. I invite you to accompany me to another floor of the castle, to brush away the cobwebs and peer out through a different window at gender politics—at the common ground women and men still share.

I was born in 1963, three years before the National Organization for Women was founded in the United States and nine years before its counterpart, the National Action Committee on the Status of Women, was established in Canada. My mother was 16 years old when she got married and 18 when she gave birth to me, the first of her three children. She never finished high school and has spent her paid working life cooking, cleaning, and waitressing. My father is an auto mechanic. Oil and grease have seasoned his hands and discoloured his fingernails. He works for a company that owns school buses and, on bitterly cold winter mornings when they worry about whether or not the engines will shudder into wakefulness, he still punches in extra early.

Even before I left my parents' home and their rural community, I was an activist. I wrote hot-headed articles for a local newspaper and was accused of being unpatriotic, antireligious, and a Communist. I sent elected officials letters protesting nuclear waste, and formed an environmental group in my high school. I attended meetings in support of native land claims and, while native classmates travelled to the nation's capital for a demonstration, organized a local picket in support.

When I was in my early 20s and living in the big city, Gloria Steinem came to town to promote her first book, *Outrageous Acts and Everyday Rebellions*. Together with my now-sister-in-law, I lined up to see her, wishing I'd bought a few more copies in order to give away the precious autographed volumes as gifts. When it was our turn to approach the platform where she sat, I swallowed my nervousness long enough to tell her I thought she was 'wonderful.' She replied in her calm, measured way, "I think we're all wonderful." My high lasted for days.

Also around that time, I attended an information evening on midwifery—not because I had plans to become pregnant any time soon but because Michele Landsberg, one of Canada's most prominent feminists (whose feisty newspaper columns I greatly admired), was a guest speaker. After viewing the documentary film *Not a Love Story*, I became convinced pornography was harmful to women. I bought my mother a copy of *Our Bodies, Ourselves* and donated feminist books to public libraries.

I enrolled as an undergraduate at the University of Toronto and went on to complete a double major in English and women's studies. I took courses on women and the law, women in western political thought, women and religion, British women writers, and so forth. The women's studies department gave out two awards. I received one of them, the Helen Gregory MacGill Prize, in my first year. Later, I graduated *magna cum laude*.

Consequently, I know a good deal about feminism, and about why this movement was so necessary. I know that Aristotle considered women inferior because they supposedly lacked qualities men possess, and that Thomas Aquinas viewed female persons as defective males. I know that women used to be prohibited from owning property, and that religious authorities routinely advised women to be ruled by their husbands. I know that Saudi Arabian women still are not permitted to drive and can't travel outside the country without their spouses' permission. I know that women are beaten, raped, and murdered by violent males.

I'm one of those people who, on a regular basis, turned up at pro-choice events to support free-standing abortion clinics during the bitter struggles of the 1980s. I've been a union shop steward, a peace activist, and an International Women's Day organizer. I currently sit on the board of directors of the Canadian Civil Liberties Association. I've long been a proponent of female self-defence training and my articles on this topic have appeared in Canada's most prominent newspapers as well as in the *Canadian Woman Studies* journal.[64] When I got married, I kept my own name.

In short, my personal history attests to the fact that I am neither an anti-feminist, a racist, nor a right-winger. Nor would it be accurate to describe me as "a good girl whose opinions are dutifully in line with prevailing prejudice." Nevertheless, I've been called such things recently, either directly or by implication, because some of the columns I now write for *The Toronto Star* (Canada's largest daily newspaper) have dared to criticize certain trends in the North American women's movement.

And frankly, I'm getting ticked off.

As a social activist, my first allegiance has been to principles such as reason, fairness, and justice. I haven't devoted energy to feminist causes just so that a group I belong to could amass privileges for itself. My aim has been to make the world in general a better place. What's of immediate benefit to women and what's reasonable and fair aren't necessarily the same thing. Since males aged 15 to 40 commit most rapes,[65] it might benefit women if all males of that age were herded onto army bases and forced to remain there during those years. But such a course of action would be unreasonable and unjust. It would punish millions of innocent men, denying them basic freedoms and disrupting their lives unconscionably. No one who believes in fair play could support such a proposal, however strong a feminist she might be.

Which is why people who criticize the women's movement aren't automatically its enemies. There *are* individuals who'd like to return us to a world of rigid sex roles in which women remain barefoot and pregnant in the kitchen, but large expanses of society have rejected such attitudes. Public opinion polls today tell us that young men are even more relaxed about having a female boss than older women are.[66] When we look back at all the thousands of years of human history, we have to admit that the few generations currently inhabiting the industrialized world have moved in the right direction on these issues at breathtaking speed. The idea that women are men's equals has triumphed. Things are far from perfect, but the Bastille has been stormed and it has fallen—and remarkably few lives have been lost during the course of this revolutionary change in beliefs and attitudes.

Now it's important that we regain a sense of perspective and proportion. We have to remember that it's *justice* for which we've fought. When feminism gets tangled up in confused thinking we have a moral duty to protest. The only way those who do so can be considered enemies is if the women's movement never was about justice but was just a plot to replace one oppressive social order with another.

Feminism must be as open to criticism as everything else. It must be judged by the same standards. We must acknowledge that a lie is still a lie—even when it's told by feminists with good intentions.

In this book I argue that today's North American feminism is giving female equality a bad name, that it is extremist, self-obsessed, arrogant, and intolerant. While such elements have always been present, I argue that it's now impossible to distinguish them from the mainstream. I show how popular feminist spokespersons and the mainstream feminist press have embraced personalities with hardline, bigoted opinions—and how dubious ideas have been elevated to feminist dogma. Moreover, I demonstrate the alarming manner in which such perspectives are permeating popular culture, influencing public policy, and receiving official sanction from our social and political institutions.

It is precisely because such thinking isn't confined to the pages of obscure journals, but is instead having a profound effect on ordinary people's lives, that feminism risks generating a backlash far worse than the one we're told occurred during the 1980s. Sooner or later, a society inundated with loony feminist ideas is going to slam on the brakes. When that happens, the general public may harden its heart and grow cynical. It may begin to dismiss all feminist protest out of hand. Since a climate in which the notion of female equality has lost its respectability would be more dangerous to women, it behoves those of us who care about such matters to try to prevent this from occurring.

In its broadest sense feminism can be defined as a belief that women should have the same social, political, and economic rights as men. But just as there are many kinds of Christians—pacifist Quakers, Jehovah's Witnesses, and conservative evangelicals all call themselves by this name—there are also different kinds of feminists. This book is concerned with mainstream feminism, with the people who are considered legitimate feminist spokespersons. I call these people 'establishment' feminists.

Over the past few years, a growing number of women have written books critical of feminism. Among them are Rene Denfeld, Amy Friedman, Christina Hoff Sommers, Noretta Koertge, Camille Paglia, Daphne Patai, and Katie Roiphe. I call these women 'dissident' feminists. While I have my disagreements with some of them, they have all influenced my thinking and their voices have sustained me during dark moments of despair. These women are accused of being attention-hungry narcissists. We're told they've jumped on a bandwagon in order to cash in on a media backlash against feminism. But it should come as no surprise that women of different ages and in different parts of North America have been looking at the same trends in a movement we care about and have been arriving at similar conclusions. It should come as no surprise that a number of us have, independently of one another, spent the past few years gathering our research material,

25

refining our arguments, and then writing books such as this one. My own work has questioned feminist assumptions and practices since early 1991, before I'd heard of any of my above-mentioned sisters. And I have often felt like a voice in the wilderness.

But this is more than a book about what has gone wrong with the women's movement. I believe it's possible to intercept the pendulum in mid-swing, before it reaches the outer limit and then slices through all of us on the rebound. In Part Two, I argue that old ways of looking at gender issues are now inadequate. I argue that it's time to take the next logical step, to re-examine our assumptions about men, women, and sexual politics—to give a fair hearing to the ideas percolating in the emerging men's movement.

Because once you become used to questioning prevailing social norms, something unexpected can happen. You can begin to observe that, while women often have a difficult time, life isn't necessarily a walk in the park for men, either. Yes, women's options have been restricted by society's expectations of us, but men are also affected by gender stereotypes.

As late as the 1970s in North America, many girls and women weren't permitted to wear trousers to school or work. These policies changed after they were challenged by feminism. Women, it was argued, weren't going to lose their femininity simply by wearing clothes society had arbitrarily designated as 'masculine.'[67] Now, a woman can get up in the morning and, depending on her mood, can don a floral print dress, a miniskirt, a hot-pink belt, a three-piece suit, pantihose, blue jeans, an oversized shirt with leggings, high heels, or thigh-high boots. She can wear lots of makeup or no makeup. She can carry a purse or not. She can tie a floppy hat on her head or wear a baseball cap backward. A woman can walk down the street dressed in any of the above and no one is going to suspect her of being homosexual, mentally unstable, or a sex offender.

But how many of those options are open to someone who happens to have been born male? The suit, the blue jeans, and the baseball cap. Fewer than one-third. If the sexes were reversed, if society were telling women they were permitted only one choice for every three men enjoyed, feminists would be raising the roof. Clothing restrictions have virtually disappeared for the female half of the population, but have remained firmly in place for males. And even though this skewed state of affairs is all around us, few of us have even 'seen' it.

How is it that a society set up to benefit men at the expense of women (as feminism insists it has been), continues to enforce male clothing taboos long after it stopped dictating such nonsense to women? If the clothes we wear are about personal expression, why does male personal expression continue to be so narrowly defined in a world men have deliberately designed for their own advantage?

On prom night in May 1993, an 18-year-old Knoxville, Iowa, student was arrested at his own high school for trespassing. His crime? Showing up in the red, sequined, spaghetti-strap dress his sister had worn to her prom the year before. According to the media, the school had been aware of the young man's plans a day in advance and had tried to discourage him. The decision to involve police, therefore, wasn't made in the heat of the moment by a flustered chaperone. Instead, one public institution (the school) called on another public institution (the police) to use a third public institution (the courts) to enforce a sexist social convention—a convention that discriminates against males.[68]

In October 1994, a teenager in Barrie, Ontario, was walking home from a dance club with his girlfriend when a group of harassing, taunting young men began to follow them. The couple ducked into a convenience store, hoping to shake them off, but the group was in hot pursuit. Shortly afterward, the 16-year-old male was attacked. He was punched and kicked so severely that his jaw was broken in two places, necessitating surgery. Police officers (I spoke to them directly at the time) were able to discover only one reason for the assault. The victim was wearing a kilt.[69]

Men have it all, don't they? The world is their oyster. Everything has been set up to promote their freedom and convenience. Or maybe it's more complicated than that.

In recent decades, women have asserted our right to an increasing number of choices. We've demanded a share in all those things that had been considered off limits simply because of our sex. We've insisted that society stop viewing us as 'female' and start treating us as 'human'—that it abandon conventional notions of what women like, want, or are. But feminism has been so preoccupied with the 'women are getting a bad deal' perspective, we've denied that other windows in the castle even exist.

Just because women's lives have been twisted by their historical sex role doesn't mean men's haven't, as well. Both these things can be true at the same time. Nor is this a contest. It may be that women have borne the brunt of the injustice in the world. If you could tally up all the terrible things that have happened to women throughout history because they were women (dying in childbirth, rape, infanticide, forced prostitution) and compare it to all the terrible things that have happened to men (being blown apart in rat-infested trenches during wartime, perishing in mining accidents hundreds of feet below the surface), perhaps women would be the 'winners'—or, rather, the losers. But that isn't particularly relevant. Human suffering is what any moral person is opposed to.

It seems that we feminists, who've declared ourselves experts on sex-role stereotyping, have missed a few things. And perhaps we shouldn't be too hard on ourselves. Many of our mistakes and excesses were understandable in a young movement full of energetic but inexperienced and politically naive individuals. But feminism isn't an infant any longer and it can no longer be excused for acting like one, for making incessant demands while remaining oblivious to the needs, rights, and hurts of others who share the same planet.

I believe it's time to make a small but significant perceptual shift: to release our minds from the category of 'women's rights' and to start thinking about the broader notion of 'gender issues'—about how the accident of being born male as well as female can warp people's lives. We need to acknowledge that the world includes both ponds and streams, delicate crocuses and stout hollyhocks, frogs with melodic voices and with grating ones. Just because women suffer doesn't mean men don't, too.

Let us reaffirm our commitment to truth, reason, and justice. Let us journey forward together, arriving at a new understanding of our parallel gender experiences.

Part 1:
Whither the Women's Movement?

Looking back over my life, which has now lasted sixty-six years, what I see is a succession of great mass events, boilings up of emotion, of wild partisan passion, that pass, but while they last it is not possible to do more than think: "These slogans, or these accusations, these claims, these trumpetings, quite soon they will seem to everyone ridiculous and even shameful."[70]
Doris Lessing

1 - Ann Landers and the Lunatic Fringe

In January 1995, newspaper advice columnist Ann Landers published a letter from a LONGTIME READER IN ST. LOUIS. After 53 years of marriage, ST. LOUIS' wife had died. His letter included a list of things he wished he'd done more often while she was alive. In addition to encouraging her to play the piano, take walks with him, and travel more frequently, the grieving widower wrote, "I should have told her I loved her every day, without fail, kissed her more often and brought home flowers for no special reason."

A month earlier, Ann had printed a query from SYD, asking whether it was appropriate to offer to contribute money toward the babysitter after inviting a woman who had children out on a date. Perplexed about what is and isn't proper behaviour in the confusing '90s, but wanting to do the right thing, SYD explained, "There are times when the sitter costs more than the dinner check. I'd like to chip in and help the woman out."

On another occasion, CHINO VALLEY, ARIZ. told Ann that although her husband isn't as romantic as she would like, he is dearly cherished. "This wonderful guy got up at 5 a.m. last week and put new tires on my bike," wrote CHINO.

"He does the dishes every night so I can rest up from my day, even though his might have been tougher. And he is a fabulous father to our three children."

In September 1994, PEGGY IN O'FALLON wrote about how she'd learned "honesty, respect, courage, faith, responsibility and kindness" from her father, who'd grown up in the Depression and had been forced to join the work force before completing grade eight. "I thank God every day for giving me such a fine role model," said PEGGY. "I am happily married to a man who is very much like my dad."

Readers of Ann's column also heard, on the same day, from STILL IN LOVE, who wrote: "After 29 years of marriage I realize that I am no longer Number 1 in my wife's life." LOVE said he felt he came somewhere after the houseplants, the pet cats, and the couple's two adult children on his wife's list of priorities. His final paragraph read: "Actually, I don't believe it's necessary to be Number 1 every day. As long as I am on her list, I am satisfied."[71]

In these letters, males are flesh and blood. They are loving husbands and fathers. They are single men sensitive to the financial circumstances of their dates. They are also people who have made compromises with life that strike some of us as sad. This isn't the only view of men one gets in Ann Landers, of course. Here, as elsewhere, there is no shortage of alcoholic or philandering husbands, 39-year-olds afraid to tell their parents they're living with someone, and men who beat their wives and rape their acquaintances.[72] But the point is that that's not *all* they are.

In the world according to Ann Landers, men are diverse creatures. If the only thing you knew about human males was what you'd read in Ann's columns, it would be difficult to say anything about them as a group. While some behave badly, others conduct themselves admirably. Some are cowardly, others are honourable. Some are aggressive, others are passive. Some are callous, others are self-sacrificing. In short, men—because they are first and foremost human beings—run the gamut.

So, too, do women. Many of Ann's correspondents praise

women to the heavens: they are strangers who perform touching acts of random kindness, teachers who inspire children
to look forward to school each day, loving mothers, and
people described as "fine, strong [and] lovely" by their ex's
new spouse.

It's also abundantly clear that women have plenty of
negative qualities. They are grandmothers who emotionally manipulate those around them, causing marriage
breakdowns while destroying "every vestige of joy" in their
homes. They are mothers who neglect their children in favour of soap operas. They are housewives who cause their
hard-working husbands unending grief with their irre-
sponsible use of credit cards. They are people who secretly
make duplicate keys and let themselves into their grown
children's homes to snoop.[73]

In late 1994, Ann published a letter that accused her of
fabricating a correspondence from a woman who'd been
surprised by her daughter's 17-year-old boyfriend while
skinny-dipping in the family pool. The woman reported that
she was infatuated with the young man, who had kissed
her and now wished to begin an affair. Ann insisted she
hadn't made it up. "I've received stacks of letters from
teenage girls who view their mothers as serious competi-
tion," she responded. "Moreover, some girls have stated
frankly that their mothers are extremely aggressive and
'up to plenty.'"

A few months previously, a middle-aged man from
GAINESVILLE, FLA. had described his alcoholic wife of 20
years: "Her constant arguing has given me high blood
pressure and headaches," he wrote. "I have heard her pray
for me to die. She's told me many times that she hates me.
Several weeks ago, I set up an appointment with a marriage counselor, but she canceled it."

There was also the May 1994 letter from SEEN TOO
MUCH, the brother of a man married to an abusive wife.
She "trashed my brother's car, shredded his clothes, threw
bleach in his face and tried to run him over with her car,"
wrote TOO MUCH. "She swears she is going to kill him even

if she has to hang for it." Although the couple had been separated for a year, the woman continued to stalk and attack her husband.[74]

Ann Landers, the thousands of people who write to her, and the millions who read her column faithfully know that, as well as being sugar and spice and everything nice, the female half of the population has its darker side. Like men, the group of people we call 'women' encompasses marvelous individuals as well as broken, nasty ones.

It isn't possible to reach a conclusion that's even remotely scientific from the anecdotes appearing in these columns. But the fact that Ann Landers has been a long-standing fixture in hundreds of respectable newspapers suggests that the issues she chooses to highlight strike a chord with a significant portion of the North American population. Ordinary people consider the world she reflects to be a reasonably authentic one.

In Ann's universe, men *and* women bring other people immense joy and cause them intense pain. That diverse, nuanced view is starkly different from the one being disseminated by mainstream North American feminism. Social movements always have their lunatic fringe. The peace movement, civil rights campaigns, pro-life forces—all attract people who make outrageous, fanatical statements. It isn't fair to judge a social movement by its few inevitable nutbars. But when the mainstream of the movement refuses to distance itself from extremist elements—when, in fact, it embraces them—there's a problem.

If people object to the tone of feminism these days, the inevitable response goes something like this: *There may be some feminists who are a little unhinged, who bash men, but that's not what feminism means to most people. Feminism, for most of us, is simply about fairness.* In the words of one woman responding to a newspaper column, it's about "equal opportunity, equal respect and equal partnerships with men." The majority of men, says this writer, "are honest and decent."[75]

This is the sort of feminism to which I also subscribe. But are these the messages emanating from mainstream feminism in the 1990s? I invite you to turn to a book titled *The War Against Women*. Published in 1992, it was written by Marilyn French, who is described on the cover as a best-selling "author and feminist scholar." French's 1977 novel, *The Women's Room*, had an important impact on my own thinking and functioned as a consciousness-raiser for a generation of women.

Her thesis, in *The War Against Women*, is that men have been waging a centuries-long global attack on half the population. According to her, men have a "need to dominate women" and therefore carry out a "purposeful policy" of oppression against them, up to and including murder.[76] She claims that "all male violence toward women is part of a concerted campaign," that controlling female reproduction "is a silent agenda in every level of male activity," and that men have a "deep, unacknowledged sexual hatred of women."[77] Her book is full of statements such as:

> Most films and television shows are produced by men for men. Their main purposes are to show white males triumphant, to teach gender roles, and to cater to men's *delight* in male predation and victimization of women. [my italics][78]

Although French says her comments aren't directed against individual men—and admits that any specific male may allow his "affectionate respect" for a woman to overcome his "drive to control her"—that doesn't stop her from alleging that female oppression is maintained by ordinary men "with a fervor and dedication to duty that any secret police force might envy."[79] Arguing that it isn't necessary to physically assault women in order to keep them down, French provides a list of ten things she says the "*vast majority of men in the world do one or more of*" (original italics). I've paraphrased it here, rearranging the order to make it easier to analyze:

1. Not hiring women for well-paying jobs
2. Paying women less than men for doing the same or more work
3. Beating their spouse
4. Murdering their spouse
5. Raping women they know or women who are strangers
6. Sexually molesting female children
7. Failing to pay child support
8. Treating women 'disrespectfully' at work
9. Treating women 'disrespectfully' at home
10. Expecting spouses to be their servants[80]

While it's true that many men make decisions regarding the hiring and pay rates of female employees, most men do not. My father, who has punched a time-clock throughout his working life, has never been in a position to commit the first two crimes that appear on this list. For every manager making such decisions, whether in a bank or a steel plant, there are many more employees who have no opportunity to do so.

What about the next four? Battering, murdering, raping, and sexually molesting. Some men do commit these crimes, but most men do not. Think of the males in your family, your neighbourhood, or your workplace. If French wants to argue that the majority of men are guilty of these horrors she's going to have to provide more convincing evidence than her own say-so. Most people's experience of the world tells us this is false. Anyone who wants you to disregard the evidence in front of your nose needs to meet a high standard of proof.

Point number seven: not supporting one's children. There's no question that some men financially abandon their offspring. We call them 'deadbeat dads,' a term that makes it clear society disapproves of such behaviour. But if French wants to claim that most of the men who father children refuse to support them we need hard data—not data about how many divorced men are in arrears, but what percentage of *all* fathers this represents.

Points eight through ten, treating women disrespectfully at work or home and expecting spouses to act as servants, are a little trickier. I've behaved disrespectfully toward people who happen to be women, and have sometimes expected my husband to perform more than his share of the household chores while I've struggled to meet deadlines. How many of us could plead innocent to treating our mothers —to whom we surely owe as much consideration as our spouses—as servants? If French is talking about the kinds of minor offences that characterize everyday life then, without a doubt, most men *as well as most women* are guilty of the last three transgressions.

But none of this demonstrates that the majority of men domineer over the women in their lives. In several of the Ann Landers letters cited above it was women who set the tone in the home. An abusive wife, a manipulative grandmother, or a woman who considers her husband less important than her houseplants isn't being oppressed by the men around her. It's also worth noticing that French's book frequently employs a rhetorical sleight-of-hand by using Third World examples to disparage the men living in industrialized nations. My younger brother, who prepares the majority of the meals he and his fiancée eat at home, should not be lumped in with Kenyan men who, French tells us, "gamble, buy liquor, and rent prostitutes, while their families starve"—or with Afghani males who want to eliminate female education and paid work.[81]

From this perspective, and this perspective only, French is probably right: most men around the globe likely treat women terribly. It's only recently that people living in select parts of the world have begun questioning centuries-old ideas about male superiority. But if she needs to resort to mixing apples and oranges in order to condemn as hopeless misogynists most of the men with whom her readers share their lives, her conclusion is tenuous.

French admits women possess some power—in families, as well as when they help foster the inflated self-image of men. She also devotes four sentences to acknowledging that women are capable of cruelty and abuse—as compared with 200 pages cataloguing male sins. But she never permits these ideas to influence her big-picture opinions.[82] Instead, she consistently interprets male behaviour in the worst possible light. According to her, men never go to war to protect their families and communities, but because male culture has turned them into bloodthirsty monsters. Divorcing fathers don't fight for custody of their children in court because they've been involved with them from the delivery room onward and can't imagine waking up in the morning without them, but merely in order to cause trouble for their ex-wives.[83]

Women, on the other hand, have only the purest of motives. She tells us that they mutilate the genitals of millions of African girls for altruism's sake, to "save them from being social outcasts." In her words, "women only seem to be in control of the practice [since] men will not marry an unmutilated girl."[84]

The War Against Women, then, tells us that men are violent and depraved, and that they use their power to victimize women. It holds men fully responsible for the fact that the world's a mess. When women behave barbarically, it says that's the fault of men, too.

In democratic societies people have the right to hold all sorts of opinions and to share them with others via newspapers, magazines, books, television, computer networks, and so forth. So I'm not suggesting that her ideas should be censored. But I seriously doubt French would have found a publisher for *The War Against Women* if she'd been employing similarly loaded language about any other identifiable group—Jews, gays, or the disabled, for example.

How did mainstream feminism respond to *The War Against Women*? Did other feminists dissociate themselves from a book that paints half the human race as violent brutes? Did the feminists we think of as being reasonable and moderate have a problem with statements that compare ordinary men to secret police? Did they get queasy over lines such as: "In personal and public life, in kitchen, bedroom and halls of parliament, men wage unremitting war against women"?[85]

The defender of feminism I quoted earlier said most feminists recognize that "the majority of men are honest and decent." French's book includes no such recognition. But that didn't prevent it from being embraced with open arms. The paperback edition of *The War Against Women* carries an endorsement on the front cover from Gloria Steinem—North America's most respected and influential feminist spokesperson. According to Steinem:

> If you can read only one book about what's wrong with this country, *The War Against Women* is it. Marilyn French writes about the state of the world as if women mattered—and (suddenly) we do.

Ms. magazine (the publication most readily associated with mainstream feminism), described *The War Against Women* as an "impressive marshaling of facts" and a "powerful indictment of patriarchy." Its brief review was entirely positive. Eighteen months later, when *Ms.* sponsored a round-table discussion about women and pornography, French was one of four guest participants.[86]

The respectability French enjoys in these circles isn't an isolated phenomenon. Other fanatically-minded individuals receive equally warm receptions. Law professor Catharine MacKinnon is a prolific writer who travels the continent delivering passionate speeches about how women are victimized by pornography. Her influence, not only within feminism but radiating outward to society at large, is significant. In the early 1990s, MacKinnon co-authored a brief whose arguments were later adopted by the Supreme Court of Canada, thus fundamentally altering legal notions about what kind of sexually explicit material is acceptable within Canadian borders.[87] She says versions of anti-pornography legislation she helped draw up have been introduced in Germany, the Philippines, and Sweden.[88]

In October 1991, MacKinnon was the subject of a glowing cover story by the *New York Times Magazine*.[89] She has been interviewed by *Ladies' Home Journal* and invited to appear on television shows such as *Donahue* and *Today*. During the Anita Hill—Clarence Thomas U.S. Supreme Court hearings, MacKinnon provided live analysis for NBC TV news. She has also participated in television panel discussions on topics such as date rape.[90]

In women's studies courses, MacKinnon's work routinely turns up as required reading.[91] This wouldn't be a problem if her ideas were being vigorously debated in such classes. But too often, students are simply told this is what feminism is and what feminists believe.[92]

MacKinnon not only writes for *Ms.* magazine, she's frequently cited with approval in its pages.[93] One 1991 article complained that MacKinnon's colleague Andrea Dworkin—with whom she drafted the anti-pornography legislation—is "sometimes" required to defend this legislation when speaking at U.S. colleges.[94] Imagine that. People attending institutions of higher learning wanting to challenge ideas rather than blindly accepting them. Naomi Wolf's 1990 feminist bestseller, *The Beauty Myth*, cites MacKinnon as though her ideas are entirely uncontroversial.[95] And when the National Organization for Women was asked about its position on pornography recently, it sent out a packet that included photocopies of MacKinnon's work.[96]

The fact that mainstream feminism has made no attempt to put distance between itself and MacKinnon is distressing, because the kinds of opinions she has been expressing for over a decade are ones few feminists who enjoy healthy, active sex lives are likely to be comfortable with.

MacKinnon has become famous for her insistence that, in a society where the sexes aren't equal, women are afraid of men or depend on them for economic survival and so aren't in a position to genuinely refuse sexual intercourse. This means that women can never be viewed as having given consent of our own free will. Anyone who thinks this is a distortion of MacKinnon's views is invited to turn to her

1989 book, *Toward a Feminist Theory of the State*, in which she declares:

> Compare victims' reports of rape with women's reports of sex. They look a lot alike. Compare victims' reports of rape with what pornography says sex is. They look a lot alike. In this light, the major distinction between intercourse (normal) and rape (abnormal) is that the normal happens so often that one cannot get anyone to see anything wrong with it.[97]

In her 1987 essay, "Feminism, Marxism, Method, and the State," MacKinnon writes:

> Instead of asking, what is the violation of rape, what if we ask, what is the non-violation of intercourse? To tell what is wrong with rape, explain what is right about sex...Perhaps the wrong of rape has proven so difficult to articulate because the unquestionable starting point has been that rape is definable as distinct from intercourse, when for women it is difficult to distinguish them under conditions of male dominance.[98]

Elsewhere, she states: "Consent means that whatever you are forced to do is attributed to your free will."[99] MacKinnon suggests that "free speech" and "women being used" are interchangeable terms. She says that "sexual freedom" really means "the freedom to abuse."[100]

If MacKinnon were routinely qualifying these statements with phrases such as "in a sense" or "in some situations" or "from a certain point of view, you could say that..." her opinions wouldn't be so disturbing. She might simply be thought of as an academic who gets carried away with her own theories. But as a lawyer, she's well aware that the way things are phrased is important. If what she really means is that sex is a horrible experience for *some* women *some* of the time, she could say so. But she doesn't.

MacKinnon considers the Miss America Pageant and the most violent pornography to be directly connected to one another.[101] Despite there being no evidence that violence against women is less prevalent in Islamic countries where porn is strictly prohibited, MacKinnon is nevertheless convinced that pornography causes sexual abuse and that it must be eliminated from North American society.

Whether or not you agree with her views, there's no disputing she's on a crusade. Like other evangelists, she is an intense, emotionally persuasive, and charismatic speaker. She paints a world of moral absolutes in which there is no middle ground, no room for ambiguity or debate. Either you see things her way or you're helping to promote violence against women. Feminists who disagree with her are dismissed as "collaborationist" individuals who are "fronting for male supremacists."[102]

This is the kind of thinking with which mainstream feminism is now associated. This is what the women's movement has come to.

Yes, thousands of women are sexually assaulted each year. But anyone who zeroes in on a sub-category of violence and obsesses about it to the exclusion of everything else is a zealot. It's as though MacKinnon has taken an image of rape and magnified it to hundreds of times its original size. In the process the image has become so blurred she has trouble distinguishing acts of brutality from consensual love-making.

MacKinnon is looking out at the world through one window only. She insists that this window is reality, that everything can be reduced to violence against women. (Indeed, she vigorously rejects the notion that her views are simply a "point of view.")[103] In her July/August 1993 *Ms.* magazine cover story about rape in the former Yugoslavia, she doesn't talk about the cities that are in rubble, the historical treasures that have been lost, the children who are having their psyches moulded by destruction and cruelty. She doesn't talk about civilians starving to death after being cut off from food and water, or about the thousands of promising young men who've died in this war and what a loss this is for all of humanity. Without acknowledging this larger context, MacKinnon zeroes in on the fact that one element of the practice known as 'ethnic cleansing' being perpetrated in this conflict reportedly involves the systematic rape of female prisoners and the videotaping of some of this violence.

Does she care about real human beings? Or is she a crow feasting on the carnage, interested only because these events provide her with new ammunition? MacKinnon begins the second paragraph of her article with the following:

> In what is called peacetime, pornography is made from rape in studios, on sets, in private bedrooms, in basements, in alleys, in prison cells, and in brothels. It should be no surprise to find it being made in a "rape theater" in a Serbian-run concentration camp...Still, it comes as a shock, a clarifying jolt.

A page later she adds, "As it is in this war, prostitution is forced on women every day; what is a brothel but a captive setting for organized serial rape?"[104] Comparing wartime rape to pornographic videos produced by film companies employing consenting adults—or by amateurs using camcorders in the comfort of their own homes—is outrageous. Women working in Nevada's government-licensed brothels, or those who turn tricks in the inner city to pay for their next drug fix aren't in the same category as the victims of ethnic cleansing.

The absence of qualifiers in the above quotes suggests that both MacKinnon and the editors at *Ms.* believed she was preaching to the converted. MacKinnon doesn't say that *some* of the videotaping that goes on in private bedrooms is coerced. She doesn't say that in some parts of the world—such as Thailand or the Philippines—girls and women are imprisoned in brothels against their will. Rather, she implies that all pornography "is made from rape" and that all prostitutes are having sex against their will.

We need to be clear about the role of *Ms.* here. In this article MacKinnon makes the kind of sweeping overgeneralizations she's known for making, and *Ms.* does everything it can to help her spread the word. The magazine chose this article to be its cover story.

According to MacKinnon, pornography tells us that:

> what men want is: women bound, women battered, women tortured, women humiliated, women degraded and defiled, women killed. Or, to be fair to the soft core, women sexually accessible, have-able, there for them, wanting to be taken and used, with perhaps just a little light bondage.[105]

Elsewhere, she writes that men "just want to hurt us, dominate us and control us, and that is fucking us."[106] So much for the kind of feminism that believes "the majority of men are honest and decent."

If all sex is really rape, then it must follow that all (heterosexual) men are rapists. Which is even more egregious than Marilyn French's contention that most men treat women badly. If all men are rapists, all women are rape victims—even though many of us *know* we were the ones to initiate sex on numerous occasions. MacKinnon says it doesn't matter if the women who pose for sexually explicit photos have signed release forms. She knows what's a perfect stranger would really prefer to be doing.

In other words, we women don't have minds of our own. Our interpretations of our actions don't count. If MacKinnon were running the world women would be considered legally incompetent, on the level of a child or a mentally disabled person, when we signed certain kinds of papers—papers that would nevertheless be legally binding on men.[107]

Surely the danger here is self-evident. If we can't be trusted to know our own minds where sexual activity is concerned, what prevents us from being coerced into other

46

things? Are we following our true inclinations when we mark our Xs at the ballot box? Or when we decide to seek an abortion? Feminism can't have it both ways. Either wo‐ men are assumed to be in full possession of our faculties— or not.

The fact that MacKinnon enjoys such a cozy relation‐ ship with *Ms.*, despite her condescending views toward other women *and* her extravagant male-bashing, indicates that the lunatic fringe has taken over mainstream feminism. Moderate, sensible feminists aren't found in one place while extreme thinkers are off in a corner somewhere else. The two have become indistinguishable.

But maybe we're jumping to conclusions. Maybe it's worth spending a few minutes flipping through other back issues of 1990s *Ms.* magazines to double-check whether the picture I've sketched is accurate. Surely there are rea‐ sonable voices?

Actually, the coverage of international news in *Ms.* is often solid. The magazine devotes considerably more space to letters to the editor than most publications, something I view as a plus. Regular contributions from the Boston Women's Health Collective, which produces the feminist classic *Our Bodies, Ourselves*, are high points. Nor do I have any desire to criticize the fiction, poetry, and artwork.

But this is a magazine that readers send to U.S. Su‐ preme Court justices in order to educate them about femi‐ nist issues.[108] Well-modulated, sensible articles should be the norm. While *Ms.* wouldn't be doing its job if it weren't challenging people's assumptions on a regular basis, there's a difference between being thought-provoking and being ri‐ diculous. In 1991, *Ms.* published a three-page article titled "Orchids in the Arctic: the Predicament of Women Who Love Men." Written by Kay Leigh Hagan, a former heterosexual turned lesbian, it seeks to give women who still sleep with men guidance about living life with "the oppressor."

It tells us that by having sex with men we are being "intimately colonized," and that those of us who think we are married to exceptional men are "in denial." The author

47

says that if she keeps one rule in mind ("If he can hurt you, he will"), she finds her own interactions with men "improve considerably." She recommends the use of condoms —not for reasons of safe sex, but so there's always a physical barrier when we sleep with the enemy. She urges us to get a room of our own "with a door that locks."[109]

Ms. began 1992 with a cover emblazoned in red and white lettering. "RAGE + WOMEN = POWER," it proclaimed.[110] Strange, isn't it? Throughout recorded history, people have warned us about the destructive influence of anger. According to Horace, the ancient Roman poet, "Anger is a short madness." St. Augustine said that "Anger is a weed; hate is the tree." George Jean Nathan, the American critic, wrote that "No man can think clearly when his fists are clenched." And the Old Testament warns: "Be not hasty in thy spirit to be angry: for anger resteth in the bosom of fools."

Even in the *Star Wars* movie trilogy, anger is a negative quality. The evil emperor, who tries to corrupt Luke Skywalker by turning him to the 'dark side,' urges the young man to surrender himself to rage. "Good, I can feel your anger," the emperor says. "Use your aggressive feelings, boy; let the hate flow through you." Luke's lightsabers are blue and green, colours associated with cool-headedness and reason. Darth Vader, on the other hand, has a red lightsaber—a colour associated with passion and rage.

It says something about the arrogance of contemporary feminism that we think we can ignore with impunity the wisdom of the ages, that just because the feminist poet Adrienne Rich wrote about her "visionary anger" in 1973, rage is an emotion we should be cultivating. To paraphrase Betty Friedan, the wise men of history may have been wrong about women, but they weren't wrong about everything.[111]

Yes, women have often been expected to be meek and mild. Yes, psychoanalytic theory holds that expressing anger is healthy. But when rage is considered a legitimate political tool, when we insist that one of the seven deadly sins is really a virtue, we condemn ourselves to an endless cycle of injustice and still more anger. It is only when we're able to set aside feelings of rage that wars can end.

On other occasions, *Ms.* has told its readers that North American women live in "a society saturated by violent misogyny"—and declared it a myth that rape is "perpetrated only by an aberrant fringe" of men.[112] It has advised readers that "your husband, lover, son or brother may be a terrorist in waiting." It has announced in large type that "A man beats a woman because he *can* do it. He calls it love and so does everybody else" (italics in the original).[113] Two male writers inform us that:

> men who batter and men who don't are not that different. Male violence is normal in our society and vast numbers of men participate. Men batter because we have been trained to; because there are few social sanctions against it...[114]

On another occasion, after claiming that people deny the true nature of contemporary North American women's lives just as many "denied the reality of the Nazi Holocaust," *Ms.* has insisted that women "live in the midst of a reign of sexist terror comparable in magnitude, intensity, and intent to the persecution, torture, and annihilation of women as witches from the 14th to the 17th centuries in Europe."[115]

It has told us that gang rape "is a key feature of male bonding rituals within patriarchal societies." It has characterized the traditional nuclear family not as a place where violence and abuse sometimes occurs but as a structure that keeps "its members in terror."[116]

Regarding women (all assumed to be truthful) in child custody battles, another *Ms.* article asserts:

> A custodially embattled mother is not unlike a runaway African slave in the nineteenth century; a Jew in Nazi Europe; a peasant, a professor, a housewife, or a child in flight from the world's gulags, killing fields,

and torture chambers. Except there is no "north"; no "Israel"; and no "United States" to shelter a woman in flight from male domestic violence.[117]

According to another article in *Ms.*, young women—who may be understandably hesitant to identify with feminism due—are said to fear "commitment to something larger than the self that asks us to examine the consequences of our actions." Readers are informed that such women avoid the women's movement because they "don't want to be called to account."[118]

In another piece, the magazine criticizes the Holocaust Memorial Museum in Washington, D.C., on the following basis:

> No use was made of feminist work on sexual abuse or bodily invasion and violation—neither the substance of this knowledge nor the strategies used to create the safety in which women can bear remembering...This museum did not become a safe place for women's testimony about the sadism of sexualized assault.[119]

While trashing the length and breadth of modern civilization, and criticizing practically everything for being tainted by tyrannical male norms, some of the solutions and personalities *Ms.* offers as alternatives fall rather short. Early in 1995, for example, *Ms.* profiled in its arts section Zsuzsanna Budapest, a writer who claims to be genetically descended from a long line of witches. Her books are recommended enthusiastically by the magazine. One, titled *The Goddess in the Office*, is described as "a marriage of common sense and magic" that includes:

> runes (ancient magical symbols) to use in managing an unruly computer, herbs to purify the workplace, and spells for getting a raise or a promotion. If you are being harassed, Budapest recommends using your full range of powers—from organizing and seeking justice

through legal avenues to performing a hex that would reform Clarence Thomas.[120]

Critical thinking, it seems, isn't something to be applied to feminism (or, at least, not to those feminists *Ms.* likes). If you, as Budapest apparently does, spout the right lines about patriarchy and female oppression, no one notices how preposterous your other ideas are.

Regrettably, a great deal of feminist analysis is being incorporated into criminal law, educational regulations, and police guidelines. This worldview influences the way the media present certain topics, and how people in positions of power gauge voter opinion. It helps us decide which problems are important, which projects receive assistance (often in the form of tax dollars), and which don't. If the extremists and the mainstream are one and the same, we need to be clear-eyed about what this means in the wider world.

Anyone who thinks feminism has had little effect on people's attitudes should consider the matter of pornography. In the 1970s 'dirty' magazines were viewed as harmless fun by mainstream society. Some people objected to them on religious grounds, but in popular culture those who got agitated over sexually explicit material were considered prudes who needed to lighten up. Few men worried they'd be causing offence if they admitted, in mixed company, to subscribing to *Playboy*. Many people considered it a sign of sophistication to have a copy on the coffee table since this signalled a repudiation of strait-laced, 1950s attitudes.

Then came anti-pornography feminists such as Catharine MacKinnon. Within not much more than a decade attitudes have swung 180 degrees. From television sitcoms to Ann Landers' columns,[121] when people talk about porn these days they're likely talking about something noxious. Rather than a celebration of sexual liberation, diversity, and experimentation, rather than a symbolic rejection of earlier ignorance and shame, porn is now considered degrading. In a public opinion poll conducted in April 1993, 55 percent of Canadians (64 percent of women and 45 percent of men) answered 'Yes' when asked: "Do you think that adult magazines are discriminating to women?" [sic]. When people were asked whether such magazines should be available in corner stores, the majority of respondents (56 percent) said 'No'.[122]

This rapid shift in public attitudes took place at the same time that many people were preaching tolerance toward homosexuality. How bizarre that, while large numbers of feminists were defending diversity in the form of lesbian sex, they were simultaneously trying to re-stigmatize expressions of (straight) male sexuality. There are now many workplaces where it would be foolish for a man to admit he was stepping out over his lunch hour to return the pornographic video he'd rented. He'd become a social pariah among many male, as well as female, co-workers.

If the feminist ideas having such a profound impact on everyday life merely promoted fairness and equality, there'd be little cause for concern. If the feminism increasingly affecting people's everyday lives were consistently driven by the belief that "the majority of men are honest and decent," I would never have written this book. But the objectionable feminist attitudes I've highlighted above are working their way into some rather high places. Once there, they are accepted at face value and given official sanction by some of our most powerful decision-makers.

Which brings us to the Canadian Panel on Violence Against Women, something I consider a national embarrassment. The panel was struck in the wake of what has become known as the Montreal Massacre, in which 14 female engineering students at the École poly-technique de Montreal were murdered in 1989 by a gunman who first separated them from their male classmates and declared that he hated feminists.

In July 1993, the panel's final report was released. It cost $10 million, took two years to complete, and represented the efforts of nearly 100 individuals—including nine full-time panellists, 18 advisory committee members, and a staff of 58. The nine central personalities, one of whom was male, all had experience and expertise in the area of violence. For example, they'd run crisis centres or been associated with the family court system.[123]

The press release distributed by Status of Women Canada, a federal government body, called the 500-page report "the world's first comprehensive national study of violence against women." The Tory government of the day—which feminists attacked for its "neo-conservative" agenda and its "devastating" impact on women's lives[124]—couldn't praise the report enough. It was called a "powerful" document that "brings us to a new level of awareness and understanding about violence against women and its links with women's inequality."[125]

But the self-described "feminist lens" through which the report's authors chose to view the world was hopelessly skewed.[126] Anyone who believes that the kind of extremist thinking discussed above is confined to individuals on the margins of society should consider the following passage, from this document's introductory pages:

> Canada's image abroad is that of a country with a high standard of living—a country dedicated to promoting peace in the world; a country where women have access to post-secondary education, and freedom of expression; a country where women are free to pursue the occupation they choose and to move about without constraint. But the panel learned that Canadian women are all too familiar with inequality and violence which tether them to *lives few in the world would choose to lead.* [my italics]

This doesn't say that *some* Canadian women are victimized by violence and therefore suffer terribly. Rather, it declares that being a woman per se in 1990s Canada means being consigned to a life "few in the world would choose to lead." If this is really the case, why does the panel devote an entire chapter to the special problems faced by immigrant and refugee women after they reach our soil? If being a contemporary Canadian woman is so dreadful an experience that few people would choose it, why not simply declare that immigrant and refugee women are mistaken to view this country as an improvement over what they left behind?

But that's only the beginning. Elsewhere we read that verbal abuse is part of "the strategy of men to control women," and that the fact that children witness wife abuse isn't an unfortunate by-product of domestic violence but "a powerful tool in reinforcing already overwhelming patriarchal norms of male dominance, female submission and the use of violence."[127]

The report declares: "In a society whose very structure condones male violence, all men, whether or not they are violent, derive substantial benefit from its institutionalization."[128] The allegation that all men 'benefit' from the current arrangement of our society is common in feminist literature. Hand in hand with the suggestion that males sat down and deliberately designed matters (as opposed to our society having assumed its present form due to competing historical, political, and economic forces) is the implication that those who benefit are also morally responsible for it.

Nowhere have I seen anyone acknowledge that there is an enormous difference between these two ideas. I benefit from the fact that I was born in an industrialized country in the late 20th century. My life has been one of the most privileged in the history of humanity. I have never gone hungry. I've always had a roof over my head and clothes on my back. Despite what the violence report's authors might think, hundreds of millions of people from the around the globe would change places with me in an instant. But am I personally responsible for this accident of fate?

If not, what is the point of implying that my husband— who, by another accident of fate, was born with a pair of testicles rather than a pair of ovaries—is responsible for the flawed state of the society he inherited as surely as did I? This is one of the ways in which feminist thought has led to decent men being blamed not only for the violence committed by their outlaw brothers, but for the sins of their fathers as well. No matter how caring and compassion- ate a man is—no matter how many pro-choice marches he's attended, dirty diapers he's changed, dishes he's washed, or toilet bowls he's scrubbed—he's male. Ergo he's derived 'substantial benefit' from our unequal system. Ergo he's guilty.

Indeed, he may as well behave like a violent brute, be- cause he's never going to get any credit from the sort of people who wrote the above quote. He may have tried his entire life to treat others with kindness and respect, but in their eyes he isn't a unique individual with his own per- sonal history. All that matters is that he belongs to a group—a group they've decided is feral.

This is stereotype. This is sexism. This is what femi- nism started out protesting.

This wretched report doesn't stop there. When it in- forms us that "the concept of patriarchy" is central to its analysis,[129] it becomes evident that the panel cares more about feminist dogma than the bruises and broken bones of real women. We're told that the 500 pages that follow address not violence against women per se but "violence women suffer because of their gender."[130] The panel makes a point of letting us know it's firmly rejecting the more in- clusive term "family violence" (which it calls inaccurate and misleading) in favour of "woman abuse."[131] Woman abuse, says the panel, is committed by men. Over and over again, we hear about "male power," "male violence," "vio- lent men," and "men's authority to be violent toward wo- men."[132]

Marilyn French, Catharine MacKinnon, and *Ms.* maga- zine all insist it's men who do horrible things and that it's women who get hurt.[133] They urge us to focus not on the violence itself but on the sex of the perpetrator because they want us to view these incidents as part of an over-arching male conspiracy to oppress women.

In some parts of the world, young unmarried women suspected of engaging in sexual activity (and, therefore, of dishonouring their families) are killed by male relatives who use violence to enforce rigid gender roles. Men who batter their wives sometimes say the women "stepped out of line" in ways that are connected to behaviour expected of them as women. This *is* one piece of the domestic violence puzzle.

But it isn't the only one. The problem with feminist tunnel vision is that it renders invisible the violence women suffer at the hands of other women. It pretends that the trauma experienced by a 32-year-old Toronto woman with a mental disability—who received broken ribs and a dislocated shoulder during the year she lived with an abusive female roommate—doesn't exist. The roommate, who was sentenced to 18 months in jail in 1994, reportedly choked her victim, kneed her in the groin, struck her in the face with a drinking glass, burned her with cigarettes, banged her head against a wall, assaulted her with a belt, drugged her, forced her to cook and clean, and threatened that she'd be "beaten beyond recognition" if she went to the authorities.[134]

If you're a frail grandmother, or a 15-year-old who has the bad luck to be assaulted by a woman rather than a man, there's no room in this panel's report for you. Your pain doesn't count. It's whitewashed out of the picture. If you happen to be murdered by another female, as was American Grammy-award-winning singer Selena early in 1995, your tragedy doesn't matter.[135]

Canadian taxpayers paid $10 million for a study that was supposed to be about female anguish. Instead, it turned out to be, first and foremost, about male misconduct. This is where extremism leads. A society that embraces feminist dogma dons a set of blinders. It *chooses* to tell only part of the truth about women's lives.

Elsewhere the violence report declares:

In a relationship, society has given the man the power over a woman from the point of earliest acquaintance. Men exercise this power not only in intimate relationships and not only in sexual matters but in any social context where contact between women and men occurs.[136]

Men are always in positions of power. They're never nervous, unsure of themselves, frightened, or worried about measuring up in the presence of *any* woman *ever*. Really. Have these people never seen a pimply-faced young man reduced to tongue-tied blushing in the presence of a self-assured young woman?

Are males in a position of power when their teachers and professors are females who mete out passing or failing grades? Are they in a position of power when the boss for whom they can't seem to do anything right is a woman? Are they in a position of power when they see a well-dressed, beautiful woman on the street and believe that they themselves are too unattractive, earn too little money, or are too short even to stand a chance with her? Are they in a position of power when, like the man whose brother wrote to Ann Landers, their wives stalk them and threaten them with death?

Many of my women's studies professors (who, as rigorous scholars, never allowed their feminism to distort the truth) wouldn't have accepted such simplistic twaddle from a first-year student. But this report has received the stamp of approval from Canada's federal government. And tangible, real-life consequences ensue from this fact.

For example, when I inquired, as a journalist in early 1995, why two Ontario government ministries had spent a total of $15,000 in taxpayers' money funding a controversial feminist conference (at a time when other worthy projects were being hit by cutbacks), I was informed that the decision to do so had been based on the findings of this very report.[137]

What further use will be made of this document in the coming years, how many more dubious decisions it will be used to defend, is anyone's guess. Subsequent to its release, however, copies were distributed to public libraries across the nation. An accompanying video, intended for rental by schools, churches, and public service organizations, was also produced.

Many people (some of whom will be young and impressionable) who read parts of this report or watch the video will hesitate to question the underlying assumptions in materials that have, after all, been given high official sanction. A Community Kit is being distributed, the contents of which are supposed to help concerned, well-intentioned individuals educate those around them about women and violence.[138]

In this way, sloppy thinking spreads like a virus. It infects the air that people who've never heard of Marilyn French or Catharine MacKinnon breathe. This extremist view of relations between the sexes, of who's to blame and who's not, of who commits violence and who doesn't, lodges inside people's hearts and minds. It becomes part of us.

If feminists defend irrationality they are in no position to complain if men resist all evidence and go on believing until the end of time that women are inherently weak, unreasonable and given to fits of the vapours...It is only through insisting that the evidence should be looked at carefully that women are able to attack the prejudices of men. Feminists cannot possibly support irrationality in any form.[139]
Janet Radcliffe Richards

2 - He Says, She Says

Try to visualize this scene: a young woman with freckles and auburn hair is strapped down to a bed. Thick, belt-like restraints encase her ankles. Others are looped around her wrists and secured near her waist. The woman, whose name is Gretchen, is not struggling.

Five other people are in the small room, gathered around, watching. She has been injected with a barbiturate—sodium amytal—long discredited as a 'truth serum.' A man sits by Gretchen's bed asking questions. "Lets finish this," he says.

She knows what he wants to hear. She believes her life will improve if she co-operates. Finally, in an agonized voice, she says the things for which he's been waiting. At last, she provides the details he's been trying to pry out of her for months. The man continues in a flat voice. He registers no shock, no surprise, at what she's revealed. It's clear he knew all along what was coming.

But then Gretchen begins to pull at her restraints, to thrash and writhe. Her face becomes contorted, her voice hoarse. She is now hysterical. Her struggles are so violent that the other people in the room grasp her limbs and hold her down. The entire episode is filmed. Later, Gretchen is shown the video. Again she becomes hysterical and again she is restrained. This, too, is filmed.

Welcome to mental health care in the '90s. The above scenario is called 'therapy.' It took place in 1992, in a psychiatric hospital in Texas. Gretchen's story represents the first 30 minutes of an hour-long documentary film about multiple personality disorder (MPD). This is an illness in which two or more distinct personalities are believed to inhabit a person's body.

The film was released in 1993 by Home Box Office and was broadcast as part of TVOntario's Mental Health Week in early 1995. The health care professionals who appear in it share three assumptions:

- One thing causes MPD—childhood sexual abuse
- This abuse was so terrible that patients such as Gretchen have 'repressed' their memories of it
- The way to treat/cure MPD is to help patients 'recover' these memories so they can be consciously confronted

Two years after being diagnosed as an MPD sufferer, and during the course of a four-month stay in a specialized psychiatric ward that "focuses on recovering repressed memories," Gretchen has finally retrieved images of being sexually abused in a bathroom as a child. We're told, at the end of the segment, that she "now feels she knows who her abuser is."

What the film doesn't disclose is that, although MPD was officially recognized by the American Psychiatric Association in 1980, debate continues over whether the illness truly exists. The World Health Organization, for instance, remains unconvinced, and some experts argue that there hasn't been a single documented case in which a person who had not previously undergone therapy—or who hadn't heard about this disorder via the media—developed MPD on their own. They contend that some mentally ill patients are highly suggestible and are being cued (often unconsciously) by their therapist to behave as though they possess different personalities.[140] Some of these personalities are apparently unicorns, angels, lobsters, gorillas, and demons.[141]

Prior to 1970, only two hundred cases of MPD had been diagnosed worldwide. In 1973, the bestselling book, *Sybil*, was published—about a woman who'd experienced childhood sexual abuse and who, after 2,300 therapy sessions, displayed 16 separate personalities. A film starring Sally Field followed in 1977. Since then, an estimated 30,000 cases of MPD have been identified. Many of these diagnoses originate with a small coterie of U.S. specialists.[142]

Even if MPD does exist (it's possible therapists were so unfamiliar with the illness in the past that they didn't recognize it when their patients displayed symptoms), what causes it is another whole debate. And even if it were agreed that MPD is the result of childhood trauma—as opposed to a chemical imbalance, for example—there's a third area of dispute over what kinds of trauma might trigger it.

Currently, there appears to be no good reason to believe that, of all the distressing things that happen to people as youngsters, sexual abuse alone produces this condition. Another famous case of MPD—involving a woman known as Eve White, whose story is told in the 1957 book *The Three Faces of Eve*—had no abuse whatsoever in her background. She had been traumatized by seeing a drowned man at the age of two, by touching her dead grandmother's face when she was five, and by witnessing an injury to her mother's arm.[143]

Nevertheless, the idea that MPD is invariably linked to sexual abuse has been adopted by an influential segment of the mental health community. More significantly for our purposes, it has also been embraced by mainstream feminism. The film discussed above, titled *MPD: The Search for Deadly Memories*, is co-narrated by Gloria Steinem, who provides no indication that she's troubled by how Gretchen is being treated. Near the beginning, referring to MPD patients, Steinem asks:

Why have they become tormented and broken into different personalities? What is the childhood pain that lies buried in the unknown depths of their minds? How can they search for the deadly memories that hold the secrets to their past and the promise of their healing?

Gretchen is obviously disturbed. She regularly experiences panic attacks, triggered by common sights and sounds such as the noise of a vacuum cleaner. Her body is, in places, a mass of scar tissue—the result of "hundreds" of self-inflicted lacerations. There's no denying she needs professional help. But does the kind of help she's receiving qualify as responsible mental health care? Surely there's cause for concern if, rather than adjusting the therapy to fit the unique circumstances of the patient, a therapist compels one patient after another to conform to a pre-established script.

If the only way a therapist can get a woman to admit she was sexually abused as a child is to strap her down and shoot her up with a hypnotic drug—which the film tells us "acts like a truth serum" but instead produces a state similar to alcohol intoxication[144]—surely we should be asking what is going on in North America's psychiatric wards.

Near the beginning of the film we learn that the reason Gretchen is trudging across town by foot and cannot afford a car is because "all the money she has goes to therapy." Later, she frets over the fact that the abuse she's been working so hard to remember bears little relation to her conscious memories. Prior to the sodium amytal scene—the first occasion in which specific details of abuse emerged— she says of the suggestion that she was sexually molested:

That doesn't fit with what I *know* that I experienced and that I saw and that I heard. Everything fits but it doesn't fit. I had a wonderful life. I have lots of happy memories. I had lots of wonderful things in my childhood. [original emphasis]

Although Gretchen is mentally ill, she's not stupid (we're told she's an honours student in college). She's desperately trying to understand what's the matter with her. "I don't want people to think I'm crazy," she says at one point. "I don't want to appear abnormal in any way. I want to fit in."

She's therefore particularly vulnerable when someone who calls himself an expert tells her he knows what will cure her. She wants to believe. She wants to get better. And when everyone she encounters during her four-month stay in the specialized psych unit not only insists there's a magic key but tells her exactly what it is, should we be surprised that 'memories' of childhood sexual abuse have begun to surface?

How can this be considered acceptable mental health care? Why is it okay for therapists who may be doing her more harm than good to take all her money? Why is it permissible to destroy the image Gretchen and thousands of other women (an estimated 90 percent of those diagnosed with MPD are female)[145] have of their childhoods on the basis of a highly controversial psychiatric theory? And what is North America's most prominent feminist doing not only applauding it all, but making a video to let the world know she applauds it?

This wasn't a situation in which Steinem agreed to be part of a project and then couldn't back out despite later reservations. Rather, we're informed at the end of the film that it was all her idea. One assumes she'd be the first to protest if it were publicly known that appendectomies were being performed on mostly female patients by doctors with fervent conviction but little evidence that such a procedure would cure acute depression. What's different about this?

No reasonable person would deny that childhood sexual abuse is an ugly reality. Nor can it be disputed that, until recently, such abuse remained unrecognized by society at large. This meant that victims could expect little help from the authorities or others in whom they might confide. It meant they suffered alone and felt ashamed, sus-

pecting that they'd somehow brought the abuse on themselves. Victims also worried, often justifiably, they'd be rejected by family and friends who were wholly unprepared
to cope with such revelations.

Sadly, these tragic facts have become more grist for the
feminist mill. Today, child sexual abuse is seen as just one
more example of how men deliberately cripple female lives.
Marilyn French, remember, lists sexual molestation of female children among her ten things the "vast majority of
men in the world do one or more of." She says, further,
that:

> All patriarchists exalt the home and family as sacred,
> demanding it remain inviolate from prying eyes. Men
> *want privacy for their violations of women*...All women learn
> in childhood that women as a sex are men's prey. [my
> italics][146]

Journalist Sylvia Fraser, Canada's most famous incest
survivor, reports that her memories, which came flooding
back to her at the age of 47, weren't induced by a therapist. We have no reason to disbelieve this statement—or
her insistence that she was abused by her deceased father.
But feminist Fraser goes well beyond such claims when
she writes, in a March 1994 magazine article:

> I was, in reality, *bred by my parents* as my father's con-
> cubine...What we take for granted as the stability of
> family life may well depend on the sexual slavery of our
> children. What's more, this is a cynical arrangement our
> institutions have colluded to conceal. [my italics][147]

The Canadian Panel on Violence Against Women also insists that domestic privacy increases "women's vulnerability." It adds:

> We are taught, encouraged, moulded by and lulled into
> accepting a range of false notions about the family. As

a source of some of our most profound experiences, it continues to be such an integral part of our emotional lives that it appears beyond criticism. Yet hiding from the truth of family life leaves women and children vulnerable. [my italics][148]

Catharine MacKinnon, too, maintains that "the private is a sphere of battery, marital rape and women's exploited labor."

In this way, privacy and family are reduced to nothing more than elements of the male domination master plan. The real reason our society cherishes privacy is because men have invented it to conceal their criminality. Those people who think families are about love and mutual aid are "hiding from the truth." The family isn't a place where battery and marital rape sometimes happen but where little else apparently does. Sick men don't simply molest their daughters, they operate in league with their wives to 'breed' them for that express purpose.

The fact that child sexual abuse remained a dark secret until recently is considered proof of a conscious plot to ensure a steady supply of victims. But this view overlooks the fact that it's only during the past few decades that our society has become more aware of, and sensitive to, all sorts of social issues. We don't call people 'bums' any more, we call them 'the homeless.' Interracial marriages are more common (and accepted) these days. 'Crippled' children's hospitals have been renamed, and openly homosexual politicians run for office (and get elected). All these changes are so recent that they have taken place within my lifetime. Even the physical abuse of children is discussed with an openness today that was unheard of before an influential paper on "Battered Child Syndrome" was first published in 1962.[149]

North American society has undergone a tremendous amount of consciousness-raising in the last while, and we're all better off as a result. Back in 1970, Canada's landmark Report of the Royal Commission on the Status of Women, for example, failed even to mention violence.[150]

While domestic abuse was surely occurring back then, many feminists were apparently unaware of its existence. Rather than the issue being kept quiet as the result of a male conspiracy, it seems more likely that society as a whole needed to be educated. Now that the highest levels of government have acknowledged that child sexual abuse exists, feminism is going one step further and trying to convince us that it's everywhere.

Let's return to the film. After learning about Gretchen, we are then introduced to John, a 40-year-old police officer. Steinem calmly informs us that John shares his job "with several personalities who have different abilities. He switches when different police skills are needed and is *always* aware of what his other personalities are doing" (my italics).

One personality is apparently good at driving in high speed chases. Other 'alters' have different styles of marksmanship. We are shown a clip of John's commanding officer, who says he makes a fine policeman, and are told that John has received "many awards and commendations" during his 13-year career.

Steinem tells us that John remembers a stable childhood home and being well provided for as a youngster. But he has always heard 'voices' inside his head and has now been diagnosed as having 20 personalities, "many of [whom] are frightened children who appear only in therapy."

According to these children, John was actually viciously abused while he was growing up. In addition to being shoved down a staircase and tortured with electrical currents, he was also, says Steinem, "sexually abused by both male and female perpetrators." In response, his psyche apparently "created a personality whose job it was to have sex." Steinem tells us he has a history of depression, unexplained mood swings, and difficulty controlling his temper. John himself admits that no physical evidence (such as scars or medical records) exists to corroborate these allegations, and he concedes that he wouldn't be able to prove any of this in a court of law.

Unlike John, neither Gretchen nor Barb—the film's third MPD sufferer—is aware of what's happening when her other personalities manifest themselves. Indeed, Gretchen says:

> I requested, when we started this, that please, when someone is out, will they please write the date, the day and the time [in her journal] and where they were and who they might have seen. If they would please give me an idea of where the body's been.

Barb's various personalities take drug overdoses, punch walls (breaking her hand in four places), inflict burns on her face, write hundreds of dollars' worth of bad cheques and, on one occasion, set her car on fire with her inside (she woke up in intensive care, on a respirator).

John's awareness obviously presents an inconsistency. When the film was released in 1993, the American Psychiatric Association's definition of MPD had two parts. Part A required a person to possess two or more distinct personalities. Part B decreed that these personalities must "recurrently *take full control of the individual's behavior*" (my italics).[151] If what Steinem tells us is true, if John is "always aware of what his other personalities" are doing, he doesn't meet the second requirement—and therefore isn't a real MPD patient.

There are a few possible explanations for this startling discrepancy. The first is that Steinem was mistaken about John's true self always being in control—a rather significant error, considering the nature of the work he does. The second is that this clearly disturbed police officer suffers from some other mental illness and was misdiagnosed, leaving Steinem in the unenviable position of commending his maltreatment by the mental health profession. The third is that Steinem, as well as others involved in the production of this film, weren't in possession of the most basic facts concerning MPD, even though three high-profile MPD experts—who would be as familiar with the APA's requirements as I am with the back of my hand—are listed in the film's credits. The fourth is that some of the people involved in the making of the film *knew* John didn't qualify, but a decision was taken to stretch the truth a little—in a documentary intended to 'educate' the public.[152]

Whatever the case may be, Steinem's reputation as a reliable, credible source of information is tarnished by this film, as is feminism's reputation by extension.

Carrying on, the film's third case study is 34-year-old Barb, who has a history of severe depression. We're told she has few memories of her life prior to her early twenties. Her therapist explains that Barb developed MPD in order to cope with the disparity between what was really going on in her childhood home and its outward appearance. Her father (who is not identified by name but appears in a photograph) was a prominent dentist and university professor. According to Barb's various alters, her father tortured her with his dentist drills (in her mouth, but also on other parts of her body) and "burned up a grey cat." Intones Steinem's male co-narrator: "Barb's father was not her only abuser. He frequented the local bars where he made friends that shared his interests." Barb informs us that "a lot of men" were eager to have sex with a young girl and were willing to pay her father in order to do so. We're told she had several abortions, the first when she was 13, and that she developed ulcers as a child.

What we don't hear is whether or not there's one iota of documented proof of any of this. Since Barb's father is dead, he's not in a position to dispute these horrific allegations. Yet the filmmakers don't seem to think independent verification is important. They apparently accept these accusations at face value and assume we will too.

Maybe these events really did happen. They aren't impossible. But what if they're merely the result of a profoundly ill patient being led to believe that a sexually abusive childhood caused her illness? What if Barb's tormented psyche simply made this stuff up? What if her father's good reputation is being dragged through the mud unjustly? Those responsible for this film don't appear to have asked themselves these questions. Instead, Steinem closes with the following:

> Multiple personality disorder shows the extraordinary capacity of the mind to invent ways of bearing the unbearable. And these people also show us that when allowed to give up its secrets, the human mind can heal itself.

Except, we don't know that these people have been healed. Gretchen may be. We're told that, following her stay in the psychiatric hospital, she returned to school and finished her degree. But we don't learn what has happened to her since. If all her problems have been resolved, we aren't informed of it.

John is anything but healed. At the end of the film we can only surmise that he continues to 'switch' personalities on a regular basis, and that he continues to visit his therapist, where he sits cross-legged, hunched over a teddy bear, speaking in children's voices about horrific victimization. When we last see Barb, despite the fact that she's apparently been aware of her former abuse for some time, she hasn't recovered either. On the contrary, she's checking herself into a psychiatric hospital out of concern that she might harm herself or her three young daughters. Says the narrator, "We were with Barb and her family when a dangerous time had come again."

This theory about how to cure MPD is an interesting one, but the examples provided by Steinem's own film don't support it.

Catharine MacKinnon thinks women who consent to pose for porn should be considered legally incompetent. I think a stronger case could be made that these three mentally ill people were not the sort of individuals who should have been asked to participate in a film that, among other things, involved the taping of intimate one-on-one sessions with their therapists. I'm astounded that the three therapists apparently had no concerns about what effect the production of this film would have on their patients' progress. Gretchen tells us she wants to fit in. Being followed around by a film crew—to class, her art studio, and the library—is unlikely to have assisted in that regard. And is it not possible that knowing a film crew was present when she was injected with sodium amytal put even more pressure on this disturbed young woman to 'retrieve' the kinds of details her therapist wanted to hear?

We're given to believe that Gretchen had no conscious memory of what she said under the influence of this drug. The first time she finds out that she has 'remembered' abuse is when she's shown the video of it later. Is it ethical to film the reactions of someone being informed of such a terrible thing for the first time? Is this not exploitation? And isn't it possible that Barb's condition has deteriorated because having a film crew in her life was too much of a strain?

What sort of judgment has Steinem exercised here? Although usually mindful of the abuse and misuse of power in our society, she remains untroubled by the fact that John is being permitted to walk around with a police-issue revolver. She is apparently unperturbed by the knowledge that, while still sorting out his own relationship to such issues, he's investigating child abuse cases and is a member of a task force on the subject. Although she suggests that John's child alters emerge only in therapy, this isn't true of all of them. At one point during the documentary we see him, in his own living room, with no therapist in sight, 'switch' to a 10-year-old who has trouble reading the words in a news clipping. Is it appropriate to allow an unsupervised 10-year-old near a loaded gun?

Steinem appears blissfully unaware that, according to one researcher, patients "frequently become suicidal and attempt to mutilate themselves" *after* they're diagnosed with MPD.[153] Nor does she seem to care about the dozens of studies, dating back to the 1930s, that have determined that sodium amytal is anything but a truth serum. Declares one recent examination of the available evidence:

The degree of agreement in the literature...is striking: numerous studies were reviewed for the present article but *not a single investigator* endorsed this procedure [amytal injection] as a means of recovering accurate memories of past events. Barbiturate-facilitated interviews intended to uncover memories of childhood sexual abuse may be worse than useless, because they may encourage patients' beliefs in completely mythical events. [my italics][154]

Gloria Steinem not only took part in the production of this film but further agreed to be the keynote speaker and guest of honour at the 1994 annual conference of the International Society for the Study of Multiple Personality and Dissociation—the organization that bears a good deal of responsibility for the fact that women are now being strapped down, doped up, and badgered until they tell therapists what they want to hear.[155] Gretchen's mother claims she has written to Steinem, both at *Ms.* and at her home address, but reports that Steinem (like HBO) has declined even to respond.[156]

Sometimes, when you're a true believer convinced of the righteousness of your cause, you don't worry too much about ethics. You think the ends really do justify the means. That your good intentions are sufficient in themselves. That the harm you do isn't real harm. Mainstream feminism seems to have a full-blown case of this malady, and nowhere is it more in evidence than in the way in which it responds to sexual abuse, MPD, repressed memories— and, to add a further twist, allegations of something called Satanic ritual abuse. In their laudable desire to have the terrible tragedy of child sexual abuse acknowledged, addressed, and prevented, feminists are gambling the credibility of the entire movement. Their propensity to view 'women and children' as victims has created a situation in which any and all claims of abuse, no matter how far-fetched, must be believed.

Ms. magazine's January/February 1993 issue provides a prime illustration of this. Its cover consists of a drawing of a naked infant caught up in the coils of a monstrous serpent. "Believe It! Cult Ritual Abuse Exists" reads the headline. Inside, six pages are devoted to a first-person account written under a pseudonym. The author tells us that, while in therapy, she started talking about the Satanic cult she'd belonged to when she was four to five years old. She accuses this cult of altering her "thought patterns" through "brain-washing and severe psychological abuse," and assures her readers that "cult leaders are knowledgeable about how to perform ritualistic abuse so it will not be detected."[157] She writes:

> cult members are smart; there was a doctor in our cult who taught members how to "discipline" children so as to leave no scars. Some examples are torture with pins and needles, forcing a child to take mind-altering drugs, and submerging a child in water, particularly as part of a satanic baptismal ritual. Other tactics include withholding of food and water, sleep deprivation, and forced eating of feces, urine, blood, or raw flesh.[158]

The author tells us her mother and her own best friend were strapped to an altar and ritually gang-raped. She says she witnessed the ritual murders of two children, one of whom was her baby sister:

> My mother became pregnant a few months after I was inducted into the cult. About seven months later, the cult decided she was carrying a girl child. Her labor was induced and the infant delivered prematurely by the cult doctor at our house.[159]

We're told the infant was decapitated a few days after being delivered and eaten by cult members. Since its birth wasn't recorded, we're advised, its death went unnoticed as well. Aside from their Saturday night rituals in the woods, she describes her family as being an "otherwise ordinary middle-class" one, living in a small city. Did friends and neighbours not think it odd that a woman seven months pregnant would suddenly lose her child but never be hospitalized? Did the writer's paternal grandparents, whom she says weren't part of the cult but lived "in the same town" and saw her family frequently, not find it strange, either?[160]

The article quotes from a Los Angeles County Commission for Women task force report on ritual abuse which claims, among other things, that "most victims dissociate their memories" of cult abuse. This is another way of saying they repress them. The *Ms.* article maintains that people who've been abused by Satanic cults may not be consciously aware of this fact, and that those who've had cult contact at a young age are more likely to develop MPD than other victims.[161]

Not one piece of corroborating evidence accompanies this fantastical tale. Since the author, her family, and the community where these events allegedly occurred aren't identified, there's no way to verify any of it. As with the film about MPD, we're just supposed to take *Ms.*'s word for it. But it's actually worse than that, because the article hints, none too subtly, that if you remain unconvinced you're aiding and abetting this horrific abuse. Near the end, it declares: "[b]ecause society tends to doubt stories of ritual abuse, this attitude carries over into the court system." A few lines later, a quote from a publication produced by the Illinois Coalition Against Sexual Assault alleges that children "are revictimized because people cannot face the truth." The *Ms.* article continues:

> The truth is that *ritual abuse exists*...It exists because violence is perpetrated against women and children, and then passed on to the next generation. Ritual abuse is at the extreme end of a continuum of abuse... Society's denial makes recovery much more difficult for survivors. Those who have suffered from ritual abuse need the

same respect and support that would be given to survivors of any tragedy. [original italics][162]

According to the available evidence, however, there is currently no rational basis for believing that Satanic ritual abuse is real. A 1992 report prepared by the U.S. Federal Bureau of Investigation (FBI) admits that while the notion of "a few cunning, secretive individuals in positions of power somewhere in this country regularly killing a few people as part of some satanic ritual, or ceremony and getting away with it is certainly within the realm of possibility," hard proof remains elusive.[163] As the report's author, Supervisory Special Agent Kenneth Lanning, would later tell a journalist: "There is not one single scrap of evidence for the existence of these cults. Not one. Nowhere. Zero."[164]

Lanning says it's extremely difficult to commit crimes on a large scale without becoming careless and leaving at least some physical evidence behind. Human nature being what it is, he says, the more people who are involved in ongoing and blatantly illegal activity, the more likely it is that internal conflicts will arise within the group, which will prompt some members to make self-serving disclosures to the authorities. His report concludes, in part:

> The explanation that the satanists are too organized and law enforcement is too incompetent only goes so far in explaining the lack of evidence. For at least eight years American law enforcement has been aggressively investigating the allegations of victims of ritual abuse. There is little or no evidence for that portion of their allegations that deals with large-scale baby breeding, human sacrifice and organized satanic conspiracies. Now it is up to mental health professions, not law enforcement, to explain why victims are alleging things that don't seem to have happened.[165]

When the National Center on Child Abuse and Neglect in Washington, D.C., made the findings of its own investigation into ritual abuse public in 1994, its conclusions were wholly consistent with the FBI's. The following quote, which relates to part one of a five-part study, is represen-tative:

> In summary, a very small group of clinicians, each claiming to have treated scores of cases, accounted for most of the reports of ritualistic child abuse. Reports by adult survivors were particularly extreme, involving acts such as murder, which should have left some traces of hard evidence. However, hard evidence for satanic ritual abuse, especially abuse involving large cults, was scant to nonexistent. Evidence for lone perpetrators or very small groups (e.g., two people) who abuse children in ways that include satanic themes was uncovered, al-though such abuse was infrequent.[166]

Declared Dr. Gail Goodman, who supervised the research team that compiled data on more than 12,000 cases of al-leged ritual abuse: "If there is anyone out there with solid evidence of satanic cult abuse of children, we would like to know about it."[167]

A similar report, prepared for the Department of Health in Great Britain, was also released in 1994. Al-though it cautions that there is a "considerable difference between North American and British cases" since there have been no allegations involving pre-school children in Britain (as sometimes happens on this side of the Atlan-tic), it too found no evidence of Satanic abuse. Rather, it describes people who claim that such things happened to them in their youth as "damaged individuals, with a known history of various forms of abuse, neglect or family problems." The report further says:

> Three substantiated cases of ritual, not satanic, abuse were found. These are cases in which self-proclaimed mystical/magical powers were used to entrap children and impress them (and also adults) with a reason for

75

the sexual abuse, keeping the victims compliant and ensuring their silence. *In these cases the ritual was secondary to the sexual abuse which clearly formed the primary objective of the perpetrators. The rituals performed in these cases did not resemble those that figured in the allegations of the other 81 cases.* [original italics][168]

Early in 1995, Randy Emon, a retired, California police sergeant, made the following public declaration on an Internet discussion group:

As a retired cop who totally believed in the SRA [Satanic Ritual Abuse] phenomenon, I actively searched for hard evidence. All I ever received were the anecdotal accounts of the "survivors." I perpetuated this myth by participating in the following videos: *In the Name of Satan: Devil Worship – the Rise of Satanism; America's Best Kept Secret;* [and] *Halloween, Trick or Treat.* I can state with absolute certainty, that if you review what I said in those videos and then ask me to prove what I said in a court of law, I could not provide any corroborating evidence to support what I had said...The fact is—I succumbed to the same hysteria as many of my colleagues have also done. The evidence I have totally proves the existence of teen involvement, and the loner criminals using Satanism as an excuse to commit a crime. Everything I said in those videos and at police seminars (I've taught about 5,000 cops) regarding [Satanic Ritual Abuse] was provided to me from "survivors" who went through therapy, visualization, who read a book or were involved in 12 step therapy programs. Yes, that's what I based my expertise upon—unverified rumors.[169]

True believers, many of them feminists, remain unimpressed by the above. Agent Lanning says his findings have been dismissed by persons who insist he's really a Satanist "who has infiltrated the FBI to facilitate a cover-up."[170] Medical anthropologist Sherrill Mulhern notes that those who believe in ritual abuse have responded less than sensibly to the absence of concrete proof:

> The lack of corroborative material evidence for the satanists' monstrous crimes simply proved that they [satanists] were far more sophisticated than the police. Doubters were portrayed, at best, as examples of society's refusal to recognize the horror of child sexual abuse and, at worst, as cult collaborators.[171]

One feminist, writing in a Canadian newspaper, recently compared people who express scepticism about the existence of ritual abuse to those who dispute the Holocaust. "Ritual abuse deniers, like Holocaust deniers, are trapped in an untenable position," wrote Judy Steed. "The Holocaust really did happen."[172] People who doubt the trustworthiness of 'recovered memories' have similarly been accused by feminists of displaying "authoritarian opposition to women having equality in our society" and of "covering up the crimes of incestuous parents."[173]

In its Fall 1992 issue, the Canadian feminist magazine *Herizons* devoted a special section to ritual abuse that included two first-person accounts. A note from the editors makes it clear they feel they are "breaking the silence" on a taboo by publishing this material, just as earlier feminists had "peeled back the protective layers of patriarchal violence." (I'm not certain *Herizons* can be considered a 'mainstream' feminist publication, since Canada has no equivalent to *Ms.*, but this example demonstrates that a belief in ritual abuse isn't uncommon among Canadian feminists.)

R.J., a 25-year-old woman who admits to long term psychiatric problems, hospitalization, and self-mutilation, 'recovered' her memories of cult ritual abuse in therapy. She says these involved images of: "little boy babies hanging from their genitalia (presumably dead), as well as visions of a blond woman in a white gown, stretched out on a stone table—a man in black held a dagger above her heart."

Amethya, the second person to tell her story, says her memories were retrieved four months after she began going to a feminist therapist. Soon afterwards, she was diagnosed as having MPD. She claims her abuse began when she was *less than a month old*, that members of the Satanic cult she belonged to were often punished by "being closed in a coffin with [a] mutilated dead body," and that she witnessed her 10-year-old best friend being impaled on a stake and burned alive. She also recalls:

> torture, electrical shocks, drowning attempts, being buried in deep pits with human bones, sadistic sexual abuse... Other experiences we suffered were cannibalism, child and adult prostitution, pornography, drugs, and witnessing countless rapes, tortures and deaths of other victims.[174]

In response to these articles, a Canadian feminist named Marjaleena Repo submitted a critique to *Herizons* in which she asked: "Since when does being a 'feminist' mean being either gullible, brain-dead, or both?" She ended her impassioned challenge to much of what the magazine had printed with the following, which I have her permission to reproduce here:

> A number of years ago I worked in a mental hospital where I met many people, men and women, with serious and elaborate delusions about their lives. They were being persecuted and tormented by sinister people in this world—the Mafia and the KGB among them—as well as aliens from outer space. Some thought of themselves as Christlike figures who continued to experience crucifixion. They pointed at their scars and injuries to "prove" that they had been tortured by laser rays and unwanted "operations." I listened to their stories with empathy, because they were obviously suffering and clearly believed in what they were saying. But...at no time did I go along with, or encourage, their delu-

sions, which I came to see as metaphors for their life experiences.

Something similar is needed with the current crop of "ritual abuse survivors." Instead of going along with disturbed and either highly manipulative or easily manipulated, suggestible individuals, true feminists—and feminist publications worth their salt—must refuse to be hoodwinked into believing every impossible and irrational story so long as it's being told by a woman and implies female victimization. We women have enough real problems to deal with, without having to invent new ones. And these problems of substance will be ignored and unsolved, if our energies and empathies are pulled into the direction of nonexistent crises in our midst.[175]

Herizons declined to run Repo's piece. The rejection letter she received began: "It is clear that you and the editors of *Herizons* have a different opinion on the experience of the women in the articles on Ritual Abuse. We stand by our initial articles and will not be publishing yours." It went on to say that the magazine would continue to print articles on abuse that explore the "different realities" of women experience.[176]

In addition to the *Herizons* coverage, a Vancouver feminist newspaper published an article sympathetic to ritual abuse survivors in June 1995.[177] Ritual abuse was also recognized by the Canadian Panel on Violence Against Women, which turned the issue into an 'all or nothing' proposition. According to the panel, there "is a clear parallel between the long-standing disbelief of sexual abuse survivors and the present disbelief of ritual abuse survivors."[178]

Apparently, one isn't entitled to make intelligent distinctions, to separate that about which there is no dispute (child sexual abuse) from that about which there is a great deal (Satanic ritual abuse). Feminists, it seems, are supposed to suppress our critical faculties whenever a controversy that involves women arises. Nor are we supposed to feel any uneasiness when the sidebars accompanying the *Ms.* ritual abuse cover story tell us that some therapists don't consider MPD "a disorder at all, but a very effective coping technique" and recommend a book that "encourages multiples to 'see themselves as the creative, sturdy, smart survivors that they are.'" We aren't supposed to be troubled when *Ms.* also recommends *The Courage to Heal*, the highly controversial 'survivors' bible, noting that it contains "an excellent short chapter on cult abuse."[179]

A subsequent issue of *Ms.* reports that *The Courage to Heal*, written by Ellen Bass and Laura Davis, has been called one of the 20 "most influential women's books of the last 20 years." Lawsuits were filed against the authors by two women who alleged that the book caused them to 'remember' childhood abuse that never happened. When the lawsuits were quashed, *Ms.* called it a victory that countered "the backlash against the concept of recovered memory."

I don't support lawsuits against book authors. I don't think rapists should be able to blame pornography for their actions, and I don't think authors should be held legally responsible for what people do with the information they provide. But *Ms.*'s lack of concern over the possibility that this book may be harming female lives seems astonishingly cavalier. The magazine ends its short bulletin by saying that, with the lawsuits out of the way, "survivors can get on with the healing."[180]

But parts of *The Courage to Heal* seem to have far more to do with manufacturing illness than healing it. Precisely what sort of healing is being encouraged when readers are assured: "If you are unable to remember any specific instances like the ones mentioned above but still have a feeling that something abusive happened to you, it probably did."[181] On page 22, readers are advised: "If you think you were abused and your life shows the symptoms, then you were." They're also told:

If you don't have any memory of it, it can be hard to believe the abuse really happened. You may feel insecure about trusting your intuition and want 'proof' of your abuse. This is a very natural desire, but it is not always one that can be met. [page 82].

What kind of health flows from chapter headings such as "ANGER - THE BACKBONE OF HEALING"?[182] Pointing to passages such as the following, one of the book's critics has observed that its authors "prescribe a cultivation of rage" to their readers:[183]

If you're willing to get angry and the anger just doesn't seem to come, there are many ways to get in touch with it. A little like priming the pump, you can do things that will get your anger started. Then, once you get the hang of it, it'll begin to flow on its own. [page 124]

You may dream of murder or castration. It can be pleasurable to fantasize such scenes in vivid detail. Wanting revenge is a natural impulse, a sane response. Let yourself imagine it to your heart's content...Suing your abuser and turning him in to the authorities are just two of the avenues open...Another woman, abused by her grandfather, went to his deathbed and, in front of all the other relatives, angrily confronted him right there in the hospital. [pages 128-29]

The Courage to Heal, it must be noted, is only one of many such self-help books. This publishing niche has grown rapidly in recent years, and it isn't uncommon to find several volumes on this topic in any moderate-sized bookstore. They bear titles such as *Secret Survivors* (which has a glowing endorsement from Gloria Steinem on the cover),[184] *The Right to Innocence*, and *Incest and Sexuality*. As feminist Carol Tavris has observed:

the authors of these books all rely on one another's work as supporting evidence for their own; they all endorse and recommend one another's books to their readers. If one of them comes up with a concocted statistic...the numbers are traded like baseball cards, reprinted in every book and eventually enshrined as fact. Thus the cycle of misinformation, faulty statistics and unvalidated assertions maintains itself.[185]

What constitutes sexual abuse can also be alarmingly broad in these books. For example, Beverly Engel, the author of *The Right to Innocence*, tells us that her alcoholic mother occasionally gave her "wet" kisses on the mouth, walked in on her while she used the bathroom, and looked at her in ways that made her feel uncomfortable when she was undressing. "It was not until very recently that I came to terms with my mother's behavior," Engel writes, "and saw it for what it really was—sexual abuse."[186]

The assumption that any woman who claims to have been sexually violated *was violated* is the one that guides rape crisis centres. When a woman phones a hotline or shows up for a consultation, she's looking for empathy and support. Disbelief is therefore suspended. It isn't the role of sexual assault counsellors to cross-examine women about what really occurred. That's the job of the police and the courts. Mainstream feminism in the '90s wants to chain us to that one window sill. It wants us to pretend that there aren't any other ways of thinking about these matters. We're all supposed to act like perpetual rape crisis counsellors, to believe any allegations that come out of the mouths of female persons.

Some of us consider this unreasonable. In Tavris' words: "If a woman suspects that she has been abducted by UFOs, that the FBI is bugging her socks or that a satanic cult forced her to bear a child that was half human and half dog, must she (and we) likewise assume that 'it probably really happened'?"[187]

At its best, feminism has been about asking questions, about challenging supposed societal 'truths,' about exposing the logical fallacies behind sexist beliefs. But feminist responses to issues such as MPD, recovered memories, and ritual abuse demonstrate that this tradition has been abandoned. Intelligent inquiry finds itself trampled into the dirt by a stampede of careless emotion. When faced with complex issues, feminism tries to shut down debate and stifle objections. It demands that 'true' feminists abandon rational thought and accept—on faith alone—highly suspect allegations.

But poor thinking has consequences in the real world. One of the *Herizons* articles says that rape crisis centres are "becoming more experienced in working with ritual abuse survivors." Amethya, who claims her abuse began when she was less than a month old, is identified at the end of her piece as a "counselor working in the area of violence against women." The editors of *Herizons* preface the ritual abuse section with this warning: "If reading these articles provokes extreme reactions or triggers memories, you may want to find someone to talk to about your reactions, or *call a crisis line*" (my italics).[188]

In February 1992, Columbia University established its own rape crisis centre in response to criticism from students that it wasn't doing enough to address the problem of violence against women. During the first semester it was in operation, 79 people used its services. Only about 10 percent of those were seeking assistance regarding a recent occurrence in their lives. The rest wanted to talk about earlier incidents, many of which involved childhood sexual abuse.[189]

In 1993, an independent consultant was asked to assess the Sexual Assault Centre in the city of Hamilton, Ontario. The centre had been criticized in the local media, and its funders (two levels of government, plus the United Way) wanted a review of the program they were supporting to the tune of half a million dollars a year.[190] The report, written by people obviously familiar with and sympathetic to feminist concerns, identified the childhood abuse cases as a serious problem. It pointed out that more than 80 percent of the centre's caseload involves clients "who were sexually abused as children."

According to the consultants, this causes two main difficulties. The first is that the reason the centre exists, is so generously funded, and enjoys broad public support is because it has a mandate to assist women who've suffered a recent sexual assault. Childhood sexual abuse clients are draining its resources. At the time the report was written, no priority was being given to recently assaulted women. This meant that women who'd just been raped were looking at a nine to 18-month-long waiting list in order to get into a support group at the centre. Such women complained that centre personnel were "too busy" to accompany them to court or didn't stay with them for "as long as they were needed."[191]

The second difficulty identified by the report is that, despite the dramatic shift in the kinds of cases it deals with, the centre had failed to modify either its staff training or its programs. Centre personnel were, therefore, prepared to deal with only 20 percent of the people who walked through their door. Although the centre appears to have assumed that the same kinds of responses are appropriate for both types of clients, the independent consultants disagreed. They concluded that:

> although there are similarities between the needs of recently assaulted women and women who are survivors of child sexual abuse, the differences far outweigh the similarities.
>
> Counselors who work with child sexual abuse require training in specific skills for this task.[192]

In other words, both groups of women were being short-changed.

What the report didn't talk about are the implications of publicly supported rape crisis centres being pulled into the childhood sexual abuse/MPD/recovered memory vortex. There are many reputable, responsible mental health professionals who'd never dream of pressuring their clients into conforming to a set script, who'd never strap someone down and shoot them full of 'truth serum' in order to extract memories of sexual abuse. But the problem is that some people clearly do operate this way—and they have influential champions such as Gloria Steinem. The problem is that women who read books such as *The Courage to Heal* may become convinced they were abused (despite having only the vaguest idea how) and then call up a rape crisis centre. Which means that people who believe they were abused by Satanic cults since they were infants are having their delusions taken seriously *and reinforced* by publicly funded rape crisis centres. This is not an appropriate use of tax dollars—or of charitable ones.

These matters should be receiving far more attention than they do. Every crisis centre on the continent should have a clear policy. It would be a great loss if these centres were to forfeit their public support and their funding because they aligned themselves too closely with questionable childhood sexual abuse claims.

These matters aren't academic. They have profound implications for real people in the real world, especially alleged perpetrators. Feminists aren't supposed to have any sympathy for these people. In our perpetual-rape-crisis-counsellor mode we're always supposed to side with the 'victim,' to accept her story no matter how preposterous. But the accused are also human beings—who may themselves be victims.

In late 1993, I attended the annual convention of the Ontario Criminal Lawyers' Association, held in Toronto. That year's conference focused on false sexual abuse allegations and the intricacies of human memory. It was picketed by feminists with signs that bore messages such as: "Please beware of the childish and abusive and disrespectful use of language re: children and women's lives." According to the pickets (whom I went out to talk to), some parts of the conference were offensive. They singled out, for example, a presentation listed on the program: "Child Sexual Abuse Syndrome—Not!" being given by a Florida psychologist, Dr. Harry Krop.

What they seemed unaware of is Krop's genuine sympathy and concern for bona fide abuse victims. It was Krop who, in 1977, established the first child sexual abuse treatment program in the state of Florida. Since then, he has counselled thousands of such victims and doesn't need to be reminded that real instances of abuse are all too common. But Krop is one of a growing number of professionals who are now expressing concern about the danger of false allegations and unjust convictions at a time in our history when sexual abuse accusations are mushrooming. After I'd told the pickets I considered the conference important because some accused persons are innocent and deserve to be represented by lawyers aware of the issues, they responded with that old feminist standby: only a small minority of those accused of sexual violence are truly innocent.

None of these people would have suggested that the experiences of South Asian immigrant women aren't important because such women represent only a tiny percentage of the North American population. Instead, they would have argued that these women are entitled to sensitivity and understanding from society at large. Moreover, all of these feminists would consider rape intolerable—even if it happened to only five women a year.

We need to be consistent. Either we're compassionate human beings, who value justice for its own sake, or we think that the suffering of some people is less important than the suffering of others. Anyone who's comfortable with this last option is invited to step right up and join the front of the line of those that society has decided not to give a damn about this week.

Sadly, even Ann Landers, an eminently sensible woman, has fallen into this trap. In September 1993, she published a letter from a man falsely accused of date rape. He reported:

Just before the case was to go to trial, all charges were dropped. Prosecutors found conclusive evidence that the woman was lying. So after 14 months of a living hell and nearly $20,000 in legal fees, my ordeal is over.

He ended his letter by saying he's convinced that many other men are currently serving prison sentences for sexual assaults they didn't commit. "My heart goes out to all of them," he wrote. Ann's response?

So does mine, but I'll bet an equal number of men who are guilty of rape are free as the breeze. Too often, the woman is reluctant to file charges and risk the publicity, so she keeps quiet. Or she files, the court is not convinced of the man's guilt and he's off the hook.[193]

Ann doesn't say anything that's untrue. But her response is the equivalent of telling someone who's just broken their arm that they should stop whining because the person across the street broke their leg. Surely both injuries deserve similar amounts of medical care, as well as compassion.

Ann devotes just three words to men who have been falsely convicted *by the state;* who may have lost their reputations, their savings, their homes, and their families because the state came and arrested them, tried them, convicted them, and is now keeping them behind bars. It does victims of sexual violence no good whatsoever to jail innocent people. All it does is add more anguish and sorrow to a world that contains too much of these things already.

Many people are never actually charged with offences such as child sexual abuse, but that doesn't mean their lives aren't shattered. As a journalist, I've received letters from parents in their seventies who say their adult daughters sought therapy for depression, or following a marriage breakdown, and subsequently ended up accusing their families of Satanic ritual abuse. These 'victims' frequently cut off all contact with their relatives, effectively abandoning their elderly parents and depriving them of access to their grandchildren. This is a heavy burden for people to bear in their later years.

In fairness to Ann Landers, she later responded sympathetically to people who claimed to be falsely accused of sexual abuse. In December 1993 she printed a letter from LITTLE ROCK, ARK., who wrote:

> As a father who has been unjustly accused, I can testify to the shock, pain and grief that results from the accusation by an adult daughter. Estrangement from my children and grandchildren followed. A therapist had convinced my daughter that all her problems were the result of "repressed" anger at me for having abused her sexually 25 years ago.

Ann tells him she's received "hundreds of letters" similar to his and, after printing another, advises readers that not all sexually dysfunctional adults were abused as children and that false memories are more common than people believe. She continues:

> Unfortunately, anybody can say anything about anyone, and the accused is then in the position of defending himself. All too often, if the maligned individual is a high-profile personality, the feeding frenzy begins, the headlines are a foot high, and the TV coverage is relentless. By the time the true facts are made public, the victim is thoroughly discredited and his reputation in shreds.

Ann had already printed another such letter, a month earlier, from TULSA. It included the following:

> My sister has literally torn our family apart with her unfounded accusations of sexual abuse. She decided to latch on to this as the reason for her teenage promiscuity and her failed marriages. She made her devastating accusations against our father publicly, but privately

has admitted that she doesn't really have any actual memory of these events. Her excuse is, "They must have happened because my life is such a mess."[194]

Laura Pasley spent half a decade convinced she was the victim of severe sexual abuse that her therapist insisted was really ritual abuse. Her story, published in *Skeptic* magazine, said that the women in her therapy group weren't even permitted to discuss the effect such allegations might have on their families:

> The visions in my head were of severe physical and sexual abuse. The images were so incredibly bizarre, yet they seemed so real. My picture of my family became distorted. Was it the drugs the doctors had me on, was it television shows or traumatic events I had witnessed over the years, or was it actual memories? I did not know but Steve [her therapist] said they *were fact* and to deny them meant that I did not want to get well. He said I was in denial, I was running, I was "protecting" my family, I was staying sick to "cover up" for my family. [original italics]

Pasley tells us that patients were often advised to write hostile letters to their parents which accused them of horrible acts and effectively divorced them. These letters were written with and read out loud to the other members of her therapy group. She says she was told the group was her "new family" and that she wouldn't be able to recover if she didn't move away from her "dangerous" relatives:

> Steve had me believing my mother had been trying to kill me for years. Not in an obvious attempt, but in the things she would do for me. I was bulimic. If Mama bought us groceries and any of them were easily ingested "binge foods," Steve said it was to kill me. At one point, I took some badly needed groceries back to her, threw

the bag and asked her if she was trying to kill me because there were some cookies and chips in the bag.

Pasley also neatly encapsulates the dilemma that people accused of long-ago sexual abuse face:

My family's response to accusations I made would not have mattered. If they said nothing, it was because they were guilty. If they cried innocence, they were trying to hide something. If they did not remember something the way I remembered it, they were in denial. There was always an answer.

Near the end of the article, Pasley describes her therapy as "the con job of all con jobs":

All my energy, all my money, everything I had went to them. When I woke up, my daughter was 12 years old and I [had] missed it. I missed some of her most precious years while searching endlessly for the next "memory."

Many 'survivors' have yet to wake up. When they do, some of them discover a new albatross around their neck—the crushing guilt they feel over the strain they've placed on innocent family members' health. Pasley tells us about one woman in her therapy group who falsely accused her parents of Satanic ritual abuse but reconciled with them a short time before her mother died of a heart attack. The woman remains wracked by guilt "each and every day."[195]

The issues of child sexual abuse, MPD, and recovered memories are complex ones fraught with moral hazard. But there is little or no acknowledgment of this within mainstream feminism. Gloria Steinem's MPD film doesn't concede this. *Ms.* magazine doesn't. To its credit, the longest of the three articles in *Herizons* spends four lines cautioning that not everyone who claims to be a Satanist is necessarily a ritual abuser. If people "lose sight of that fact," it says, "we just might find ourselves in the midst of a modern-day witchhunt."[196] How strange that this author is more concerned about stereotyping people who belong to a fringe religious group than in the harm being done to those falsely accused of cannibalism and of molesting their one-month-olds.

A women's movement that insists all accusations of sexual violence must be believed no matter what—and that calls people who express reservations about such matters 'backlashers'—is a feminism that cares more about its own dogma than real women's lives.

Gretchen, Barb, R.J., Amethya, and Laura Pasley all turned to people in the mental health field for help. If these women have suffered any abuse, it isn't difficult to argue that much of it may have been at the hands of 'experts' whom they trusted. There's more than one way to victimize women. When mainstream feminism actively applauds such victimization, its credibility vanishes.

If you prick us, do we not bleed? If you tickle us, do we not laugh? If you poison us, do we not die?

William Shakespeare

3 - Double Standards, '90s Style

In April 1994, around 11 o'clock at night, three men burst into a trendy Toronto cafe where more than two dozen patrons were enjoying gourmet coffee and decadent desserts. These people were ordered to hand over their cash and other valuables. When the robbers left, a 23-year-old woman named Georgina Leimonis lay dying from a gunshot wound to the chest.

By American standards, Toronto is a clean, safe place to live. This kind of apparently random violence might happen in New York City, but it's not the sort of thing to which Canadians are accustomed. In the aftermath, the media declared that Toronto had "lost its innocence" that night. Members of the public stopped by the shut-down cafe to pay their respects with bouquets of flowers, which soon overflowed onto the sidewalk.[197]

The three robbers, as it happened, were black. There was resulting concern, in certain quarters, that the incident might undermine race relations in the city. Newspaper editorials stressed that it was unjust to view these robbers as representative of the black community. A high-profile black spokesperson delivered a speech in which he pointed out that most blacks lead quiet, normal, law-abiding lives. "The whole community shouldn't be criminalized by the actions of a few," he said. "I am appalled at anyone who would do that."[198]

Unlike the United States, Canada doesn't compile race-based

crime statistics. Following the cafe shooting, a few commentators called for this, but the suggestion went nowhere. Others argued that even if such figures showed that blacks commit more crime than other groups, this still wouldn't demonstrate a "cause-and-effect relationship between race and crime."[199] While they'd have the potential to besmirch an entire community, they'd tell us little about *why* and nothing about how to correct the problem.

Which is all well and good. But on each December 6 since 1989, Canada—with the vocal support of practically every segment of its population—has been commemorating the deaths of the 14 female engineering students gunned down in the Montreal Massacre. Speeches are made in Parliament, rallies are held across the country, and the media is flooded with angst. In this case, people have little compunction about saying that gunman Marc Lepine *is* representative of *all men*.

When we talk about this event we don't say Lepine was a profoundly troubled individual whose behaviour tells us little of importance about the group to which he happened to belong. We don't say that most men lead quiet, normal, law-abiding lives.

Admittedly, Lepine made it easy for us. He told us he was committing these offences because he hated feminists. He apparently believed he hadn't been accepted by the engineering school because female students were taking places that should have gone to men. He baited the line— and we swallowed it, along with the hook and the sinker. As dissident feminist Amy Friedman has observed:

> The act itself was named by the killer, and we accepted his explanation. Marc Lepine said he was out to get feminists, and we took him at his word. We allowed Lepine to write the scenario for us.[200]

Let's suppose that the men who took part in the cafe robbery had gone to the trouble of articulating their thoughts and feelings. Suppose they'd muttered, while threatening people and shooting one of them: "You're middle class scum. You suckers get up in the morning and go to work. We hate people like you, with your smug, stable lives."

Would we, in such a case, have allowed these ravings to become the focal point, the lens through which we viewed the entire incident? Would we still be referring to them five years later? Or, after duly reporting such comments, would we have relegated them to the sidelines, collectively deciding that the life that was lost was the important thing, not the twisted logic of the criminals?

To use another example, Susan Smith, the South Carolina woman who confessed to drowning her two young sons in 1994 (after falsely telling police she'd been car-jacked), may say she did so because her boyfriend told her he wasn't able to face the responsibilities associated with a ready-made family.[201] Should we allow this excuse to dominate what we write and think about this tragedy? Or do we conclude that Smith is a sick woman whose pathetic explanation doesn't deserve much attention, that what really matters is that she deliberately snuffed out the lives of two beautiful little boys?

Yet Marc Lepine's stated rationale has been enshrined as the correct, final interpretation of his horrific acts—as the thing that deserves to be remembered. Why? Because feminism's explanation for his behaviour happens to coincide with the man's own ravings. Although most feminists would denounce in an instant anyone who said the *black* robbers in the cafe were merely acting out the violence that blacks as a group are more prone to committing, many consider it an article of faith that Lepine was merely acting out the violence to which men as a group are more prone.

This is a double standard of the worst kind. It is logically inconsistent and morally offensive.

In late 1994 a man wrote an opinion piece in the country's national newspaper defending the decision to spend more than a quarter of a million dollars not on violence prevention but on 14 pink granite benches in Vancouver, each bearing the name of a slain female engineering student as well as "a small hollow that will gather rainwater, the tears of and for the women who were murdered that day, and who are murdered every day."

The political and social climate being what it is, he also defended the inscription accompanying these benches, which reads, in part: "In memory, and in grief for all the women who have been murdered *by men*" (my italics). Later in the article, he declares that to remove the word 'male' from 'male violence' is to render it "a causeless phenomenon, like the weather."[202]

The report prepared by the Canadian Panel on Violence Against Women explicitly rejects the notion that men who commit violent crimes are troubled individuals who should be viewed as such. It criticizes Canadian institutions for regarding men's violent acts as "individual pathological responses by 'sick' men." It says that a man who uses violence is really "affirming his power, which he wants to preserve at all costs and which makes him neither monstrous nor sick."[203]

From this perspective, men never lose their cool and lash out angrily at whoever is nearby. They are always calmly and deliberately carrying out a political agenda of oppression whenever they mistreat female persons. The report says that violent men "make conscious choices including their choice of victim, the places and circumstances of their violence and the degree of force they use."[204]

Do the authors of this report live in the real world? Surely we can all agree that there's sometimes a political subtext to male violence, that some men do believe they are entitled to punish and control women. But *most* men grew up being told they weren't supposed to hit a girl. They were raised to view males who assault females as despicable bullies.

Men often feel trapped, inadequate, overwhelmed, confused, resentful, and unappreciated. Those who haven't developed constructive strategies for dealing with these emotions may behave horribly, but the reasons for their behaviour are surely part of the complex tapestry of everyday life. The idea that men are always acting on a single, identifiable political impulse whenever they behave violently toward someone who happens to be female honours neither truth nor humanity.

The panel says it's interested in dispelling myths. Accordingly, it insists it's a myth that women are in any way responsible for the violence committed against them:

> One of the most pervasive is the myth that places responsibility for violence on the victim rather than on the perpetrator: women provoke, tease and taunt men, invite their sexual advances and then push them away. Women annoy, disobey and confront, thus leading or contributing to the violence they encounter. They were wearing the wrong clothing, drank too much alcohol, walked alone at, night, etc.
>
> We flatly reject any analyses that place *any degree of responsibility* for violence on the women themselves *no matter what their actions*, appearance, demeanour or behaviour. [my italics][205]

I'm as outraged as the next feminist by the idea that some man would think that by merely being out on the street late at night, I'm asking to be raped. But is it reasonable to say that nothing I *ever* do can be viewed as contributing to crimes that may be committed against me?

As dissident feminist Camille Paglia has argued, if you drive to New York City, leave your keys in plain sight on the hood, and someone then steals your car, that person should be tracked down and punished. If you sleep with your doors wide open and someone comes in and burglarizes your home, that person, too, should be brought to justice. But this doesn't change the fact that you have behaved stupidly.[206] Is it reasonable to maintain that you haven't *contributed* to what has transpired, to assert that someone else is 100 percent responsible?

Let's say my husband and I get into a raging fight. I slap him in the face and threaten him with a frying pan.

Am I not somewhat to blame if he grabs my wrist and, in the struggle, it becomes sprained? Women aren't in the right all the time. Feminism may have dragged us down off our Victorian pedestal, but it now appears intent on placing us back up there.

A couple of pages later, the Violence Report continues:

> Men who are violent bear *sole responsibility* for their violent actions...Abusive behaviour cannot be explained away by loss of control or unfavourable circumstances. Problems with relationships, stress, alcohol, anxiety, depression and unemployment may contribute to violence against women, but they are neither acceptable excuses not root causes. [my italics][207]

If that's the standard we're going to hold men to, why do women who commit violence against other women get to 'explain away' *their* inappropriate behaviour? Why do lesbians who batter other lesbians get to blame it on the stress that a society hostile to lesbians places them under? What's so unique about this sort of pressure that nothing remotely approximates it? The report reads:

> Although research into the incidence and prevalence of [lesbian battering] is virtually non-existent in Canada, women who spoke to the Panel contend that it is the result of institutionalized heterosexism which isolates lesbians and adds pressure to their relationships.[208]

This is one of the rare occasions in which the panel is forced to acknowledge that women can be victimized by people born with ovaries rather than testicles. And how does it respond? First, by neglecting to mention that U.S. research on this problem does exist and that it suggests lesbians batter their partners at about the same rate as men batter their wives.[209] (The panel cites U.S. sources—including *The Courage to Heal*—elsewhere, so why not here?) Second, it accepts an excuse from women it has already said won't be tolerated from men. Stress made her do it.

The double standards don't stop there. In its section devoted to native women, the panel suggests that native women who commit criminal offences shouldn't be held accountable for their behaviour the way other people are, since they're really just victims of the system. Indeed, the report reads: "For Aboriginal women in conflict with the law, a prison sentence is the final act of violence imposed on them by a society that has oppressed them since birth."[210]

The panel urges the development of an alternative justice system that would respond to criminal acts by native women within the context of their own cultures. But when native men are discussed, the report brazenly reverses itself. It says that taking an aboriginal man's heritage into account amounts to racism:

> Aboriginal culture should not be considered in determining whether or not to lay criminal charges. Nor should it be used by law enforcers to decide whether or not to act on a complaint of spousal abuse. This is systemic racism because different standards of treatment are applied to Aboriginal people than to non-Aboriginal people.[211]

Elsewhere, the Panel declares:

> Women who have committed crimes need healing models identical to other women and correctional environments that allow them to regain power over their lives. They have more in common with other women than with male perpetrators of crime.[212]

Men are supposed to be afraid of going to prison because it's an unpleasant place where people are deprived of "power over their lives." But female prisons should empower inmates.

As we've seen, these state-sanctioned feminists aren't the only ones who embrace double standards. In the introduction to *The War Against Women*, Marilyn French protests against prejudice—which she defines as the "prejudgement of people based on their inherent, unchangeable sex or color." She then spends the next couple of hundred pages pre-judging men based on their sex while making excuses for women. In the context of talking about women who abuse alcohol or drugs while pregnant, she says:

> A society that was really concerned about this behavior would address the causes for the hopelessness. Most of the babies harmed by self-destructive maternal actions are part of the underclass that society condemns to death every time it chooses to spend money on weapons rather than social programs.[213]

Feminism consistently tells men to shape up, to stop being jerks, and that they're the problem. As Wendy Dennis writes of the contemporary North American male in her book, *Hot and Bothered: Sex and Love in the Nineties*:

> Even though he's been bending over backwards to adjust to [women's] ever-changing needs, over the years he's taken a fair bit of flak for behaving like the male creature he was raised to be. He has also heard—and endured in manly silence—interminable lectures about how he must mend his ways. In fact, the story of his life in the aftermath of feminism has largely been a story of censure, blame, belittlement and distaste for the male person that he is.
>
> For one of the implicit, if unadmitted, tenets of feminism has been a fundamental disrespect for men.[214]

Men hear about women's rights and their own responsibilities. Among the Canadian violence panel's recommendations is one that says schools "must create the strongest possible equality model" by "emphasizing the rights of girls and women and the responsibilities of boys and men to respect these rights."[215]

Feminism's message to women is: 'There, there, it's not your fault.' In *The Beauty Myth*, Naomi Wolf argues that women know, instinctively, that if we dress in certain ways we have a better chance of getting what we want from people who are male. This is often the case. But she then proceeds to argue that women therefore don't have a choice about how we conduct ourselves. She says a woman who puts on spike heels and lipstick before asking "an influential professor to be her thesis advisor" shouldn't be considered "a slut" because she's merely doing what a woman has to do in a hostile world.[216]

Isn't this a grave insult to all those women who've managed to work their way up academic and corporate ladders without sleeping with their bosses? We always have choices. Even if all the cards we've been dealt are low ones, we still select from among them and decide in which order to play them.

If a knife-wielding man threatens me as I'm getting into my car in a parking lot, I can yell loudly and try to attract attention, give him a shove and attempt to run away, or do what he says and get inside. Even if I choose the latter, I can still try to lean on the horn or exit by the passenger door. I can struggle violently, remain calm until he lets down his guard, talk to, scream at, or ignore him. If he tries to force me to perform fellatio, I have the option of complying or chomping on his penis. Women aren't rag dolls being pulled this way and that by forces immune to anything we might say or do. We spend our lives around other human beings, not caught up in the grip of King Kong-sized adversaries. We have the ability not only to affect our own destinies but to make history.

Contemporary feminism, though, accepts this idea only sometimes. It *does* say that women should organize and agitate and demonstrate. But then we have Wolf telling us that women won't really have a choice about whether to dress provocatively until we've either rewritten the last several hundred years (an impossibility) or advanced a few more hundred into the future. She says, of her hypothetical graduate student:

> She will have a choice when a plethora of faculties in her field, headed by women and endowed by generations of female magnates and robber baronesses, open their gates to her; when multinational corporations led by women clamor for the skills of young female graduates; when there are *other* universities, with bronze busts of the heroines of half a millennium's classical learning; when there are *other* research-funding boards maintained by the deep coffers provided by the revenues of female inventors, where half the chairs are held by women scientists. [original italics][217]

This pretty much condemns women who are alive here and now to perpetual victimhood—and the excuses feminism never tires of making for their frailties, faults, and misdeeds.

Feminism doesn't tell women who suffer from anorexia to get a life, to stop obsessing about superficial matters such as their appearance, and to start putting their energies to better use. Feminism doesn't demand that women who are being battered stand up for themselves the very first time and every time a man tries to push them around. It doesn't demand that they leave abusive situations (even if that means going on welfare) because they have a responsibility to ensure that their children don't grow up in such circumstances.

Feminism doesn't tell young women that giving birth to a child when you're 15 is a one-way ticket to poverty. It doesn't say there's no excuse for not using birth control in the '90s. It doesn't tell teenaged girls it'll take longer to close the gender wage gap if they keep dropping out of school and settling for low-paying jobs.

Instead, we say that anorexics, battered wives, young single mothers, and high school dropouts all deserve understanding and compassion. We demand programs to assist them and blame the school system for being a 'hostile environment.'

When I think of friends who have been anorexic, I know it's callous even to suggest that this problem can be dismissed. But what's good for the goose is good for the gander. Why don't men deserve the same consideration? Why, at a time in history when everyone insists women are men's equals, do women still get a shoulder to cry on and men get a cuff upside the head? Why do we bend over backward trying to understand *why* women behave in less-than-perfect ways but don't spare a tear for men who end up as basket cases? Why are men held fully responsible for their defects but not women? Why is it okay to be nasty to men as a group but not to women as a group?

In 1991 *Ms.* magazine published a piece by novelist Alice Walker (*The Color Purple*) about Winnie Mandela, the estranged wife of South African president Nelson Mandela. Ms. Mandela is a controversial figure. In May 1991, she was found guilty of four counts each of abduction and of being an accessory to assault—activities that ended tragically in the death of a 14-year-old boy.

Since the publication of Walker's piece, Ms. Mandela has been suspended from an African National Congress position amid allegations of fraud, and continues to be a source of mortification to her husband.[218] While it's possible, as Walker suggests, that Ms. Mandela is the victim of an elaborate plot to discredit her, it appears just as likely that she's an unstable person who has let the celebrity of being the wife of the revered Nelson Mandela go to her head.

In a classic case of the appalling double standards that prevail in the women's movement, the *Ms.* article leaves the reader with the distinct impression that even if Ms. Mandela had helped her bodyguards kidnap, confine, and assault the four young men in question, even if she herself had slit the throat of the youth who died, she shouldn't be held accountable. Are crimes are only crimes when they're perpetrated by people whose politics you disagree with? I doubt the family of the slain 14-year-old finds such thinking comforting.

While *Ms.* runs a "No Comment" column that calls attention to the sexist attitudes displayed in mainstream advertising, it has no compunction about printing, in large lettering, in its 'international news' section, a Saudi Arabian proverb that reads: "Trusting a man is like trusting a sieve to hold water." Or another from Sweden that declares: "A woman's heart sees more than ten men's eyes."[219]

These double standards are important because they spill over into mainstream culture. Feminists are experts at insisting loudly that the female experience of the world is far worse than the male experience. That message seeps into our consciousness, it influences how we all view social issues.

How many times have we heard that three to four times more teenaged girls than boys attempt suicide? How often have we put down a newspaper or magazine after reading this figure convinced that the world is an inhospitable place for females?[220]

In truth, this statistic tells only part of the story. What it doesn't reveal is that many more young males than females actually kill themselves. According to 1992 U.S. data, *six times* more males aged 15 to 24 took their lives than females. In Canada, 1990-1993 figures reveal that *five times* more males than females in this age group committed suicide.[221]

Only in a topsy-turvy world could actual deaths receive less attention than *attempted* suicides. Dead bodies are the end of the line. There are no more chances with a dead body, no more opportunities to work things out.

Unless we want to argue that young women are more incompetent than males of the same age, we have to conclude that most young women who attempt suicide don't mean to kill themselves. They're trying to signal their desperation; they're calling for help. Partly because males are socialized to believe that admitting they have problems is the same as admitting that they're failures, suicidal young men don't appear to believe help will be forth-coming, or that they are entitled to it.

We haven't heard about the suicide crisis that's rob-bing North America of its young men because feminism has played into and helped to reinforce pre-existing, sexist double standards. Our society has never considered men's suffering to be as important as women's. It has always been assumed that 'real men' take stress, abuse, danger, fatigue, and so forth in stride. Men have been trained to view such things as challenges to be met, trials by which to gauge one's self worth, rather than conditions to com-plain about. They grow up knowing that, in the event of a natural disaster, it's women and children who get seats in the lifeboat first.

Men's activist Warren Farrell refers to football, which high school boys learn they will be considered manly for playing, as "smashface."[222] I thought this was a tad ex-treme until the Toronto Argonauts of the Canadian Foot-ball League ran a series of advertisements in 1995 featur-ing slogans such as:

• Disabled list? Hey, if it ain't broke, they're not trying.
• There's nothing like seeing a gory blind-side tackle to the kidneys to really make you feel alive!
• It's like slowing down to look at a gruesome road kill. For 3 hours.

There's no female parallel in our culture. There is no con-text in which the pain and damaged bodies of living, breath-ing young women is blatantly celebrated.

In 1993, 208 females of all ages were murdered in Canada. In that same year, 488 males aged 15 to 24 took their own lives. Two-and-a-half times as many. The media devoted loads of coverage to violence against women yet barely mentioned young, male suicides.[223]

Only so much air time and only so many pages of print get devoted to social issues. If a society is told again and again that women are the ones who are having a terrible time of it, other concerns recede into the background. Communities have limited dollars and limited numbers of volunteers with which to address social problems. When these resources are concentrated overwhelmingly in one direction, others are neglected.

Nor are suicide rates the only indicator that males are faring poorly. As Betty Friedan has recently pointed out, American women currently live eight years longer than men do. (In Canada, the gap is six years.)[224] Imagine the outcry from feminists if these numbers were reversed: if five times as many women were taking their own lives in their youth, and if those who managed to reach retirement age were going to their graves seven years sooner!

Similarly, the attention paid to female health issues, and the accusations of bias in the medical profession (according to Marilyn French, "many doctors...take pleasure in mutilating women's bodies")[225] obscure the fact that men die more often than women do from all 15 of the leading causes of death in the United States. From heart disease to motor vehicle accidents, it is men—not women—who are over-represented.[226]

This doesn't mean research into women's health problems shouldn't continue, or that the male medical establishment can be absolved entirely of charges of insensitivity toward their female patients. But it does tend to cast doubt on the notion that a massive male medical conspiracy bent on victimizing women has been underway. If such a conspiracy exists, it's surely one of the least effectual in memory.

Now let's look at violence. Despite everything we've been hearing, the truth of the matter is that American men were four times more likely than women to be murdered in 1992. In Canada in 1993, twice as many men were robbed and murdered.[227] This means that the world writ large is less dangerous for women. As John Fekete says, in *Moral Panic*, a good deal depends on the framing:

Many women would be relieved to hear that they need not worry about getting knifed or even hurt; and that [statistically] their abrasions in life, such as they are, will come from people they associate with. An acquaintance relationship that goes over the top, and a society in which this happens, are still closer to the orbit of what is understandable and predictable, and perhaps preventable, than perpetual risk from strangers.[228]

Feminists routinely concentrate on sexual assault and point out that, while men are more often attacked and murdered by strangers, women are more frequently victimized by someone they know. But in a further twist, a 1993 Statistics Canada report found that women "who were separated or divorced had violent victimization rates almost *seven* times that of married females."[229] Feminist claims to the contrary, intact families aren't the place in which women are most at risk.

Now let's turn to education. American, Canadian, and British data all tell us that boys are currently doing measurably worse in school than girls. Yes, some studies claim that adolescent girls' self-esteem plummets. Others say that teachers devote less classroom time to girls than they do to boys. Still others assert that the sexual harassment girls experience in school makes them *want* to cut classes more. But the cold hard facts are that high school girls are currently outperforming boys. The most successful boys still tend to take slightly more senior math and science courses and to score slightly higher in these subjects on standardized tests. Boys also participate in more school-related sports. But in every other area—whether you look at reading, student government, overall academic achievement or absenteeism and drop-out rates —girls are doing better than their male counterparts. Girls also report more often than boys that their parents expect them to continue their education.[230]

Feminists deserve to take a bow for much of the success girls are now enjoying. But few people are paying attention to the other side of the coin. Precious little noise is being made on behalf of these boys, innocent children who surely deserve our concern. If the numbers were reversed a chorus of feminists would be condemning a system that doesn't give girls a fighting chance, that undercuts them from their earliest years. The media can be counted on to ensure that results showing girls trailing boys make it into the headlines. Yet when the Toronto Board of Education released results of its most recent high school student survey, the media emphasized that black students and those of Portuguese descent were doing less well than others. The fact that boys from all ethnic backgrounds were performing at lower levels than their sisters was scarcely noticed. No establishment feminist I'm aware of was prepared to admit that these results indicate that young women aren't as beleaguered as we've been assuming.[231]

In an earlier time, boys who weren't academically inclined could still find high-paying, unskilled jobs. But automation, economic restructuring, the global economy, demographic shifts, and information technologies are all having profound effects on employment prospects. Today, many unskilled jobs have disappeared or are in the process of being phased out. Thus, at a time in our history when young adults need a high school diploma more than ever, the fact that boys as a group aren't keeping up with girls as a group—and will likely lead disadvantaged lives as a result—isn't receiving the attention it warrants. If a story doesn't conform to our preconceptions, if it doesn't show women being short-changed or victimized, it's not considered news.

Incidentally, some of those high-paying jobs that poorly educated young men perform are also unpleasant, dangerous ones. In the United States, men accounted for 94 percent of occupational fatalities during the 1980s. According to 1993 Canadian data, 96 percent of those killed on the job were male, while men suffered three times as many non-fatal injuries at work as women did.[232]

In *The Myth of Male Power*, Warren Farrell points out that young men are 24 times more likely to be killed while performing farm labour than are young women. He further notes: "The more a worker's beat requires exposure to sleet and the heat, the more likely is the worker to be a man."[233]

Feminists rarely acknowledge these realities when they complain that women remain concentrated in pink-collar ghettos. Nor do they acknowledge that women's widespread expectation they'll marry a man who earns more than they do emboldens them to pursue career options that are less lucrative. Given a choice between repairing power lines outdoors in all weather or supervising children in a daycare centre for less than half the pay, many women *choose* to do the latter. Says Farrell:

> We frequently hear that women are segregated into low-paying dead-end jobs in poor work environments such as factories. But when *The Jobs Related Almanac* ranked 250 jobs from best to worst based on a *combination* of salary, stress, work environment, outlook, security, and physical demands, they found that 24 of the 25 worst jobs were almost-all-male jobs. Some examples: truck driver, sheet-metal worker, roofer, boilermaker, lumberjack, carpenter, construction worker or foreman, construction machinery operator, football player, welder, millwright, ironworker. All of these "worst jobs" have one thing in common: 95 to 100 percent men. [original italics][234]

When Canada was making its most recent appointment to the Supreme Court in 1992, three women declined the position before it was awarded to a man. We can talk about glass ceilings and structural discrimination. We can say there are too few women in positions of power. And yet, these three women reportedly turned down a chance to rise to the absolute pinnacle of their profession because the job demands would be too disruptive to their families.[235]

In the last few pages, then, we've scanned suicide rates, life spans, leading causes of death, violent crime, education, occupational fatalities, and unpleasant jobs. This data can't be denied or manipulated out of existence. In many significant areas, males—not females—are losing out.

Yet feminism continues to self-obsess. I think it's time we started asking why feminism closes its eyes to the above facts, why it refuses to admit that males often get a raw deal, too. Why can't we just acknowledge that the universe contains both ponds and streams?

A worldview that dismisses male disadvantage out of hand doesn't deserve our allegiance. In late 1993, Letty Cottin Pogrebin, a founding editor of *Ms.*, began a column in that publication with the words: "Have you ever noticed that whenever women take center stage, someone rushes into the social control booth and yanks the spotlight back to men?" Pogrebin goes on to insist that questions about why the *Ms.* Foundation's Take Our Daughters to Work day didn't include boys are merely "Me-Too" and "What-About-Us" reactions on the part of selfish males who can't bear to see girls enjoy "their one moment in the sun."

She then presents the self-esteem studies and refers to eating disorders, depression, and the lack of female occupational role models as proof girls are in more desperate need of encouragement than boys.[236] The data we've just looked at is utterly absent from her analysis. It doesn't exist. From the feminist perspective, males are never, ever worse off than females.

Feminism used to be about making sure all the relevant data was taken into account, about ensuring that female experiences and perspectives were added to the information already under consideration so that a balanced perspective was possible. Today, feminism is about cherry picking the facts and figures that make your argument while ignoring everything else.

Which brings us back to questions of clothing. In *The Beauty Myth* Naomi Wolf complains that career women are sometimes hassled, judged, and denied opportunities because of the way they dress, how much they weigh, and whether or not they wear make-up. Marilyn French similarly notes that rules regarding female attire are a means by which gender conformity is enforced.[237] In 1992, hundreds of feminists across Canada demonstrated for the right to go topless in public after a young woman was arrested and convicted of committing an indecent act by walking bare-breasted along some of the main streets of a small university city in southern Ontario. They based their position on the fact that men don't face criminal charges for similar behaviour.[238] When sexist conventions hurt women, feminists make their views known.

Let us cast our minds back to the two young men discussed at the beginning of this book—one of whom was arrested and the other who was assaulted for wearing 'women's' clothing. To my knowledge, feminists failed in both cases to declare their solidarity with these young men. Nor do they seem to mind that male elected representatives to Canada's national parliament aren't permitted to participate in debates while wearing turtlenecks, even though women are.[239] Feminists similarly remained silent when, in 1994, a male Canada Post employee was threatened with dismissal for refusing to cut his hair and trim his beard.[240]

If true gender equality is our goal, surely sexist conventions deserve to be protested *all* the time, not just when they work against women. Feminists, of all people, should know that being forbidden from doing something solely because of your sex is anything but liberating. Which means we shouldn't stand for arguments that say men actually have it better than women because they don't have to worry about make-up and because no one notices if they wear the same suit to the office twice in the same week. This is similar to arguing that women were lucky when only a handful of jobs were open to them, since it wasn't so difficult to decide what they wanted to do.

Perhaps the most telling example of how comfortable feminists are with sexist double standards is the military one. In the United States, young men are still required, by law, to register for the draft when they reach the age of 18. Those who refuse to do so may be jailed for up to five years and fined up to $250,000. They can also be restricted from holding government jobs and, in some states, are prohibited from attending certain schools or receiving student loans.[241]

In 1967, world heavyweight boxing champion Muhammad Ali refused, on moral grounds, to fight in the Vietnam War. He spent the next four years of his life in a prison cell. Not only was he deprived of his liberty, but a period of time that should have figured prominently in his athletic career was taken from him. Other young men became draft-dodgers who, to this day, have yet to receive official pardons. Both former U.S. vice-president Dan Quayle and President Bill Clinton have been forced to explain why they didn't fight in Vietnam. As an acclaimed documentary film series on the American Civil War reported, social pressure on men to do their military duty extends back into history. According to the series, first aired on PBS in 1990, Southern men who preferred not to join the war effort were goaded into doing so by women who made it clear they wouldn't marry men who were afraid to fight.

Women have endured none of this. They haven't been shipped off, young and scared, to risk their lives and mental health in a war they didn't understand or care about. Women haven't had to worry about whether they'd be able to pull the trigger when ordered to kill other human beings, or about disgracing themselves if they failed to behave as instructed under such circumstances. Women haven't been compelled, by their government, to kill and kill again in gruesome hand-to-hand combat. They haven't been jailed or forced to flee their homes and families for refusing to do so.

While some men clearly enjoy war, savouring the adrenaline rush and the danger, if all men were the aggressive brutes our society supposedly turns them into *we wouldn't have to threaten them with jail or ostracism* in order to get them to register for the draft and join battles already in progress.

Some contemporary feminists think today's women should be compensated for injuries their great-grandmothers suffered.[242] They would do well to remember that the righting of past wrongs cuts both ways. Half a million American males died in the Civil War. Another 100,000 were killed in World War I. 400,000 perished in World War II. And 60,000 lost their lives in Vietnam. The total exceeds one million. These figures don't include soldiers whose lives were never the same again, who returned from the fighting paralyzed, blind, suffering from shell shock, minus limbs, or emotionally traumatized past all hope of recovery. Should the US draft only women for military service and send only women off to the world's combat zones until a million American and 100,000 Canadian females have been shipped back home in body bags?

Why isn't a movement that advocates fundamental equality between women and men protesting these sexist draft policies? There's nothing remotely just about women enjoying all the privileges but not all the responsibilities of full citizenship. In Farrell's words: "Registering all our 18-year-old sons for the draft in the event the country needs more soldiers is as sexist as registering all our 18-year-old daughters for child-bearing in the event the country needs more children."[243]

Double standards tend to perpetuate double standards. Feminists who are convinced that women are the only aggrieved sex suffer from a worldview so skewed, they're prepared to believe any outrageous claim if it 'proves' female victimization. We carefully dissect 'male' data, treating it with both suspicion and scepticism. But evidence that originates from feminist sources is automatically presumed to be true. This explains the embarrassing phenomenon known as 'feminist fictions.'

In *Revolution From Within*, Gloria Steinem tells her readers that "about 150,000 females die of anorexia each year" in the United States. Steinem cites Naomi Wolf's *The Beauty Myth* as her source for this information, and Wolf's book does, indeed, provide this figure. She says it comes from the American Anorexia and Bulimia Association. But rather than quoting their literature directly, Wolf herself has found the statistic in another book.

In her words, this number tells us that "more die of anorexia in the United States each year than died in ten years of civil war in Beirut." That a disease that's claiming the lives of so many young women isn't consistently on the front pages of our newspapers is, in Wolf's opinion, just one more indication of how indifferent our society is to female well-being.[244]

She devotes an entire chapter to this topic, referring to "emaciated bodies starved not by nature but by men." She compares anorexia to a famine in the Netherlands during World War II and to the Holocaust. She declares:

> Women must claim anorexia as political damage done to us by a social order that considers our destruction insignificant because of what we are—less. We should identify it as Jews identify the death camps...

She also argues that a woman's body can't tell the difference between being an anorexic living "in an affluent suburb" and being a concentration camp inmate.

That may be. But in addition to exploiting the deaths of Holocaust victims in a scandalous manner, this is about as meaningful as saying that your body can't tell the difference between performing manual labour in a coal mine for pay and working there as an indentured slave. It's actually meaningless.[245]

The real story is that nowhere near 150,000 women die from anorexia and bulimia in the U.S. each year. Many women may suffer from these diseases, but the obvious reason why the front page of your morning paper isn't telling you that women are dropping like flies is because they aren't.

Christina Hoff Sommers is a philosophy professor and the author of *Who Stole Feminism?* Having learned in driver's ed that a total of 50,000 Americans are killed in automobile accidents every year, she found the 150,000 anorexia figure rather high. She contacted the Anorexia and Bulimia Association in order to double-check it and was told the organization had been grossly misquoted. As it turns out, a 1985 newsletter released by the group had reported that there were between 150,000 and 200,000 *sufferers* in all of the United States. In fact, American government figures show that only 54 women died of anorexia and bulimia combined in 1991.[246]

But this myth has taken on a life of its own. In April 1992, for instance, Ann Landers told her readers that "150,000 American women die from complications associated with anorexia and bulimia" every year. Ann got this information from yet another book. Since then, the bogus statistic has also begun turning up in college textbooks.[247]

Sadly, this isn't the only example of statistics that wildly exaggerate female victimization. In January 1993, *Time* magazine reported that a March of Dimes study had identified wife battering during pregnancy as a major cause of birth defects. The idea that some men batter their pregnant spouses is particularly grotesque, and is therefore cited constantly. Over the next few months, these same 'study' results made their way into several newspaper articles. But when the March of Dimes was contacted by Sommers, she was advised that no such document existed. According to her, the chain of events went like this:

> [The *Time* magazine journalist] had relied on information given her by the San Francisco Family Violence Prevention Fund, which in turn had obtained it from Sarah Buel, a founder of the domestic violence advocacy project at Harvard Law School who now heads a domestic abuse project in Massachusetts. Ms. Buel had obtained it from Caroline Whitehead, a maternal nurse and child care specialist in Raleigh, North Carolina.

Whitehead told Sommers the whole thing was the result of a misunderstanding. While introducing Buel as a speaker at a 1989 conference, Whitehead referred to a March of Dimes protocol aimed at screening pregnant women for domestic abuse. Buel apparently misheard Whitehead and afterwards began disseminating the birth defects myth both verbally and in writing, without bothering to track down a copy of the alleged document. Nearly a year after printing the false information, *Time* magazine published a correction. Observes Sommers:

> Unfortunately, the anorexia and the March of Dimes "study" are typical of the quality of information we are getting on many women's issues from feminist researchers, women's advocates, and journalists...When they engage in exaggeration, oversimplification, and obfuscation, the feminist researchers may be no different from other such advocacy groups as the National Rifle Association or the tobacco industry. But when the NRA does a "study that shows...," or the tobacco industry finds "data that suggest...," journalists are on their guard. They check their sources and seek dissenting opinions.[248]

Violence statistics of questionable merit pop up in all sorts of places, and are often distributed by prominent institutions, including governments, the police, and public libraries. Writing in *Newsweek* in 1993, Sarah Crichton tells us some college students are being given flyers containing suspect information as part of their freshmen orientation:

> As Penn State's Sexual Assault Awareness pamphlet reads, in can't-miss-it type: "FBI statistics indicate that one in three women in our society will be raped during her lifetime."

Crichton goes on to explain that the FBI's data is so out of date that no one takes it seriously. Somewhat conservative, trustworthy numbers from the National Victim Center suggest that one in seven American women are victims of forcible rape.[249]

During a five-month period in 1994, Ann Landers published letters claiming that:

- two to four million women are assaulted or raped by their boyfriends or spouses each year
- 12 million American women have been raped at least once
- "a man beats a woman every 12 to 15 seconds"
- "nearly half of all women will be battered at some time in their lives."
- 80 percent of the women who leave abusive mates are subjected to further violence from them[250]

A Statistics Canada study released in late 1993 similarly reported that 29 percent of married women had been assaulted by their spouses (this included anyone who'd ever been "grabbed" during an argument).[251] The Canadian violence panel's data, which was made public the same year, indicated that 98 percent of the females surveyed had experienced violence. (Since obscene telephone calls qualified as 'violence,' it's surprising the total wasn't 100 percent.)[252] Both these sources were subsequently cited repeatedly in *Dispelling the Myths*, a 12-page booklet about sexual assault published by the Ontario government in 1994.[253]

Much of the research from which the above numbers have been culled is seriously flawed. Often, the people who've been polled aren't representative of the population at large. If the only people who've filled out your survey are women seeking refuge in battered women shelters, you may have discovered important things about *their* situation but it's unwise to extrapolate those numbers to the rest of the population. If you've collected information from women who suffer from one type of disability, it might tell us little about *all* disabled women.[254]

On other occasions, only women are polled about violence and abuse. If we don't ask men the same questions, we don't know whether these experiences are common to everyone. When researchers *do* go to the trouble (and expense) of asking both sexes about sexual harassment and domestic abuse, they're often surprised to find the sexes have more in common than many people suppose. But this data doesn't always make it into the public arena.

In late 1991 the Ontario minister responsible for women's issues, Marion Boyd, announced Wife Assault Prevention month and disclosed details of an $858,000 ad campaign that featured the slogan: "Wife assault; it *is* a crime. There's no excuse." She also took the opportunity to inform the provincial legislature of an alarming statistic:

> Research shows that one in five men living with a woman admits to using violence against her. This violence takes many forms, including slapping, throwing objects at her, beating her up, threatening her with a knife or gun and even using weapons against her.

Those numbers came from a study conducted by a University of Calgary sociologist named Eugene Lupri. The portion that dealt with violence committed by males appeared in a Canadian journal and did appear to confirm the minister's remarks. But part two of the study, involving female violence, couldn't find a Canadian publisher. It eventually saw the light of day in a German publication. In the words of David Lees, the journalist who tracked it down, it reveals

> nothing that should surprise anyone, male or female, who has survived—or clings to—a troubled relationship or who takes the saddened view that we should be better people than we are. It documents the probability that both sexes evolved on the same planet and bring to their affairs the same disagreeable tendencies. Violence in the home, in other words, observes no gender boundary.[255]

The results:

Admitted to:	% Wives	% Husbands
threatening to hit or throw something at their partner	15.9	9.1
pushing, grabbing, or shoving their partner	13.1	11.9
slapping their partner	7.6	5.0
hitting or trying to hit their partner	9.0	5.4
kicking, biting or hitting their partner with a fist	6.3	6.4
beating up their partner	6.2	2.5
threatening their partner with a gun or a knife	3.6	2.1
using a gun or a knife against their partner	0.8	0.5

Some people admitted to doing things that fell into more than one category, but when the dust settled it was determined that 17.8 percent of the men and 23.3 percent of the women among the 1,530 people surveyed admitted to behaving in a 'violent' manner toward their spouses.[256]

The irony is that a government concerned about the violence taking place in Canadian homes spent the better part of a million dollars on an ad campaign that targeted *only* wife assault. Yet according to the research project it chose to cite, the ads should have targeted female violence if, for some reason, it was necessary to single out one gender.

Feminists respond to data such as this by arguing that it doesn't tell us anything about the *context* in which women behaved this way. Maybe they were acting in self-defence. Fair enough. But it's equally true that we don't know the context of men's behaviour, either.[257] When Winnipeg researcher Reena Sommer asked if self-defence was the issue, nine out of ten women said 'No.'[258]

Then another objection is raised. Contradicting the standard line that patriarchal society condones and encourages male violence against women, feminists now acknowledge that it's less socially acceptable for men to hit women than vice versa. Therefore, they say, the results can't be trusted because men's sense of shame is causing them to under-report or minimize their violence.[259] It's worth remember-ing, though, that no such protest is voiced as long as the findings make only men look bad.

The excuses continue. Even if women commit more do-mestic violence than men, we're told, women suffer more in-juries as a result. Perhaps. But let's acknowledge that re-liable information is difficult to obtain. Prior to the 1970s, many rapes didn't make it into the official statistics be-cause women were afraid of the shame and blame they'd be exposing themselves to by reporting them. (Large numbers of rapes continue to go unreported, even though the social climate has changed considerably.) Men may be at a simi-lar point in their history with respect to domestic assault. They may still be too afraid of being ridiculed by police of-ficers, medical personnel, and judges. As a result, when they show up in emergency wards, they have a powerful incentive to say their injuries were incurred in some man-ner other than spousal abuse.

A number of studies do suggest that women are seri-ously injured more frequently during domestic disputes than are men. As Lees observes, "greater strength brings with it a greater obligation for restraint."[260] But all of this is ultimately a side issue. If domestic violence isn't OK when men do it, it isn't OK when the perpetrators are fe-male. End of story.

The Canadian Violence Panel report includes "psychologi-cal violence" among the crimes men commit against women. This is defined as "taunts, jeers, insults, [and] abusive language," as well as a "deliberate withholding of various forms of emotional support." The author of "several land-mark books on violence against women" recently told *Ms.*: "in my view, a lot of women are battered who are never hit, because you can, you know, be subject to control without any physical violence."[261]

Here again, if such things are true when women are on the receiving end, they're equally true when men are. The 'silent treatment' can be resorted to just as easily by a woman as by a man. There is no good reason for thinking that females are less adept at emotional and psychological abuse than are males, or that they participate in it any less frequently.

One of feminism's last lines of defence is that when men *do* experience abuse, it's easier for them to leave because they aren't as economically dependent as women are. Ergo, men still don't deserve the attention and concern women receive.[262] Once again, this is beside the point. It also indicates how feminists have come to assume that the female experience is 'the norm'—something for which we've long berated men.

Most men earn more money than their wives, but many men do not. In 1992, wives were the major breadwinners in one out of every four Canadian families.[263] And while economic factors may be the biggest obstacle for a woman trying to escape an abusive relationship, they aren't the only obstacle. For a man, a more pressing concern might be that contact with his children would be sharply curtailed should he leave, since he can't count on being awarded custody.

Women tend to be more economically dependent on their spouses. Men tend to be more emotionally dependent. Farrell refers to this as the "all your emotional eggs in one basket" phenomenon. Most men have fewer emotionally significant relationships than do women. It isn't uncommon for women to spend hours talking about their problems and sharing intimate details of their lives with friends, but men are less likely to do so. Because they usually have less-developed support networks, walking away from the main source of emotional sustenance in their lives (even if it's negative sustenance) isn't easy.[264]

Feminism may be satisfied with double standards and excuses, but in the real world, women are no angels, and a significant percentage of abuse appears to be a two-way street. In November 1993, Ann Landers published a letter from CONCERNED IN MICHIGAN about an incident he'd witnessed in his rear-view mirror involving a couple in the car behind him.

"I was struck by the fact that they both were unusually good-looking," he wrote, "when suddenly, I saw the woman hit the man in the face." The letter continued:

> The guy didn't show much reaction, which suggested to me that she had probably hit him before. I could see them shouting and exchanging harsh words. When the woman bent to the floor to pick up something, the man tried to choke her. There was more shouting and tears as she broke away.
>
> The man made a move and she flinched, throwing her hands up protectively. As they pulled into the next lane and passed me, I saw her hit him again.

In June 1994, Ann printed another letter from a ST. LOUIS WOMAN who said her husband was prone to ordering her around, shoving her, and treating her roughly in bed. One day, she decided she'd had enough:

> When Ike shoved me again, I let him have it. It turned into a real fight and I beat the tar out of him. I have never seen him so mad. Over the next few months, he started a few more fights and I beat him every time. The bottom line is, our marriage is much better now.

As Ann said, if "it works for you." But in a climate where feminists insist, and society believes, that only men behave violently in the home, Ike would be criminally convicted for doing things for which his wife would never even be prosecuted.[265]

An over-the-top example of gender double standards appeared in a December 1994 letter published in 'Dear Abby,' the advice column of Ann's twin sister, Abigail Van Buren. LOOKS LIKE A BLIMP said she needed advice before she inadvertently took her mate's life. She told Abby she had a short temper, a weight problem, and a stressful job which paid three times as much as her husband's. She then explained the difficulty:

> When I get home, I feel like a volcano ready to explode, and my poor husband is usually on the receiving end of my wrath. This is dangerous because I'm bigger and stronger than my husband and can easily overpower him. I'm ashamed to admit that to spare him from my terrible rages, I've had to move him into the garage, which is really unfair to him.

I'll say. There's no question this is a bizarre letter and that people such as this are rare. But can you imagine the reaction if the genders were reversed? Can you imagine what Abby would say to a man who, rather than using his larger income to get a room somewhere, had decided it was best that his wife lived in the garage?

Abby responded at length, urging the woman to join Overeaters Anonymous. She explained the organization's philosophy, its international presence, and told readers how to get in touch with a chapter in their area. She assured LOOKS LIKE that when her appearance improved she'd like herself better and would "be kinder" to her husband as a result. That was all. There were no strong words to condemn the decision to exile someone you presumably love to the garage, as though they were the family pet.[266]

Our society insists that women must be treated with dignity, respect, and sensitivity. But males are still expected to square their jaw and 'take it like a man.'

There is a postscript to this chapter. A year and a half after the 1989 Montreal Massacre, in which Marc Lepine murdered 14 young women, wounded 13 other people, and then turned the gun on himself, the person in charge of security at the school revealed that the tragedy had claimed three additional lives.

The first was a young male student who'd been present that terrible day. He left a suicide note that, in the security chief's words, explained that "he could not accept that, as a man, he had been there and hadn't done anything about it." Unable to cope with their son's death, both his parents took their own lives several months later.

The security chief also revealed something else. He said that the 25-five-year-old killer had sat outside the registrar's office for about 40 minutes on the afternoon of the murders. He had stretched out his legs in a manner that had obstructed people's passage in the hallway, but apparently no one spoke to him.

Psychologists have since speculated that "by drawing attention to himself, Lepine was probably hoping someone would stop him."[267]

If we do not take care, we run the risk of planning a scheme in which the only freedom women get is the freedom to do what their liberators want them to do.[268]

Janet Radcliffe Richards

4 - Office Politics

Did you know that the real reason I'm writing this book has nothing to do with fairness, honesty, or compassion? Did you know that I'm not writing it because a movement I used to believe in has gone terribly wrong and I'd like to help repair the damage? Susan Faludi, author of a 1991 bestseller titled *Backlash: The Undeclared War Against American Women*, knows this.

Faludi and I have never met or corresponded. And although I've read work by her and articles about her, as far as I'm aware she's never laid eyes on one word I've set to paper. But in the March/April 1995 issue of *Ms.* magazine, Faludi says that dissident feminists such as myself are neither honest nor sincere. What we really are, she insists, is part of a "media-assisted invasion of the women's movement." We represent an "artificially engineered reproduction effort" by right-wing forces to replace "real" feminists with fake ones, *a la* the B-movie *Invasion of the Body Snatchers*. We're all just trying to "turn the media spotlight" our way, to opportunistically cash in on conservative-inspired unease over feminism. We're just pretending to be feminists so the television cameras will give us our 15 minutes of fame.[269]

On the list of women Faludi denounces as pretend feminists are writers who share many of my concerns: Rene Denfeld, the author of *The New Victorians: A Young Woman's Response to the Old Feminist Order*, and Camille Paglia, the author of *Sex, Art and American Culture*. Katie Roiphe is impugned for her book, *The Morning After: Sex, Fear and Feminism*. So is Christina Hoff Sommers for hers, the full title of which is *Who Stole Feminism? How Women Have Betrayed Women*.

People who feel passionately about certain topics sometimes say things they later wish they hadn't. But one of the advantages of being a writer is that you have an opportunity to think carefully about statements before signing your name to them. When you're doing magazine work you have a further period of time to reconsider, to call up your editor and have the petty things you've said changed before the article rolls off the presses and gets sent off into the wide world to take its place in libraries and databanks.

I can only assume that Faludi's recent *Ms.* article is an accurate reflection of her considered position, and that *Ms.* thinks this 'exposé' (which was hyped by a banner on the magazine's cover) qualifies as thoughtful debate. This is depressing because Faludi's article is little more than an insult-slinging, name-calling session.

According to her, the authors on her list are faux feminists, pseudo feminists, pod-feminists, and anti-feminists. They employ "low-rent logic." They "gleefully" pounce on feminist mistakes, and promote "erroneous, easy opinions parading as serious and daring ideas." Rather than looking "forward to creating a better future," she knows they're against improving women's lives because their views are really "just right-wing thought undercover." You get a feel for the tone of her piece from the following passage:

While the Roiphes and the Sommerses claim to be going against the cultural grain, they are really auditioning for the most commonly available, easiest parts to get in the pop culture drama: the roles of the good girls whose opinions are dutifully in line with prevailing prejudice.

If one disregards the illustrations, the headlines, and the quotes in large lettering that accompany the article, the text totals six-and-a-half pages. Faludi uses the word "conservative" ten times and terms such as "right-wing," "rightward leaning," and "far right" a further eight times in this short space. She also refers to conservatives such as Dan Quayle, George Bush, Norman Mailer, George Gilder, Phyllis Schlafly, Newt Gingrich, Clarence Thomas, Ronald Reagan, Jerry Falwell, and Pat Buchanan— sometimes more than once. Rather than discussing the ideas in these books with even-handedness, she smears the authors by repeatedly implying (but never demonstrating) a link between them and the far right.

When I was in university, I had a professor who used to say that whenever anyone tries to tell you there are only two choices—you agree with them or you're the enemy—you know you're being fed propaganda. In Faludi's mind, anyone who has serious concerns about the direction in which the women's movement is headed is the enemy. There are only two choices: accept feminism as it is or you're a right-winger.

This is either/or thinking. This is us/them thinking. This is thinking that doesn't believe in a middle ground, in compromise, in unlimited possibilities. But there are always more than two options. We can be critical of the way a school board is being run without being opposed to education.

Faludi's approach is precisely the sort *Ms.* berates others for. Rather than dealing with the substance of these women's concerns (Faludi discusses a few points only briefly and superficially), she impugns their motives, she pretends to uncover their 'real' reasons for saying the things they do. A 1992 *Ms.* editorial complained about such tactics when the woman who accused William Kennedy Smith of acquaintance rape encountered it:

> Always the interrogators thunder: "What is your real reason for coming forward? Ambition, money, attention,

scorned love, revenge? What is your real motivation?"

When rape is concerned, feminism says women always tell the truth. But according to Faludi, when women criticize feminism they're really liars with ulterior motives. The *Ms.* editorial quoted above says that women's testimony "will at first be disbelieved. They will try to deny it, denounce it, defuse it, rename it."[270] Yep.

Faludi also criticizes dissident feminists for not being sufficiently angry:

> [T]he "I am feminist, but..." crew are not feminists at all. They frown on any feminist display of political passion or anger; they are cool mouthpieces, appropriate for the cool media to which they aspire. It is this lack of heat and passion, this lack of anger, that gives them away.

Doris Lessing is a world-renowned novelist who was a Communist in her youth until she became aware of the great wrongs Communism was committing in the name of making the world a better place. In her non-fiction book titled *Prisons We Choose to Live Inside*, Lessing discusses the problem of ordinary, decent people becoming carried away by political passion, and notes they are capable of inflicting great harm while under this influence. In her words,

> One mass movement, each set of mass opinions, succeeds another...Each breeds a certain frame of mind: violent, emotional, partisan, always suppressing facts that don't suit it, lying, and making it impossible to talk in the cool, quiet, sensible low-keyed tone of voice which, it seems to me, is the only one that can produce truth.

Lessing warns us that one "learns nothing, about anything, ever, when in a state of boiling ferment, or partisan enthusiasm."[271]

Isaiah Berlin is a British political scientist whose books include *Four Essays on Liberty* and *Against the Current*. When the University of Toronto presented him with an honorary doctorate in late 1994, his acceptance speech noted that the horrors of the 20th century, the "oppression, torture, murder which can be laid at the doors of Lenin, Stalin, Hitler, Mao, [and] Pol Pot," weren't caused by "ordinary negative human sentiments"—but by ideas.

These atrocities were carried out by people whose "eyes were fixed upon some ultimate golden future" and who were, therefore, prepared to "kill and maim with a tranquil conscience." Berlin doesn't view heat, passion, or anger as positives in the political arena, either. Rather, he says:

> [W]e must weigh and measure, bargain, compromise, and prevent the crushing of one form of life by its rivals. I know only too well that this is not a flag under which idealistic young men and women may wish to march—it seems too tame, too reasonable, too bourgeois, it does not engage the generous emotions.

In reference to the revolutionary argument that one has to break a few eggs in order to make an omelet, Berlin cautions that it's precisely when we are willing to forgo being 'reasonable' that we are in danger of starting down the path toward coercion and tyranny, to:

> destruction, blood—eggs are broken, but the omelet is not in sight, there is only an infinite number of eggs, human lives, ready for the breaking: and in the end the passionate idealists forget the omelet, and just go on breaking eggs.[272]

Faludi is entitled to her opinion that those who fail to display political anger are suspect. But there are wise, learned souls who strongly disagree.

Faludi also accuses dissident feminists of proclaiming, in essence:

I don't believe women face discrimination anymore; I don't see any reason for women to organize politically; I don't think the pay gap, sexual harassment, rape, domestic violence, or just about any other issue feminism has raised are real problems.

If this is the case, why did Camille Paglia help draw up sexual harassment guidelines at the college where she teaches?[273] Why does Katie Roiphe write so sympathetically about anorexia and agree (with reservations) with much of what Naomi Wolf says about young women who suffer from this disease?[274] Why does Rene Denfeld complain so bitterly that the attention feminism is paying to goddess worship doesn't do a thing for the millions of women who "have to cope with unequal pay, lack of affordable child care, nonexistent job opportunities, raising families without health insurance"?[275] Why does Christina Hoff Sommers protest the inequities in rape crisis services?[276]

These women all call themselves feminists. They care deeply about many of the same issues Faludi does. Faludi may think she's been appointed supreme arbiter, that she gets to decide who's a feminist and who's not, but that isn't the case. The last time I checked, not only did we feminists not require identity cards, Faludi was in no position to be unilaterally revoking them.

The problem isn't that these women aren't feminists, it's that they don't believe the women's movement is above criticism. They think high-profile feminists such as Marilyn French, Catharine MacKinnon, Gloria Steinem, Naomi Wolf and, yes, Susan Faludi should be vigorously challenged when they make mistakes and highly questionable pronouncements. They think a spade should be called a spade, and that we should all be prepared to admit that the empress isn't wearing any clothes.

Perhaps the most distressing part of Faludi's piece is her insistence that red is really green, that the sun is really the moon. Within this same article she insists that the women's movement is an open, tolerant one that doesn't stifle dissent.

If that's true, why didn't *Ms.* invite each of the feminists whose work Faludi attacks to contribute a short piece outlining her own position—rather than commissioning Faludi to 'expose' them? Why does the magazine pull mostly one-liners from their work, presenting these quotes in large print minus any context? Why, rather than showing us attractive photos of these women, does the magazine employ line-drawing caricatures?

Sommers' caricature is wearing a T-shirt with percentages written all over it, Roiphe's has blinders that obstruct her vision, and Denfeld's is punching a bag that has a woman's face on it (she's an amateur boxer). Only one other person is represented by a caricature in that issue of the magazine: Newt Gingrich, the Republican.

Such treatment may be *Ms.*' idea of open and honest dialogue, of welcoming views that conflict with its own, but most people would consider it something else. Yet there's Faludi asserting that only a minority of feminists "think only their opinions are the right ones":

> for every feminist trying to dictate policy in one direction, there's another challenging her. Heated exchanges, not censorship, characterize feminists' approaches to difficult subjects like pornography, surrogate motherhood, or [the abortion pill] RU 486.

Yeah, right. Perhaps Faludi should take another look at the "RAGE + WOMEN = POWER" issue of *Ms.* By my count, the subject of pornography comes up seven times, and on *every* occasion it's considered irredeemably sexist. On page 10, a letter to the editor describes our society as one "where we raise men on pornography and violence against women." Another, on the following page, complains that men "are comfortable purchasing women's sexuality cheaply and easily at newsstands and video stores."

Pages 50 and 51 display an enormous photograph of a feminist anti-porn march. There's a large banner that reads "WOMEN AGAINST PORNOGRAPHY. STOP VIOLENCE AGAINST WOMEN." Assorted picket signs declare: "PORN HURTS WOMEN," "PORN IS VIOLENCE AGAINST WOMEN," and "PORN IS VIOLENCE DISGUISED." In a book review appearing on page 59, we're told that it's "sad" that a particular author has "buckled" and decided to part ways with anti-porn feminists. We also read that young women who don't agree with the feminist anti-porn critique are "a depressing case study in the success of backlash propaganda."

On pages 86 and 87 we find a feminist theory piece about prostitution, which criticizes those women who continue to defend pornography. Finally, the last two pages of the magazine are devoted to a guest column written by a black male who says pornography "demeans and degrades women and men," that it "corrupts our sexuality," and that it fosters "aggression and abuse." The piece ends with him saying it's time for porn to "be thrown into the trash."[277]

If this is what Faludi means by a "heated exchange" of opposing ideas, if this is what she means by one feminist pulling in one direction and another feminist pulling in another, she has a notion of these concepts that differs radically from mine. Robin Morgan, the long-time editor of *Ms.*, is the person who coined the phrase "Pornography is the theory, rape is the practice."[278] By no stretch of the imagination can it be said that *Ms.* has given equal time to feminist anti-censorship ideas, never mind pro-porn ones.[279]

In a published speech titled *The Sexual Liberals and the Attack on Feminism* (which, incidentally, is referred to positively in the *Ms.* 'rage' issue), Catharine MacKinnon makes it clear that she doesn't consider women who defend or enjoy pornography to be feminists at all. She calls them "liberals," and she regards the term as an insult.

She spends in excess of two pages disagreeing with the position of a group called FACT, the Feminists Against

Censorship Task Force. She has every right to do so, of course, but then she gets nasty. "The Black movement has Uncle Toms and Oreo cookies," she says. "The labor movement has scabs. The women's movement has FACT."

On another occasion, MacKinnon has compared feminists who oppose censorship to "house niggers who sided with the masters." She has declared that if "pornography is part of your sexuality, then you have no right to your sexuality."[280]

Faludi and MacKinnon aren't the only ones who think they get to decide who's a feminist and who's not, in this ever-so-tolerant movement in which people treat each other with respect despite differences of opinion. Robin Morgan's editorial in the May/June 1993 issue of *Ms.* declared flatly that pop singer Madonna is not a feminist and that any "attempt to characterize her as such reveals an unfortunate lack of understanding about feminism." It continued:

Madonna may be talented; she's clearly in rebellion against her Catholic upbringing; she's taken admirable stands in urging voter registration and in the fight against HIV/AIDS. But a feminist? Quite a stretch—for a performer marketing herself in the acceptable objectifying style, and acting "outrageous" in ways calculated not to undermine but to enhance the patriarchal establishment, pornographic and otherwise.[281]

There's only one way to interpret Madonna's performances, and if you didn't know that then you're obviously not a 'real' feminist. Would someone please let me in on the big secret: where are the checklists and the scorecards kept? Where can I fill them out and discover whether or not I pass the Feminist Purity test? Or do I have to sleep on a stack of mattresses and discern the pea underneath the last one? As Denfeld has commented with respect to this editorial:

The question is not whether Madonna's depictions of sexuality make her a feminist, the question is whether they prohibit her from being deemed one.

Morgan...would answer yes. Women of my generation might answer, "Who cares, and since when is it your business?"[282]

Gloria Steinem, too, pronounces on who's a feminist and who isn't. In a 1992 interview with the *Advocate* magazine, Steinem said of Camille Paglia: "Her calling herself a feminist is sort of like a Nazi saying they're not anti-Semitic. She's not a feminist. She's Phyllis Schlafly with sex added."[283]

This is an opportune moment for me to say a few words about Paglia. I think she's an acid-tongued egotist whose catty, personal attacks on other feminists aren't constructive. But when I went to hear her speak in late 1992, I spent the entire evening in stitches. Her irreverence was such a relief from the earnest, pained feminism I was used to. She was the first person I'd ever heard criticize out loud the famous-feminists-on-high.

To her credit, Paglia doesn't take herself too seriously. She admits she has a "boisterous, wisecracking, machine-gun American verbal style" and a manic personality. She acknowledges that she's "an overeater and *overstater*, a gourmandizer of the grand manner" (my italics). She jokingly says, with respect to her new lover, "I lost a big part of *my act* when I couldn't complain about my sex life any more" (my italics)."[284]

I don't have to agree with half of what Paglia writes to concur with Sommers that she's "one of the most brilliant, original thinkers" in America. She's therefore entitled to make up her own mind about whether or not she's a feminist. And, regardless of what Steinem may think, Paglia loudly declares that she is.[285]

In the same *Ms.* editorial in which Morgan said Madonna wasn't a feminist, she addressed another question she said she was being asked frequently: *What do you think of Camille Paglia?* Her response: "I don't. Why should we waste energy on a publicity-obsessed, intellectually bereft, rather pathetic person trying to revive the lie that women want to be raped."

That's not what Paglia says at all. She makes it clear that rape "is an outrage that cannot be tolerated in a civilized society," and acknowledges that acquaintance rape "has been a horrible problem for women for all of recorded history."[286] But she believes women should use common sense. Just as they wouldn't drive to New York City and leave their keys on the hood of their car, they shouldn't get drunk at fraternity parties and then go upstairs to a boy's room if they're not interested in sex. She makes comments such as, "I feel that sex is basically combat," and "You have to accept the fact that part of the sizzle of sex comes from the danger of sex. You can be overpowered."[287] All of this is a far cry from saying women *want* to be raped.

The women's movement's response to Paglia is an excellent barometer of just how closed the feminist world can be. Steinem's answer, when she was asked at a feminist gathering about Paglia, has become almost legendary: "We don't give a shit about what she thinks," she's reported to have said from the podium.[288]

Yet these people insist on maintaining the fiction that "feminists don't all think alike." Maybe so, but you can be a woman running for elected office who's pro-choice and in favour of tougher rape laws, yet still be dismissed as a "female impersonator" by Steinem because you're a Republican.[289]

You can be a novelist who writes an opinion piece for *The Washington Post* about how feminism has alienated large numbers of ordinary women and have Faludi respond in a magazine interview: "Who is she to be commenting on feminism?" while Steinem calls you "a water bug on the surface of life."[290]

You can be Sommers, who—after taping an interview about her book with CBS TV's Connie Chung—learned that Steinem had contacted Chung personally in an attempt to get the show cancelled.[291]

Feminism is supposed to belong to all women, but she who criticizes it had better have a thick skin. Not only might she be publicly reprimanded by Big Sister feminists, half the people she thought were her friends might stop talking to her, as well.

In Betty Friedan's words, 23-year-old Katie Roiphe "was virtually crucified for her [book's] attack on the excessive focus on date rape among college feminists."[292] In *Newsweek*, women's studies professor Gail Dines called Roiphe a "traitor" who was reinforcing the "white-male patriarchy."[293] Roiphe was subjected to this ugliness even though her book decries feminist intolerance. In the introduction, she writes:

> At Harvard, and later at graduate school in English literature at Princeton, I was surprised at how many things there were not to say, at the arguments and assertions that could not be made, lines that could not be crossed, taboos that could not be broken. The feminists around me had created their own rigid orthodoxy. You couldn't question the existence of a rape crisis, you couldn't suggest that the fascination with sexual harassment had to do with more than sexual harassment, you couldn't say that Alice Walker was just a bad writer, and the list of couldn'ts went on and on.

She continues: "Everything was cut and dried. It was feminists against the backlash, us against them, and increasingly I was 'them.'"[294]

Amy Friedman was born and raised in Ohio but now lives near Kingston, Ontario. As a college freshman in 1972, she was one of the first seven women to be assigned to what had previously been an all-male dormitory at Columbia University. She campaigned for the Equal Rights Amendment, participated in the women's health movement, learned car repair, and lost a job when she refused to sleep with her boss. In the late 1980s, she began writing a column for Kingston's *Whig-Standard* newspaper.

Alarmed by what appeared to be a growing victim mentality within the women's movement, she started asking questions about the direction things were taking—and found herself vilified by local feminists.

Her book, *Nothing Sacred: A Conversation with Feminism*, describes how merely expressing doubt in a public forum prompted other women to attempt to silence her. She reports that, after the appearance of a column in which she implored men and women to try to listen to one another, her supervisor at the community college where she was teaching received a telephone call from a feminist history professor who urged the college's women's studies department to demand a public apology.

On another occasion, when she wrote about being raped years earlier on a subway platform in New York City— and suggested that life goes on—Friedman was informed by other feminists that she'd dealt with her assault in "too white and too middle class" a way. While feminism used to insist that a woman's personal experience was important and legitimate, Friedman's view of the incident, her manner of coming to terms with the associated trauma, was callously dismissed on obscure political grounds.

She describes one such conversation she had around this time:

> [with] a woman on the verge of graduation from Queen's School of Law with a job secured in a Toronto law firm at a starting salary well above the average middle-income family's, a white woman in her thirties, an intelligent, well-educated, sophisticated, lovely woman, [who] talked to me about her life, her experiences, the changes she had gone through in Law School. She called herself oppressed.

When Friedman gently challenged the woman's use of such an adjective, she became hostile. Says Friedman:

I suddenly perceived something that I began to think of as the Feminist Forehand Smash. It consisted of this: I am female and I am telling you my feelings, so you must be still and listen to me.

And that seemed simply another version of the male power gambit: I am male and I can overpower you and so you must be still and listen. And if you don't...Feeling was substituted for force, but it worked the same way. This woman's feelings, obviously to her, demanded my silence...

Friedman says she is now considered "a threat, an enemy, a member of the backlash brigade, an anti-feminist." She knows, from first-hand experience, that genuine diversity of opinion isn't encouraged on either side of the Canada-U.S. border. In her words, some feminists "had given themselves the right, indeed the privilege and responsibility of pointing out just who was good and who was bad, who was the enemy and who was friend."[295]

In November 1990, journalist Danielle Crittenden delivered a speech to a Women in the Media conference in Toronto that discussed the relationship between women's issues and responsible journalism. She noted:

We are all aware that there has come to be a "political line" on women. True, this line fluctuates enormously. At one moment it is heresy to suggest that women do not yearn to pick up briefcases and emulate the career patterns of men; at another, it is heresy to suggest they do. But at any given moment there is a line: Depart from it, if you're a man, and it makes you a sexist; if you are a woman, a traitor.

Crittenden said the pressure she has felt to adopt a particular slant while writing about women's issues has not come from sexist male editors but from other female journalists. It would be a tragedy, she says, if women "fall into the trap of sternly enforcing new stereotypes upon them-selves" in the name of liberation.[296]

Margaret Atwood (the Canadian author whose novels include *The Handmaid's Tale* and *The Robber Bride*) has also written of this phenomenon. She says:

> For me, the dangers of dictatorship by ism are largely metaphorical: I don't have a job, so no one has the power to fire me. But for some members of what I now geriatrically refer to as the younger generation, things are otherwise. When younger women writers come to me, at parties or under cover of night, to whisper sto-ries about how they've been worked over—critically, professionally, or personally—by women in positions of power, because they haven't toed some stylistic or ideo-logical line or other, I deduct the mandatory fifteen points for writerly paranoia. Then I get mad...
>
> If the women's movement is not an open door but a closed book, reserved for some right-thinking elite, then I've been misled. Are we being told yet once again that there are certain "right" ways of being a woman writer, and that all other ways are wrong?
>
> Sorry, but that's where I came in. Women of my generation were told not to fly or run, only to hobble, with our high heels and our pantygirdles on. We were told endlessly: *thou shalt not*. We don't need to hear it again, and especially not from women. [original italics, ellipsis inserted][297]

Atwood reports that she, too, has felt pressured by femi-nists who'd like her to say she encountered sexism when dealing with male publishers, particularly as a beginning writer. But she insists this wasn't the case, and that she's not about to rewrite history just because other feminists claim the publishing industry is stacked against them.

Often, much of what you're not supposed to say as a

feminist writer is closely connected to issues of race. It's important to be aware of—and sensitive to—the concerns of racial minorities. But there's a difference between treating other people with respect and agreeing with everything they say. Unlike *Ms.* magazine, which declares on its 1995 subscription inserts that "anyone who has experienced something is more expert in it than the experts," I don't believe that direct experience automatically trumps everything else. We shouldn't be silenced by people who imply that skin colour dictates who should, and should not, be heard.

One of my earliest newspaper columns about the women's movement dealt with the racial politics associated with Toronto's 1991 International Women's Day (IWD) march. When the piece appeared in *The Globe and Mail*, a friend who's a veteran of the feminist trenches called to say: "I agree with you, but I think it's a good thing your number isn't listed in the phone book."

In that piece, I had expressed my uneasiness over the march's primary slogan: "Women say: Stop the racist war from Oka to the Gulf. Make the links." (The Oka Crisis took place near Montreal in 1990 when a small town attempted to extend its golf course onto land that local aboriginals claimed as their own. The town sent in the police to ensure that work could begin only to encounter armed resistance on the part of the aboriginals. The standoff lasted 78 days.) I wrote that it was overly simplistic to reduce either Oka or the Gulf War to pure racial terms. I also took issue with two of the march's three policy statements.

The first called for self-determination for aboriginal people, Palestinians, and black South Africans. The second opposed racism generally. I said that while these were worthy causes, they shouldn't be dominating a women's event. To borrow an example from Denfeld, this is the equivalent of allowing gay issues to dominate a march organized by the National Association for the Advancement of Colored People. Some African-Americans may be gay, but most aren't. A black organization that doesn't concentrate on issues common to most members of the community risks becoming irrelevant to the very group of people it's supposed to be serving.[298]

Shortly afterward, the paper published a rebuttal written by the chair of the Coalition of Visible Minority Women as well as a representative of the National Action Committee on the Status of Women. Read one passage:

> Racism is a priority for the women's movement in Canada today. It is appalling that Ms. Laframboise calls a day devoted to racism "an opportunity for solidarity lost and squandered." It is frightening that she holds a degree in women's studies. Under the banner of feminism, Ms. Laframboise sets out to maintain that celebrations in Toronto are "not relevant to most women."

The message was unmistakable: dare to disagree and you'll be considered "appalling" and "frightening."[299]

For the past several years, I haven't belonged to any women's groups precisely because I don't need the hassle of dealing with people who are likely to express hostility to what I write each week. The women's movement tries to keep people on a short leash and I'm not willing to play good puppy dog.

Because my social and professional life doesn't depend on what other feminists think of me, I'm relatively immune to the feminist office politics that end up consuming so much time and energy. While I can't think of a single friend (male or female) who isn't a feminist, when we have our differences, we agree to disagree rather than behaving like children in a schoolyard who chant: "I'm a feminist and you're not." Many women aren't so lucky. If they want to help out at a battered women's shelter or a rape crisis line they run a high risk of getting caught up in interminable political skirmishes.

It's no exaggeration to say that, in Toronto, women-of-colour issues are currently wrestling with violence for first place on the feminist agenda. I left the last pro-choice I attended in disgust when someone took the megaphone and started going on about a supposedly racist Royal Ontario Museum exhibit. What she was talking about had no connection to reproductive rights. It had no connection to the political party outside whose offices we were demonstrating. It was, instead, an example of how contemporary feminists insist that "all issues are women's issues." According to this view, there is only one 'correct' opinion in each case.[300]

Any woman who wants to call herself a feminist soon senses that she must not only bring her views into line on a whole range of immediately recognizable women's concerns, she's also expected to hold uniform ideas about gays and lesbians, racial issues, the disabled, goddess worship, the environment, the Gulf War, and the exhibit running over at the museum.

The theory is that if all the people associated with each of these different constituencies joined together in a united political front of right-thinking individuals, paradise on earth would be assured. But the reality is that the longer the list of predetermined opinions grows, the less likely it is that any one person can agree with it. The average Jane Doe might be comfortable aligning herself with a movement that stands for the first three points, but she might have doubts (some of them serious) about the next four. So she drifts away. When the united front fails to materialize, exhausted activists blame the patriarchy, capitalism, or public apathy.

In February 1995, a letter to the editor appeared in a Canadian newspaper outlining one woman's disillusionment with the women's movement in general, and the National Action Committee on the Status of Women (NAC) in particular. It read, in part:

> I am a feminist, in the sense that I believe women should have equal opportunity and should be free from all threat of discrimination and violence. But I didn't

measure up to NAC's politically correct standards because:

• I held a management position in my job. A NAC leader once told me I was "part of the problem" for women in the workplace and that my own problems as a woman manager were "of no consequence."

• I was white, middle-class, able-bodied and heterosexual. I stopped attending International Women's Day events because I got tired of being made to feel guilty for the supposed sins of my peers.

• I used new reproductive technologies to treat my infertility. NAC has viewed these new technologies as exploitation of women by the male-dominated medical-pharmaceutical complex. They have also tried to exclude the major stakeholders in the debate (infertile women and their partners).

• I stayed at home with my child. The NAC family-policy committee was sure that my baby would be better off in day care, that I was turning back the clock on women's gains.[301]

In my view, this woman is correct when she says that International Women's Day (IWD) events have been as much about guilt as anything else in recent years. As she isn't the only one who has been voting with her feet. During the 1990s, the annual IWD march has attracted 2,500 or fewer participants annually, down considerably from 5,000 to 8,000 in the 1980s. (By comparison, Toronto's annual Lesbian and Gay Pride Day parade draws crowds ranging from 25,000 to 500,000.)[302] This decline in participation has corresponded to an increasing emphasis on race. Below is a list of official Women's Day slogans:

• 1986: Women say no to racism from Toronto to South Africa

• 1987: Fighting racism and sexism together (notice which comes first)
• 1988: Women united to fight racism, sexism and economic inequality
• 1991: Stop the racist war from Oka to the Gulf
• 1992: 500 Years of resistance—recovery from discovery (a reference to the native perspective on the Columbus quincentennial)

In 1993 the official slogan, "No time to stop, our struggle must continue," was accompanied by four demands. Three of the four mentioned racial issues. Only 2,000 people participated in the 1994 Women's Day march. The media reported that one of the organizers called it an historic year because, "for the first time in Toronto, the annual celebration was organized by women of color."[303]

Not quite. As far back as 1986, the Canadian feminist newspaper *Broadside* was reporting that black feminists had had significant input into Toronto's IWD events that year. According to the paper, a group of black women had expressed dissatisfaction with "the decision-making process" employed by the IWD organizers:

> The result of the Black Women's Collective statement was that direction was taken from the leadership of Black women in every aspect of organizing the day: from the rally, to the order of contingents in the march, to the march route, to the topics at the fair workshops, to the entertainment of the day, to the kind of music that was heard at the dance.[304]

Although the Canadian women's movement is frequently accused of having ignored non-white issues, a representative of the Committee Against the Deportation of Jamaican Women addressed the first Toronto IWD rally in 1978. (Her speech resulted in a unanimous demand that deportation orders for domestic workers be rescinded.)[305]

The 1979 IWD march sent a telegram of solidarity to Iranian women protesting attacks on female civil liberties following Ayatollah Khomeini's rise to power.[306]

In 1985, the keynote speaker was African-American activist Angela Davis.[307] In 1990, a young woman named Sophia Cook was invited to be a guest speaker—apparently because she is black and had been shot by a white policeman while a passenger in a stolen car. That same year, the fact that an advertised IWD party turned out to be an aggressively black-music event prompted complaints.[308]

And in 1992, aboriginal women's insistence that alcohol was a tool of white oppression deprived the march of its biggest fundraiser when the post-demonstration dance was designated alcohol-free.[309]

When one combines this list with the IWD slogans appearing above, it becomes evident that race has received rather a lot of attention—especially considering that Statistics Canada tells us that non-whites represent only 10 percent of the overall population. (Admittedly, this figure rises to at least twice that in downtown Toronto and Vancouver.)

It's my contention that IWD attendance remained high in the short term because many of us didn't mind emphasizing race for a while. But we've grown tired of being told not only that we oppress our sisters, but that we haven't shown any willingness to share power or to acknowledge racial concerns. The history of this particular event tells a different story.

In June 1993, 35-year-old Sunera Thobani, a graduate student who'd been living in Canada for just four years, wrote a newspaper opinion column for *The Toronto Star* in which she claimed the Canadian women's movement had benefited only a minority of women. Feminism, so the argument goes, has been dominated by white, middle class women who have selfishly promoted their own agenda while ignoring the concerns of everyone else.[310]

This is absolute nonsense. During the past two decades, the central feminist issue in Canada has been access to abortion. This battle has been fought on the streets and in the courts. Feminists picketed and demonstrated. We organized fundraising events and circulated petitions. If the women's movement had merely been addressing middle class concerns this would never have happened. As we pro-choicers have been fond of telling politicians (and anyone else who'd listen), middle class women have always been able to arrange safe abortions. They've had the money and the connections to secure one quietly and locally, or to travel elsewhere. Abortion access became a rallying point because the lives of less privileged women were at risk.

White, middle class feminists poured their time, energy, and money into this struggle precisely because they recognized a social inequity and were determined to do something about it.

A similar argument can be made with respect to affordable child care, another feminist mainstay. Women who are in a position to hire nannies need this far less than do other groups. Ditto for battered women's shelters, since women with money have more options when it comes to leaving violent situations.

Thobani's article suggested that different groups of Canadian women had always been at each other's throats rather than genuinely supportive of one other. Even more disturbing was her insistence on narrowing matters down to an either/or scenario: "Either the women's movement will forge ahead *under the leadership* of the women most marginalized in society" (my italics), she wrote, or it would be seen to be slamming the door on them.

Translation: minority women would consider themselves badly treated if control of the women's movement wasn't handed over to them. She went on to say that disadvantaged women "understand our society *better* than those who live in the four walls of their relative privilege" (my italics). Translation: circumstances don't provide each of us with different perspectives, they provide minority women with a superior worldview.

Thobani wasn't talking about a mutually respectful working relationship. She was saying that the leadership of feminist organizations should be decided on the basis of skin colour. Three days after this piece appeared in the country's largest daily, she became the first woman-of-colour president of NAC—Canada's biggest and most influential feminist organization—by acclamation.

Racial politics had already left their mark on NAC before Thobani stepped into that role. A year earlier, the organization had issued an ultimatum to the Canadian Panel on Violence Against Women. Although the project was two-thirds complete by then, NAC suddenly declared that three more women-of-colour panelists should be added immediately.

Two of the people already on the nine-member panel were visible minorities. This translates to 22 percent—hardly a glaring case of under-representation. But this wasn't good enough for NAC, whose proposal would have bumped non-white representation to 42 percent.

NAC threatened to withdraw its support and do everything in its power to discredit the panel's findings if its demands weren't met.[311] The composition of the violence panel remained the same, and NAC publicly dissociated itself from it shortly afterward.[312]

In mid 1994, Canadian women were given another indication of where NAC's priorities lay when a woman named Maureen Kempston Darkes became the new president of General Motors of Canada, the country's largest company. Many of us considered this an important achievement, a wonderful symbol of how women are altering the face of the corporate world. We thought it especially encouraging that this had occurred in such a male-dominated industry.

But when a radio station telephoned NAC for its response to this historic occasion, the organization's spokesperson responded with the following: "She's white, isn't she? Skin colour brings privileges."[313]

Perhaps the most disturbing example of racial infighting in the Canadian women's movement involves June
Callwood. This journalist and social activist holds 14 honorary degrees and has written more than two dozen books.
Over the years, she either founded or helped start 24 organizations, including a home for teenaged mothers, an
AIDS hospice, and the Canadian Civil Liberties Association.[314]

In 1974, Callwood cofounded Nellie's, a hostel that provides services to battered women, ex-prostitutes, and psychiatric patients. In the early 1980s, a black woman named
Joan Johnson was given refuge at the hostel along with
her three children for about a year while she sorted out
immigration difficulties. Callwood used her connections to
help Johnson secure a permit to remain in the country legally. Johnson eventually became a member of the hostel's
collective board of directors, along with a number of other
women of colour. They formed their own caucus and came
to believe that internal policy disputes over how to respond to drug addicts and other issues were connected to
race. One journalist described matters this way:

> The situation polarized, and it wasn't pretty. It polar-
> ized around power, race, sexual preference, ideologies,
> personalities, written texts, spoken words, even body
> language—not all at once, but with the mounting force
> of implosion. The board split into three main factions:
> women with a business-as-usual approach; women of
> colour trying to show the workings of systemic racism
> at Nellie's; and their sympathizers. The staff split. When
> the Women of Colour Caucus—mostly heterosexual—
> said they would bring racism before the board, they
> were told by white women on staff: "Then we'll say
> you're homophobic."[315]

In late 1991, Johnson delivered an impassioned statement at a Nellie's board meeting in which she accused the
hostel and its staff of widespread racism. Callwood, never

147

one to mince words, responded by asking her, in essence, "Are you the same woman we helped for over a year?" This was then taken by the Women of Colour Caucus as proof that Callwood herself was a racist. She was asked to apologize and agreed to do so at the next meeting she attended because she'd violated confidentiality guidelines by revealing that Johnson had been a former client.

But Callwood was still indignant about the racism accusations and it showed. Her half-hearted apology led to more accusations of racism. She left the meeting and, within days, the Women of Colour Caucus had sent out flyers to other groups in the city seeking their support. Reports another journalist:

> The hostel collective went into disarray. Chandler, the facilitator, insisted that white members write letters of apology to the women of colour for Callwood's behaviour. The letters were deemed insufficient, and they were asked to write again. And again.[316]

In March, representatives of an unrelated women-of-colour organization attended the Nellie's board meeting with a list of ten demands, one of which was that the board request Callwood's resignation and bar her from the premises. The request was repeated later in the month. On May 1, Callwood resigned voluntarily. She says, "The accusation that I am a racist was common currency at subsequent [to February] board meetings. It also appears in letters and proclamations widely distributed by the women of color."[317]

When *Toronto Life* magazine published an article sympathetic to Callwood, its offices were picketed by protesters who insisted that the article, too, constituted a racist attack.[318] For someone like Callwood, now 70, who has devoted her life's energy to propelling Canadian society in the direction of more enlightened views on a range of social issues, these events have been painful.

"Except for deaths in my family," she says, "this is the worst thing that has ever happened to me."[319] Her sterling reputation has been besmirched by feminists who claim to be fighting racism, who say they want to improve the world, but who instead appear to have used such accusations as weapons in an old-fashioned power struggle.

In the '90s, charges of racism are just another way to stifle criticism and dissent in the manner that journalist Amy Friedman described earlier: she was expected to be silent in the face of another woman's feelings that she is oppressed. Callwood's sin was that she refused to remain silent when accusations she considered unfounded were made against the hostel and its staff.

Many Toronto feminists have drawn an obvious conclusion: disagree with what women of colour are saying and you, too, risk being branded a racist. No matter how many hours you've poured into good causes, your good name may be slandered on the flimsiest of grounds. I'm not the first person to observe that some of the feminists at Nellie's seemed more interested in race politics than in the health of the hostel itself—or the well-being of the women it exists to serve.

This is no isolated tale. Similar difficulties have reduced New York City's Women's Action Committee to a shadow of its former self after some members accused others of being homophobic because they questioned the amount of time and energy being devoted to lesbian concerns. In Denfeld's words:

[T]heir paralyzing "antihierarchical" stance, combined with...allowing extremist factions to silence debate, saw the organization's meetings degenerate into vicious insider attacks and ineffectiveness, and their membership plummeted from a claimed eighteen hundred members to a handful of women.[320]

The May/June 1995 issue of *Ms.* included articles written by three young feminists, one of whom was a 25-year-old Af-

149

rican American graduate student in women's studies named Tiya Miles. She was part of a group that began a campus feminist publication in 1991, called *The Rag*, at Atlanta's Emory University. Two years later, it had collapsed due to internal squabbling. Writes Miles:

> Class conflicts piggybacked racial discord. In other meetings that semester, a black woman who had taken a year off to work so she could pay for the rest of her education, expressed resentment at what she viewed as the insensitivity of wealthy white women. A few *Rag* parents had donated hundreds of dollars to the magazine, and one staff member had offered her family's summer house as a retreat site. The black woman, with no funds or house to offer, felt that her worth and strength as a group member were diminished by those women's economic power.[321]

Christina Hoff Sommers' book describes parallel problems at the US National Women's Studies Association. She describes its 1992 conference held in Austin, Texas, as opening with a speaker who recounted:

> a brief history of the "narratives of pain" within the NWSA. She reported that ten years ago, the organization "almost came apart over outcries by our lesbian sisters that we had failed adequately to listen to their many voices." Five years ago, sisters in the Jewish caucus had wept at their own "sense of invisibility." Three years later the Disability caucus threatened to quit, and the following year the women of color walked out.

Sommers continues:

> At past conferences, oppressed women had accused other women of oppressing them. Participants met in groups defined by their grievances and healing needs: Jewish women, Jewish lesbians, Asian-American women,

African-American women, old women, disabled women, fat women, women whose sexuality is in transition. None of the groups proved stable. The fat group polarized into gay and straight factions, and the Jewish women discovered they were deeply divided: some accepted being Jewish; others were seeking to recover from it.

Yet another conference speaker told the 500 gathered feminists about how her lesbian support group had split into black and white factions, which had then splintered further. In this woman's words: "Those of us in the group who had white lovers were immediately targeted...It turned into a horrible mess...I ended up leaving that group for self-protection."[322]

Is it any wonder that Denfeld calls the women's movement a "minefield," and that Paglia says feminism should get its own house in order before making prescriptions for the rest of society?[323]

Daphne Patai and Noretta Koertge are the authors of *Professing Feminism: Cautionary Tales from the Strange World of Women's Studies.* As avowed feminists and women's studies professors, they say they've gone public with their concerns about what's taking place in women's studies departments (there are currently about 600 in the US), partly because they provide a sneak preview of what the world might look like if it were run by feminists.

The women quoted in that book frequently requested anonymity out of fear of repercussions in their professional lives. One passage from the prologue reads:

Again and again, women told us that they had long wanted to discuss their concerns but had felt isolated and hesitant to express opinions they knew could be dismissed as the experience of one disgruntled woman unable to thrive under the new feminist regime. Many of the women who were willing to talk with us were pained or distressed. No enemies of feminism lurked

151

among them. Instead, we found sincere and thoughtful individuals, providing accounts of troubling experiences and disappointed hopes.[324]

The women interviewed reported the same kinds of political infighting, preoccupation with 'feelings,' and intolerance discussed above. One talked about attending a meeting where a black woman at the podium declared that she wasn't going to allow lighter-skinned black women to get away with denying their 'light-skin privilege.'

Another told of attending the screening of a video about sexism and MTV at a campus women's centre. Viewers were informed beforehand that, if any of them wanted to watch the video in a women-only environment, they could report to a different room. They were advised that counsellors would be standing by afterward to assist those who'd been made 'uncomfortable' by what they'd just seen. Rather than a serious intellectual debate, what followed was a discussion about how people *felt* about the video.[325]

A number of the women Patai and Koertge interviewed have been strong supporters of women's studies. They themselves have been instrumental in founding departments. But some have transferred back into mainstream academe, and others are on the verge of doing so. Still others have faced criticism from their own students for emphasizing scholarship above militancy.[326] All of this is unfortunate, because it leaves the field open to feminists who seem to have forgotten that students are paying good money for an *academic* education—not political indoctrination.

Patai and Koertge report on a women's studies professor whose idea of encouraging tolerance is to say the following to her students:

Personally, I can't imagine why any woman would want to have a relationship with a man, but since some do, we have to try to respect them.

Another professor informed fellow feminists on an Internet women's studies mailing list that she sees nothing wrong with disclosing her personal problems in class:

> I managed to get a few older students to give some personal examples. I ended with telling them about how I had had to come to terms with an excruciatingly painful past (explicitly identifying the problem as incest), and how until I could do that I had no future, only an endless repetition of old patterns. And now there is joy and hope and boundless energy.
> This was the third class meeting (one night a week). They all sat so still, with amazement and wonder on their faces. Afterward an older student thanked me for making myself so vulnerable. I told her I didn't feel vulnerable as I spoke. I felt loved.[327]

In late 1993, in a cover story for *Mother Jones* magazine, Karen Lehrman expressed similar concerns. While being careful to say that the women's studies classes she'd sat in on had varied widely, she reported that some professors and texts seemed to be "celebrating subjectivity over objectivity, feelings over facts, instinct over logic." In her words:

> Terms, like sexism, racism, and homophobia have bloated beyond all recognition, and the more politicized the campus, the more frequently they're thrown around. I heard both professors and students call Berkeley's women's studies department homophobic and racist, despite the fact that courses dealing with homosexuality and multiculturalism fill the catalog and quite a number of women of color and lesbians are affiliated with the department.[328]

In Lehrman's estimation, many of these courses seemed to be turning students into 'Angry Young Women.' She says that after attending a number of them in succession, she

153

found herself noticing, quite involuntarily, that "the sign on the women's bathroom door in the University of Iowa's library was smaller than the one on the men's room door."

She also noted that while a great deal of lip-service was paid to the notion of respecting 'diversity,' this principle didn't appear to apply to political opinions. (A survey by the Association of American Colleges found that 30 percent of students taking women's studies courses said they're uneasy about offering dissenting opinions. Only 14 percent of non-women's studies students said so.) She described many of the students she spoke to as "quite bright," but said they "seemed to have learned to think critically through only one lens."[329]

Susan Faludi responded to Lehrman's article with a lengthy letter to the editor that suggested Lehrman was afraid to question authority. Pauline Bart, a feminist sociology professor known for her research on rape, included these comments in her own letter to the editor:

> My best guess about Lehrman is that she is exploiting the market that provides instant stardom for women criticizing feminist endeavors. Move over Camille Paglia and Katie Roiphe!

For her part, history professor Elizabeth Fox-Genovese wrote:

> I finished Karen Lehrman's article with a sigh of recognition: This is, indeed, the world of women's studies that I have come to know reasonably well during the past decade. And knowing the world, I hate to think of the response the article is sure to provoke. These are not stories that we tell in public...So the rage of insiders who will dismiss her as a traitor or, worse, an antifeminist is predictable.[330]

Lehrman's observation that women's studies students are being taught to think critically through one lens only is vital. When people ask me why my opinions aren't closer to those of other feminists, particularly ones who also hold degrees in women's studies, my response is two-pronged.

First, I (like many of the women who are now express-ing their reservations and concerns) used to buy into a lot of these ideas. When I was a women's studies student, I was a true believer. I didn't attend such classes for five years of my life in order to spy on the enemy. Rather, I knew that I most definitely was a feminist, I was in my early twenties, and a lot of this stuff sounded perfectly okay back then. I remember having conversations with other women at the time who questioned my concentration on women's issues, and I remember thinking smugly that they just didn't 'get it.'

Second, I took the tools my university education gave me—such as critical thinking skills—and applied them. My ideas about the world kept evolving. I didn't chain my-self to one window sill and declare that particular view to be the only reality. As Patai and Koertge point out:

> Religious fanatics are adept at thinking and speaking critically about secular society. They are not so inclined to turn their scrutiny on themselves. The skill of Women's Studies students at...ferreting out the hand of the devil patriarchy in every sin and crime of society are not an exhibition of critical thinking at a very significant level. The fact that students have abandoned received views (and have some good reasons for doing so) is no indication that they have not, at the same time, uncriti-cally locked themselves into another framework, which is at least as deeply flawed.[331]

A growing number of women familiar with feminism— as it is practised in the real world as well as how it is be-ing taught in women's studies courses—are deeply trou-bled by what we see. We see a movement marked by extrem-ism and arrogance, a movement that embraces fanatical per-sonalities rather than distancing itself from them. We see a movement that encourages anti-male bigotry rather than condemning it. That has responded dogmatically to the controversies surrounding repressed and recovered memories, Satanic ritual abuse, and multiple personality disorder. That's prepared to overlook troubling mental health care practices in the interests of advancing the political thesis that child sexual abuse is widespread.

We see a movement that protests sexist myths and double standards that harm women while at the same time promoting double standards that malign men. We see leaders who think they're entitled to decide whether or not other women are feminists. We see attempts to silence criticism and dissent by calling people right-wingers, traitors, racists, and homophobes. We see a women's movement that is splintering and fracturing according to absurd group identities, that is paying so much attention to often imaginary slights that the positive aspects of the movement are being seriously undermined.

In short, feminism in the 1990s is a mess.

Part 2:
Flinging Open New Windows

No feminist whose concern for women stems from a concern for justice in general can ever legitimately allow her
only interest to be the advantage of women.[332]
Janet Radcliffe Richards

5 - Enter: The Men's Movement

It should come as no surprise that a women's movement
that's so ill-mannered toward its own members has responded less than graciously to the emerging men's movement. In 1992, twenty-one feminists—from American novelist Ursula Le Guin to Zsuzsanna Budapest (who advocates solving career problems by casting spells)—contributed
essays to a collection titled *Women Respond to the Men's
Movement*. The editor of this project was Kay Leigh Hagan,
whose 1991 *Ms.* article advised feminists who live with men
to get a room with a door that locks. (Evidently, none of
these contributors felt the need to distance themselves
from Hagan's extremism.)

The book's preface is written by Gloria Steinem, thus
signalling that the opinions contained within its pages are
considered more or less acceptable in mainstream feminist
circles. Steinem doesn't declare any of *these* women to be
non-feminists. She doesn't dismiss any of *them* as "a water
bug on the surface of life."[333] Nor does she take the pre-
caution of saying that, while some of this commentary is a
little hyperbolic, the dialogue is valuable in its own right.

Without question, the collection is among the most dis-
heartening pieces of feminist literature I've read. Taken
as a whole, it is condescending, derisive, and arrogant in
tone. It is a display of feminine busybodyness at its worst.
Men are repeatedly condemned for thinking they're the

centre of the universe, yet these feminists personify this in reverse.

Writer after writer declares that a 'real' men's movement should be concerned not with whatever it chooses but with women's issues. In the words of bell hooks (who says it's unfortunate men didn't request "critical feedback about the direction of the men's movement" from women), it "should merely be a segment under the larger feminist movement."[334]

Let's think about this for a minute. Feminism has focused its attention on the ways in which oppressive gender stereotypes have harmed women. Early feminists didn't hold meetings in suburban homes to tell women the reason they were miserable was because they weren't being good enough mothers and housekeepers. They held meetings at which women concluded there was something wrong with the system, not with them. Why would a men's movement not behave similarly? Why shouldn't it decide that the traditional male role is the problem, rather than men themselves?

Steinem begins by devoting a full page of her five-page preface to listing female victimization—*aka* male misconduct—statistics. She tells us that one woman in four is sexually assaulted in her lifetime, that the "most dangerous place for a woman is not in the street but in her home," that "more than half of battering husbands also abuse their children," that 50 percent of women experience sexual harassment in the paid workplace, and that divorced men are awarded custody of their children "even when there is medical evidence" of child abuse.

She says women "are literally dying" for a men's movement, but that while they want to believe in "male change," they have "little reason to do so."[335]

Young male bodies showing up at city morgues five times more frequently than young female bodies make no impression on Steinem. That's the kind of statistic one would expect a fair-minded person writing about men's issues to be discussing, but she's adamant. People who consider her stats "male bashing," who think men get a bad deal are plain wrong. In her words, the notion that men are oppressed in our society is "no more (and no less) true than saying white Americans are oppressed by racism."[336]

Elsewhere in this collection, the writer Starhawk says the men's movement should:

> be clear about the difference between spiritual malaise and oppression. Oppression is what the slave suffers; malaise is what happens to the slave owners whose personalities are warped and whose essential humanity is necessarily undermined by their position.[337]

Jane Caputi and Gordene MacKenzie suggest a link between right-wing racists and "much of the activity going on under the rubric of the 'men's movement.'"

Rosemary Radford Ruether invites us to "imagine a parallel 'white people's movement' arising that would claim to solve racism primarily by seeing it as a problem of the wounded white psyche."

Elizabeth Dodson Gray scandalously contends that the failure on the part of men's activists to talk about male violence is "like focusing on the feelings of SS guards while the ovens of genocide burn a few feet away. It is like pondering the feelings of white people while black people are being lynched just over the hill."[338]

But this analogy is fundamentally flawed. Under apartheid in South Africa, the average black person died considerably younger and was far more likely to be homeless, imprisoned, or victimized by violence than a white person. Here in Canada, statistics tell us that aboriginals commit suicide at a higher rate than the rest of the population, that they have shorter life spans, and are more likely to die violently, be imprisoned, suffer from alcoholism, or end up on the street. We say this data demonstrates that they are *oppressed*. We look at these appalling statistics and insist society at large must be at least partially responsible—

and that we should respond with understanding, compassion, and support

In order for the racism analogy to work for feminists, it would have to be true that *women*—not men—were dying eight years sooner than their spouses. That young *females* were committing suicide at a rate five times greater than young males. That *women*—not men—were suffering more from alcoholism, violence, and homelessness. That *females* —not males—were 20 times more likely to end up in a prison cell.

Let's get a grip. A true male supremacist society would have ensured long ago that women outnumbered men in all the categories we've just examined. So let's cut the male supremacist nonsense, shall we? If it's okay for women to focus on difficulties unique to their gender, males are perfectly entitled to concentrate attention on the ways in which their own sex is being short-changed by the system.

Caught up in her feminist worldview, Steinem insists it's the business of women to decide which parts of the men's movement we "trust." In order to arrive at these decisions, she says we should ask ourselves whether men's groups make us "feel safer as women" and whether they are devoting time and money to "diminishing violence."[339] She alleges that men's groups support fathers' child custody rights even in the face of apparent sexual abuse, but fails to acknowledge that some women falsely accuse spouses of child abuse during bitter custody disputes, and deliberately poison their children's minds against their dads.

Hagan's introduction to the collection isn't much better. She says the thought of men organizing on their own behalf "is so absurd as to be amusing."[340]

Another writer, who tells us she's using an "ironic satirical character voice," invites us to do an exercise to get our "blood boiling." She then asks: "Is this some kind of joke about laxatives or something?" She wonders whether men are learning how "to stop worrying about the size of their dicks" in their wilderness retreats and then refers to them as "a bunch of boys playing games with the cultures of people they don't know how to live next door to."[341] (How do you suppose women would respond to a man who wondered whether they were learning to stop worrying about the size of their breasts at feminist events?)

Starhawk declares that "something is wrong with men, and the prospect of men getting together to fix it them- selves is a happy one." She then adds, "On the other hand, our history with men doesn't generate much trust that, left to themselves, they will actually get it right."[342] Al- though she says there are men she loves and respects, that doesn't stop her from characterizing the lot of them as inferior beings in need of repair.

Here's where I draw my own race analogy. In less tol- erant times, people would make comments such as: "You really have to meet Joe. You'd never know he's a Jew, he's not like the others." Or, they'd say: "Mary's such a sweet girl. You practically forget she's coloured." When people aren't prepared to recognize the humanity of an entire group, when they'll make exceptions on an individual ba- sis but still consider the group as a whole inferior, we call them racists.

How is this different from the way feminists talk about men? Exceptions are made for individual males, yet we say things about them as a group we'd never dream of say- ing about anyone else. Can you imagine the uproar if I wrote, in one of my newspaper columns, that while I love and respect the occasional Asian person living in my neighbourhood, I'm pleased they're getting together to 'fix' themselves? Can you imagine if I added insult to injury by saying: "But you know, I'm not certain they're capable of 'getting it right' if left to their own devices"? Yet this con- temptible bigotry toward men is the order of the day among feminists, journalists, and even among some men.

"We're in trouble; men are in trouble," says John McManiman, a counsellor who works with abusive men. His quote opened an article, a full newspaper page in length, that appeared in Canada's largest daily two days prior to the fifth anniversary of the Montreal Massacre.

Elsewhere in the piece, McManiman says: "It's a great thing that feminists are holding men accountable for their behavior."

Another male therapist is quoted as saying: "We're taught that if we're not violent, we're not men." Only then, two-thirds of the way into the article, does the feminist writer proffer this tepid disclaimer: "Yet most men don't act in obviously violent ways, most of the time."[343]

Let's return to my analogy. Can you imagine someone saying: "We're in trouble; Asians are in trouble. It's a good thing society is holding us accountable for our behaviour," when the problem wasn't the Asian community in general but Asian gang violence? These would be considered ridiculous statements. As one man indignantly responded, in a letter to the editor:

"We're in trouble; men are in trouble." Really? Which men? All men? Me included? Why? The article doesn't explain the quote...Vilifying an entire gender for the transgressions of some of its members is neither fair nor constructive.

Regarding the statement that men are taught to behave violently, another wrote:

the males in my family were taught to work out their adversary tendencies in a variety of sports. My uncles were champions in several disciplines and I had 37 amateur fights until my future wife decided not to go dancing on Saturday nights with anyone sporting one or two black eyes. In my family, we were taught to respect women. They were our mothers, our sisters and (often) our better halves.

On another occasion, a man wrote a letter to *The Globe and Mail* that took issue with a female columnist who had made sweeping generalizations about men and housework. It read, in part:

I myself have never done any of the following with any frequency: left underwear in the middle of the bedroom floor, washed dishes only when there were no clean ones left, dusted only when the mantle appeared to be sagging, chosen cleanest dirty socks as an alternative to doing laundry.

Leave me and men alone for a while, or at least castigate us in a more precise way. I am not a bad person really and neither are my male friends.[344]

When *The New York Times* reviewed Marilyn French's *The War Against Women* in 1992, the top half of the page was devoted to a discussion of another book. The headlines appearing above both reviews were part of the same thought. They read: "Women Have Always Hated Men...And With Good Reason."[345]

If these are the kind of headlines that a male supremacist society produces, I'd hate to read the headlines in a matriarchal world. Kind, decent, non-violent men don't deserve to be lumped together with troubled, abusive ones any more than mothers who love their children deserve to be lumped together with Susan Smith, who pushed her two little boys, strapped into car seats, into a lake.

The feminists in *Women Respond to the Men's Movement* aren't deterred by such logic, however. They make statements such as: "men's relationships with others are held in place by the abuse of power and control" and "men are hooked on a spectrum of control that extends from not listening to violence."

Another argues that men's involvement in parenting isn't necessarily a good thing, since men raised in a patriarchal society might simply be contaminating the nursery with their ingrained sexism.[346] Still another says:

how do I feel about the mythopoetic men's movement? I feel frightened, and angry, and critical, and amused. I think that anything which is so terrifically attractive to

165

white, middle-class heterosexual men...*is probably dangerous to women*. [my italics]

That this writer consumes paranoia with her breakfast cereal is evident in the very first lines of her article, in which she blames men even for her own confused thoughts:

> It says something about the ability of the patriarchy to confuse women's thinking that I, who can usually sit down at the computer and simply state what is on my mind about almost any topic, have been for the last hour forthing and backing and deleting lines and acting as a well-trained woman in that I cannot seem to find my voice.

A little further on, she insists that men are solely responsible for domestic violence, air and water pollution, and social program cuts.[347]

Someone else complains that women have been organizing around violence issues for 20 years and "the only visible response during that time is that the violence against women has increased to proportions that can only be seen as a holocaust!" She adds: "men are in denial about *most* women's terrifying reality: imprisoned in the cage of the patriarchal family, with rape and murder a constant threat, and no safe place to go to get away" (my italics).[348]

Where *do* these people get this stuff? Where does the venom and hostility come from? What has happened to their sense of perspective? Most women are not cowering in their homes worried about being murdered and raped every minute of the day. Violence against women, as serious as it is, is not a holocaust. Women and men both vote in the United States and Canada, which means they both bear some responsibility for social program cuts. They both drive cars, use electricity, and buy pre-packaged goods, all of which might contribute to environmental degradation.

Sophisticated political analysis isn't necessarily a strong point in this collection, either. Says Starhawk:

> If there is to be a men's movement I could trust, I want to know what it is going to do about war. Because, hey, guys, you could end it tomorrow, by simply refusing to fight in it...Why don't men rise up and refuse to go to war?[349]

Nice theory. But isn't this as unrealistic as saying that women should all snap their fingers and resolve never to worry about their weight, their wrinkles, or their grey hair again? Isn't this like saying that women could overthrow the fashion, make-up, diet, and cosmetic surgery indus-tries in a day if they simultaneously decided to stop pur-chasing these goods and services?

Why does feminism expect men to accomplish things women can't? There are actually more female than male voters.[350] If we were all united, we could dictate policy to our elected representatives, who'd have little choice but to do whatever it was we wanted, including putting an end to war. Unity amongst men is no easier to accomplish than unity amongst women. Nevertheless one feminist in this collection insists that men should be held "directly ac-countable for their continued support of patriarchy," while another demands that men have "take responsibility for the actions of their own gender."[351]

Many of these feminists see suspect motives every-where. One refers to Robert Bly, the author of the 1990 bestseller *Iron John: A Book About Men*, as a "rather blustery old man, an arrogant showman" who has decided he's had enough of feminism and "by golly, he's going to do something about it, maybe even make a living off the project."

A second says Bly's writing is "not about social change" but rather "a backlash—men clamoring to reestablish the moral authority of the patriarchs."[352] Elsewhere, co-authors quote a passage from Bly, who says that when a father and son spend time together, especially in tribal cultures,

167

"a substance almost like food passes from the older body to the younger" and that the "younger body learns at what frequency the masculine body vibrates."

Bly says this is similar to the way a fetus becomes attuned to "female frequencies" while in the womb. Although Bly—who is, after all, a poet—appears to me to be making use of a benign physical metaphor, one feminist declares: "This sounds frighteningly like psychic and/or physical incest and evinces both pedophilia and a characteristic patriarchal phenomenon: homophobic eroticism."[353]

Not every essay in this book suffers from such problems, but the majority do. Which means that, once again, we're compelled to acknowledge that much of mainstream feminist thought falls into the 'highly questionable' category. If these are feminism's finest minds, the movement is in deep trouble.

Men are also told by these writers that they're supposed to "shut up and listen" to women. Starhawk says, "It's not that we want you to be perpetually silent, it's just that we want you occasionally to listen first before you speak. Just listen." Laura S. Brown declares that men have "to learn how to truly listen to the tears of others."[354]

But what are women doing, here? There's very little listening taking place on our side of the table. Instead, we're busily telling men that they've got the incorrect analysis, that they're overlooking what's really important, that they're doing everything wrong. These feminists are calling men whiners. These women are ridiculing the first feeble attempts of a movement struggling to breathe air into its newborn lungs. Robert Bly's book may be flawed, but how does it compare with much early feminist writing? More than a quarter of a century later, this wave of the women's movement is still producing more heat than light.

Feminists like to talk about how unkind the mainstream media was to the early women's movement. We like to talk about how men sneered and condescended.[355] And what are we—who should know better—doing in our turn? Instead of behaving as we wish men had behaved toward us, we're sniping from the sidelines.

Women, as a group, have gone through an enormous consciousness-raising process. We've actively and publicly questioned the old female role, identifying the things that constrained and limited us. Men, as a group, have yet to re-examine the old male role in anything approaching the same manner. They've held no lively public discussions about what to keep and what to discard, about how this role continues to circumscribe men's options and behaviour. In the words of Wendy Dennis:

> although the nineties man has certainly become more feminized through feminism, he has never (unlike his female contemporaries; whose definition of themselves has been virtually reconstructed from the ground up) undergone a collective mind-altering process of deep internal reflection, metamorphosis and transformation of his own making.[356]

Not one of the nearly two dozen contributors to *Women Respond to the Men's Movement* is able to put aside her own concerns long enough to offer men a generous, no-strings-attached blessing. No one simply wishes men well as they embark on their own journey of self-discovery. No one says, "We hope the process is as rewarding for you as it has been for us."

Gloria Steinem doesn't. The editor, Kay Leigh Hagan, doesn't. Riane Eisler comes closest when she talks about "the straitjackets of the old roles" and says that "what the women's, men's, and partnership movements are all about is exploring new frontiers of what is possible for both women and men."[357]

As a feminist, I'm ashamed of this absence of goodwill. I'm ashamed of the pettiness, sarcasm, and self-absorption in this book. We, who have been insisting on our own right to be seen and heard, remain blind and deaf to the misery of others.

169

Nor is feminist disdain limited to this collection of essays. The January/February 1995 issue of *Ms.* magazine included the following smarmy paragraph under the headline *Like a Hole in the Head*:

> Students at the Boston University School of Law have formed the Men's Law Association. Its mission? To educate "the next generation of lawyers about the impact of antimale prejudices." The group says the areas of divorce law, domestic violence, and child custody are "laden with anti-male bias." The association believes itself to be the only one of its kind in the U.S. We can see why.

A few months later, the same magazine gloated: "In case you forgot, International Men's Day came and went. Looks like everyone else forgot too. All of five men showed up for the International Men's Day convention in Toronto on February 7."[358] Charming, huh?

In my opinion, if this particular phase of the men's movement had produced no more than two specific books, it would still have made an enormous contribution to gender scholarship. The first is Warren Farrell's *The Myth of Male Power: Why Men are the Disposable Sex*. The other, by British journalist David Thomas, is titled *Not Guilty: In Defence of the Modern Man*.

Warren Farrell was elected three times to the board of directors of the New York City chapter of the National Organization for Women. As a young man, he worked on feminist issues for a decade, attempting to be a translator of sorts between feminism and ordinary men, trying to explain the feminist perspective to males. He says his speaking engagements during this period were attended mostly by women, who gave him standing ovations, warmly asked how they could clone him, and invited him to speak elsewhere, thus assuring him a degree of financial stability.

But at some point, while reviewing tape recordings of workshops he'd been conducting with both genders, he became aware of a bias on his own part. He noticed that he hadn't been really listening to men. He writes, in the introduction:

> When women criticized men, I called it "insight," "assertiveness," "women's liberation," "independence," or "high self-esteem." When men criticized women, I called it "sexism," "male chauvinism," "defensiveness," "rationalizing," and "backlash." I did it politely—but the men got the point. Soon the men were no longer expressing their feelings. Then I criticized the men for not expressing their feelings!

Afterward, he says, he started listening more closely. He began responding as openly and receptively to what men said as to what women said, and became aware of perspectives that hadn't occurred to him before. When he started incorporating these new ideas into his speeches, he says his "standing ovations disintegrated" almost overnight. He writes:

> I would not be honest if I denied that this tempted me to return to being a spokesperson only for women's perspectives. I liked writing, speaking, and doing television shows. Now it seemed that all three were in jeopardy. I quickly discovered it took far more internal security to speak on behalf of men than to speak on behalf of women. Or, more accurately, to speak on behalf of both sexes rather than on behalf of only women.[359]

No book is perfect, and Farrell's attempts at pithiness sometimes sound inappropriately glib ("men who are retired or fired are soon expired").[360] But having long had an interest in gender issues, and considering myself an open-minded human being, I picked up his work at my local bookstore one day and spent the entire weekend saying to my husband, 'Listen to this" and "Now listen to this."

My husband and I have had the good fortune of developing intellectually and politically in similar directions at approximately the same time. We met in the peace movement, when we both had objections to the testing of U.S. cruise missiles over Canada's north, and have demonstrated for abortion access together. I used to share the insights of my women's studies classes with him: "This is what the lecturer talked about today. Doesn't that make so much sense?" He typically responded by thinking of other examples that served to prove the point. Several years later, as I read snippets of Farrell's book out loud, as my mind was being set on fire by a fascinating new perspective, he was telling me that much of it rang true, that Farrell was doing a good job of capturing the male experience.

When I recommend *The Myth of Male Power* to people, I stress that Farrell relies on tried-and-true feminist methods, particularly the hypothetical gender switch. Women protested that since men weren't taking an oath to 'obey' their wives during the traditional marriage ceremony, it was outrageous that women should be required to say they'd obey their husbands. We argued that since men didn't adopt their wives' last names, there was no good reason for women to continue doing so. We said it was unfair to call a woman who slept around a 'slut' when men were admired for similar behaviour.

Farrell does the same thing. He says it's unfair that men are told there's never any excuse for domestic violence, but women get to blame their violence on PMS. He says it's unfair that the male captain of the *Exxon Valdez* oil tanker was tried, convicted, and imprisoned for his part in the oil spill that wreaked environmental havoc in 1989, while a female air traffic controller who failed to perform her job properly and was directly responsible for the deaths of 34 human beings in 1991 was shielded from prosecution and publicity and provided with counselling.

He says it's unfair that while our society knows better than to make jokes about female suffering, it considers men who have lost their jobs fair game, despite evidence

172

that many men are profoundly traumatized by this experience (in the United States, unemployed males commit
suicide at twice the rate of employed ones). He points out
that our society doesn't have as many support services for
widowers as widows even though men are 10 times more
likely to commit suicide following the death of a spouse.[361]

For me, one of Farrell's most illuminating observations
concerns the idea of good and evil. In his words:

> Feminism suggested that God might be a "She" but not
> that the devil might also be a "she." Feminism articu-
> lated the shadow side of men and the light side of
> women. It neglected...to acknowledge that each sex has
> both sides *within* each individual. [original italics]

He also argues persuasively that society has historically
been organized in certain ways not to oppress women but
because these structures made sense. He suggests thinking of human development as falling into two categories:
"Stage I" and "Stage II". The first is concerned with survival.
The second is the kind of life we, who live in the industrialized world, have enjoyed since the end of World War II:

> In Stage I, most couples were role mates: the woman
> raised the children and the man raised the money. In
> Stage II, couples increasingly desired to be soul mates.
> Why? As couples met their survival needs, they "upped
> the ante" and redefined love.
>
> In Stage I, a woman called it "love" if she found a
> man who was a good provider and protector; he called
> it "love" if she was beautiful and could take care of a home
> and children. Love meant a division of labor which led
> to a division of female and male interests.[362]

According to this line of thought, it's precisely the standard of living we now take for granted (largely the result
of male blood, sweat, and tears) that freed vast numbers of
women to think about self-fulfilment, to start questioning

whether it was right to confine women to the home when many have talents that can be put to use in the public sphere.

Farrell says most men haven't gone through a similar period of self-assessment yet, that they're mostly still stuck in Stage I, and that this has caused problems all around:

> Many marriages consummated in Stage I, then, were suddenly held up to Stage II standards. They failed. Marriages failed not only because the standards were higher, but because the standards were also contradictory. For a Stage I woman, a lawyer was an ideal candidate for a husband. For a Stage II woman, the lawyer, often trained to argue more than to listen, was an ideal candidate for divorce. The very qualities that led to success at work often led to failure at home.

Wendy Dennis puts it a different way. She says:

> You've got to feel for men on this count. I certainly do. Basically, they were sitting around minding their own business when the world turned upside down on them; the women in their lives marched through a door, came out the other side unrecognizable and started barking orders and telling them to hurry and catch up. Women have been reading them the riot act, in one way or another, ever since.[363]

I used to justify taking women's studies, studying female history and literature, for example, by saying that the rest of history was men's history. I used to say that the male perspective permeated everything, that all I was trying to do was reclaim a small corner—in an overwhelmingly masculine garden—to grow a few feminine vines. In high school, I'd found the succession of male coming-of-age novels particularly tedious. But Farrell's view on such matters is compelling. He writes:

174

Women's studies questions the female role; nothing questions the male role. History books sell to boys the traditional male role of hero and performer. Each history book is 500 pages of advertisements for the performer role. Each lesson tells him, "If you perform, you will get love and respect; if you fail, you will be a nothing." To a boy, history is pressure to perform, not relief from that pressure. Feminism is relief from the pressure to be confined to only the traditional female role. To a boy, then, history is...the *opposite* of women's studies. [original italics][364]

Farrell also raises a formidable challenge to feminist orthodoxy by questioning one of our most sacred cows: the assertion that rape is a manifestation of male power, that it's not really about sex. Again and again, one encounters this feminist dogma. A booklet titled *Sexual Assault: Dispelling the Myths*, published by the Ontario government, says it's a "fact" that "studies on the profiles of rapists reveal that they are 'ordinary' and 'normal' men who sexually assault women in order to assert power and control over them."

In June 1995, a doctor who works for a Women's Health Centre in British Columbia declared in a letter to the editor of *The Globe and Mail*:

It's both welcome and refreshing to see sexual assault's most common myth so eloquently shattered. That rape is "purely and simply an act of violence and degradation" rather than a sexual act cannot be overemphasized...[this] article does far more than sell newspapers; it educates the public.[365]

If so, Farrell asks why American women aged 16-19 are 84 times more likely to be raped than are women over the age of 50.[366] When feminists first suggested that rape was about power, they were trying to account for the fact that frail, elderly women as well as young children are some-

175

times raped. Assaults against people in these two categories strike us as particularly vile, but statistically they're the exception—not the rule. Women in their teens, who come closest to meeting our society's ideal of what's sexually attractive, are at the highest risk of being raped. Why can't we admit that sex is also part of the rape equation? What purpose are we serving by refusing to acknowledge the complexity of these issues?

Farrell, as he has mentioned, isn't so popular with the women's movement any more. It's true that Camille Paglia gave *The Myth of Male Power* an enthusiastic review in the *Washington Post* in 1993,[367] but as I've already discussed, Paglia isn't considered a 'real' feminist.

In her preface to *Women Respond to the Men's Movement*, Steinem explicitly dismisses Farrell's ideas when she maintains that men aren't oppressed. In her 1991 *Backlash*, Susan Faludi tells us about Farrell's female housekeeper and secretary (would she be happier if he'd refused to hire them because they were women?), his leather jacket, his sports car, and his vanity plates before recounting the immense contribution he's made to the organized women's movement. She then says:

> But as feminism lost its media glitter, Farrell's enthusiasm seemed to fade, too. Perhaps the changes he said he had made in himself were superficial, little more than cosmetic touch-ups to enhance his stardom in the short-lived '70s liberation drama.

Faludi describes the people who have responded positively to Farrell's work as "antifeminist fans." She suggests, in language we've seen her use elsewhere, that he's simply trying "to reclaim center stage." What's remarkable is that she insists (minus any supporting evidence) on her own narrow-minded interpretation, even though she's aware he's paid a high price for his unpopular views among people whose opinions he once cared about. Indeed, Faludi's four-page account ends with this passage:

"I see now that the ideologues of the feminist movement don't want to listen," [Farrell] says, returning to
the subject of *Ms.*'s failure to acknowledge his [1986]
book. "Gloria Steinem didn't return my phone calls,
and she used to." He studies his glass some more, then
says: "It affected me a lot to see my popularity waning
among people who saw me as an idol. When Gloria
Steinem distanced from me, that hurt."[368]

The response to *The Myth of Male Power* in the mainstream media has been mostly hostile. In addition to my
own columns, *The Toronto Star* has mentioned his book
twice. One article, by a woman, ticks off the fact that men are
over-represented in dangerous occupations, are the only
sex forced to fight in wars, and that prostate cancer research receives less funding than breast cancer even though
these diseases kill a comparable number of people. She
then says, "*Excuse me? Is this relevant?*" (original italics).

If the genders were reversed, feminists would consider
these facts absolutely relevant. Why wouldn't they be?
The writer says that, in a workshop she attended in Ed-
monton, Farrell drew an analogy between the way men
are viewed in our society and the way "the Aryans began
to treat the Jews during World War II."

Personally, this analogy makes me queasy. When deciding how harshly to judge Farrell, let us merely keep in
mind that, in the course of this book, we've already seen:

- Jane Caputi and Diana E.H. Russell declare in a
  Ms. article that women's reality is denied in the
  same way that people "denied the reality of the
  Nazi Holocaust"[369]
- newspaper columnist Judy Steed assert that ritual abuse skeptics are "like Holocaust deniers"[370]
- Gloria Steinem compare Camille Paglia to Nazis
  who say "they're not anti-Semitic"[371]
- Naomi Wolf draw a parallel between anorexia sufferers and Holocaust victims in *The Beauty Myth*[372]

177

- Vicki Noble declare, in *Men Respond to the Women's Movement*, that current rates of violence against women amount to a holocaust[373]

While grudgingly admitting that "nobody has a monopoly on pain," it's clear this writer thinks Farrell has damaged rather than improved gender relations.

The other occasion in which Farrell got ink in *The Star* was a book review, written by the poet Tom Wayman. His opening paragraph captures the tone:

Throughout Warren Farrell's *The Myth of Male Power*, the author evidently imagines himself riding to the defence of the besieged male sex, with all guns blazing. He aims to shoot down the idea of men as oppressors of women...and he has rounded up all the statistical and anecdotal ammunition he can stuff into his bullet clips, bandoliers and saddle bags.

Wayman accuses Farrell of harbouring "rage at the women's movement." He accuses him of working "into the book a lot of the agenda of the U.S. right wing," and says that if the book "is representative of an intellectual backlash against feminism, women have nothing to fear from this direction."

Since we're on the subject of analogies, Wayman offers one of his own. After (in my view, mistakenly) accusing Farrell of "denigrating inequities to which women are subject," he says:

This gives *The Myth of Male Power* the feel of one of those anti-Semitic tracts where the author claims he doesn't hate Jews—merely wants to point out how Jews control not only world capitalism but world communism as well.[374]

These are strange times, when people who attempt to discuss how male misery is inadequately acknowledged are

178

compared to anti-Semites, while those who tar all men with the misogynous brush are considered enlightened and progressive.

In *Not Guilty: In Defence of the Modern Man*, which also appeared in 1993, David Thomas talks about how men themselves erect some of the biggest roadblocks to questioning the traditional male role—how it's a sign of weakness to admit they're struggling. He describes men who refuse to see a doctor about their medical ailments until they're struck down by serious illnesses. He talks about the inability of fathers and sons to express their love for one another, and the fear some men have of acknowledging old emotional wounds.

Thomas is also disturbed by a certain kind of 'feminist' male:

> Brought up with the traditional male stereotypes, they have at some point internalized the feminist critique of men. The result is an over-riding determination to prove that they are truly penitent, that they are more willing than any woman to criticize the wrongdoings of men...Male feminism has almost become a perverse badge of machismo. It's a bit like the anti-drug campaign that featured an addict saying, "Heroin—I can handle it," as he collapsed into the gutter. The new motto is, "Feminism—I can handle it."[375]

Thomas says the industrialized world's obsession with women conflicts dramatically with a lack of concern about men. While conducting research for his book he notes that, with "the zeal of the natural obsessive," he decided to count the number of entries appearing in *The New York Times* 1991 index under the subject headings "women" and "men." The grand total: Women: 679. Men: 104.

Similarly, in the London, UK, telephone book 114 listings appear under "Women," including organizations that address rape and sexual harassment. Under "Men," there are two listings, one of which is a hairdresser.

He, too, asks why—if men are doing so well—four British males commit suicide for every British female and men live significantly shorter lives than their spouses? "The fact is," says Thomas, "people are in pain. And right now, the ones who wear trousers and stand up to piss don't seem to count for much when it comes to being healed."[376]

Thomas admits that men continue to enjoy advantages women don't. He acknowledges that a man can walk into a drinking establishment and not worry about being ogled, and that he personally doesn't feel as vulnerable as women do while out alone at night. "But," he says, a man "lacks one vital freedom. He cannot be himself."

Men, he insists, are under constant pressure to conform to a definition of masculinity that feels utterly foreign to many of them, with clothing taboos being only the most visible manifestation of this state of affairs. He writes:

> A modern woman can, like my little daughters, play any number of roles in her everyday life. Her persona is as flexible as her wardrobe. But you do not have to venture far from the beaten path of masculinity before becoming trapped in the thickets of what society sees as effeminacy or perversion. Men have to keep any internal deviations from the straight and narrow locked up within their psyches. It is no surprise that so many men, unable to express themselves in normal circumstances, turn instead to deviancy and perversion. Countless broken lives, and careers cut short by scandal, testify to the damage that is done as a result.[377]

Like Farrell, Thomas sees both sex roles as offering pluses and minuses—not the 'men-all-plus, women-all minus' world implied by so many feminists. Stephanie (whose name used to be Keith prior to a sex-change operation) observes in an interview with Thomas that males now treat her more as an accessory to the man she's with than as an individual in her own right. She also admits that, in the professional world, life might be easier for men. But she also says:

> on an emotional level, life is much, much richer for a woman. Women can let down barriers and can get much closer to people. Men have to maintain barriers. As a man, you can't go and cry on a best friend's shoulder when things go wrong. The first thing he'd do is edge away if you touch him.[378]

Graham is another Thomas interviewee. Having worked in a nightclub dressed as a woman (apparently indistinguishable from the female waitresses), he says that while men condescend to women, they also treat them with greater overall kindness, consideration, and courtesy.

Thomas further quotes from a magazine article written by a female journalist who spent time undercover as a man:

> I felt cut off from other people, distanced from them simply by the assumptions they made about manhood. As a person I had a sense of pitching from further back, needing to be louder and tougher in order to be acknowledged.[379]

Similar views were expressed by BEEN THERE, in a letter that Ann Landers published in July 1994. The writer suggested there was a link between male violence and the fact that males are expected to keep so many of their emotions under such tight control. It read, in part:

> emotionally, men are at a disadvantage. It is socially acceptable for women to cry, scream, kiss or hug other women, act flaky or flirty and indulge in all sorts of behavior that would cost a man his job, marriage and reputation. "Real men" aren't permitted to do any of the above. A man who cries, screams or hugs a member

of the same sex is immediately suspect. If he is overly sympathetic, he is considered a wimp.[380]

Thomas also challenges the feminist assumption that disparities between the sexes are always the result of patriarchal oppression. He points out that a feminist-inspired insistence that female tennis players deserve to be paid as highly as male players has led to a situation in which the women's prize money at Wimbledon is "within 10 percent of the men's."

This may appear to a just state of affairs, but in reality it's profoundly unfair—to men. Male tennis players are more abundant, which means the winner must defeat more competitors and play more games in order to become a contender for the championship. Thomas observes that the 1991 men's Wimbledon championship was won by Michael Stich—after he'd played a total of 257 games that year. The women's was won by Steffi Graf, who claimed the prize money after playing only 128 games—half as many.

Feminists rightly protest when women are required to work longer hours to earn the same pay as men, but when the opposite is true they don't even notice. Thomas adds that the current state of affairs can't be justified by the revenues the sport generates, since more television viewers choose to watch the men's Wimbledon finals than the women's, and the men's games command higher spectator ticket prices.[381]

We all say we support equal pay for equal work, but few people are concerned that male fashion models are paid significantly less than female ones. This is the case even though males are already disadvantaged by being unable to supplement their income with lucrative cosmetics contracts.

Four-year, $5-million deals signed by the likes of Christy Turlington with Maybelline are out of the question for male models who, Thomas reports, earn no more than $5,000 for a show while women routinely pull down fees in the five figures. He writes: "Everyone understands that our culture is not particularly interested in looking at men who aren't actually doing something, or who haven't already established a reputation in another field."[382]

One achieves a brighter future through moral consistency—not by playing favourites. If a daughter and a son are raised in the same home by parents who consistently take the daughter's side even when her injuries are imaginary, the son may not grow up sympathetic to the hurts of other females. Rather, he may grow up bitter and resentful that his own abrasions mattered so little.

Thomas further challenges the feminist notion that crime is solely a male problem. (Remember the Canadian Panel on Violence Against Women, which implied that the only real criminals are male?) He points out that, in Great Britain, the segment of the population most at risk of being murdered are children under the age of one.[383] These murders, frequently committed by women, are classified separately as 'infanticide,' which then distorts the number of homicides for which women are deemed responsible. Criminal charges are laid in only a small fraction—less than 15 percent—of these deaths. (In Canada, children in their first year of life were also disproportionately represented among homicide victims in 1993 and 1994. According to the available data, however, it appears this country has a better record of holding perpetrators accountable.)[384]

In Ontario, wife battering is taken very seriously, to the point where police have been issued written directives to lay criminal charges "in all incidents of wife assault." Officers are further advised that they "should not be influenced" in such situations by factors such as the "likelihood of obtaining a conviction in court."[385]

Let's look at the hypothetical situation of a couple married for many years. In the course of a heated argument, the man—who has never done so before—angrily grabs his wife. If the woman picks up the phone, dials 911, and says she's been assaulted, the police are going to arrive. Sometimes it doesn't matter what the man says, it's the woman

183

who's believed. And if the man is honest enough to admit that, yes, things got out of hand and he did grab her, it's game over. He's handcuffed and taken out to the cruiser in front of his children and his neighbours.

At the police station he's confined to a cell. When he's able to get in touch with a lawyer (it might be the first time he's ever needed one, and so he doesn't have the first clue who to call), the lawyer will help arrange bail. But according to the authorities I checked with, prosecutors "routinely" ask for, and judges "frequently" impose a restraining order that says he can't return to his home until the charge is dealt with (except on one occasion, accompanied by a police officer, to pick up a few things).

It might take a year for the case to come to trial, during which time the man has had to find another place to live (an expense he might not be able to afford). Meanwhile, his family, friends, and perhaps, even his wife have gone into shock at what happens once the criminal justice system gets involved. Then there are the thousands more dollars needed to cover his legal fees. And all because he grabbed another, fully-grown, adult.

Yet women who snuff out the lives of utterly helpless infants might not even get charged in Great Britain? Writes Thomas:

> Could it be that the legal system simply finds it intolerable to contemplate female perpetrators? The notion of a mother who kills her own child is profoundly horrifying. These days we talk about post-natal depression, or baby blues, as a means of explaining acts which are otherwise inconceivable. Yet, purely by virtue of the intimacy of their relationship, the stress imposed on the mother and the amount of time that mother and child spend together, it would not seem unreasonable to suppose that the majority of small babies are killed by their mothers. Unfortunately...the numbers dry up once men stop being the bad guys.[386]

In other words, when no charges are laid, little information about these crimes makes it into the public record. This makes it even easier to believe that it's solely men who commit horrific acts.

Not Guilty isn't without its flaws. Its lack of footnotes makes it difficult to verify many of Thomas's claims. He also occasionally overlooks a legitimate alternative perspective. For example, while discussing sexual harassment allegations in the U.S. Navy, he remarks that a female lieutenant complained that the person called in to investigate had asked her out and referred to her as "Sweet Cakes." Thomas says he "fears for the future of the free world if it is to be protected by naval personnel who take fright at being called Sweet Cakes."[387] But surely the lieutenant's point was that someone assigned to investigate allegations of sexual impropriety should keep matters strictly professional.

That said, the book provides a valuable male perspective on many 'feminist' issues. This is important, because until both sides are doing as much listening as talking, the chances of achieving a more just society are remote. Shouting at people, nagging them, or threatening them with the coercive powers of the state are inferior ways of solving difficult problems. Writes Thomas:

> The last thing that the world needs now is another bunch of whining, self-proclaimed victims, and no one should close this book thinking that I spend my whole time feeling miserable about being male. I have been privileged in every aspect of my life...But that doesn't mean that I don't get angry or hurt or perplexed by some of the things that I see happening to the men around me.

He argues that, if "we are to have a healthy society, our sons need to grow up with a sense of self-confidence and self-respect."[388] In my view, this point can't be stressed enough. Gender harmony depends on well-adjusted human beings who believe they are valued in their own right, and that their needs and concerns are taken seriously. Young men currently inhabit a world in which people have little good to say about maleness, and even less sympathy for masculine anguish.

Wendy Dennis, who interviewed hundreds of people for her book about sex and love, observes:

> I have come to realize that women all too often have their guns out of the holster when they encounter men, and those guns are getting in the way. Women need to listen to men more often; like women, men are hurt and confused right now, and they have something valuable to say about their hurt and confusion.

Elsewhere, she notes that her research has taught her "that a sense of humor will take a woman farther with a man, both in and out of bed, than a sense of superiority, that listening will take her farther than a lecture."[389]

Women have been saying that men just don't get it. But there's a lot that we, too, don't understand. Much of what we imagine we know is a mean-spirited feminist stereotype—a narrow way of looking at complex individuals in a complex world.

A colleague of mine at *The Toronto Star* is an Anglican minister whose column on religious and ethical matters appears each Sunday. His name is Tom Harpur and, on New Year's Day 1995, he wrote about the necessity of forgiving others for their transgressions, as well as the necessity of forgiving ourselves for wrongs we've committed. He wasn't writing about gender issues, but his remarks apply here. He says:

> Show me a person who is at this moment holding some grudge or brooding over some sense of having been victimized by this or that person or circumstance of life and I'll show you an unhappy man or woman.

A bit later, he adds:

> It's one thing to examine one's life and conscience and
> accept blame where it is due, together with a decision
> to make amends; but it's quite another to indulge in
> exaggerated or ongoing self-flagellation for past mis-
> takes. That results in misery and saps the energy needed
> for moving on.[390]

If both women and men could be guided by such principles we might be able to climb over the mountain of refuse
we've been slinging at each other. We might emerge at a
place where the air is a little clearer. It wouldn't be a perfect world, but it would be one in which we viewed ourselves as individuals rather than as mere 'victims' and
'oppressors' in a drama of someone else's design.

The mass of men lead lives of quiet desperation.
Henry David Thoreau

6 - Men and Power

In 1994, an unlikely novel made its way onto the British bestseller list—George Eliot's *Middlemarch*. First published in 1871 under the now famous pseudonym, the novel was the creation of a woman named Mary Ann Evans. Described by feminist Virginia Woolf as "one of the few English novels written for grown-up people,"[391] *Middlemarch* is a masterpiece of Victorian literature more commonly found on college reading lists than front-racked in local bookstores. The 900-page work's renewed popularity was sparked by a BBC television miniseries production, which PBS broadcast to North American audiences later that year.

Middlemarch's opening scene takes place in 1829. This was a time in which women were thought to be ruled by their emotions and were therefore considered too irrational to vote. They weren't allowed to attend university since it was believed their ovaries would shrivel up if they directed their energies toward academic endeavours. (Decades later, they were still prohibited from practising law or sitting on juries, their ears being too sensitive for testimony involving violence or profane language.)

Although working class women toiled long hours under dangerous conditions in mills and factories, society considered 'woman' to be fragile, weak, and in need of protection. This was also a time in which reliable contraceptives were nonexistent, and many women didn't survive childbirth.

Even feminists who have little good to say about contemporary society have to admit that women's lot has improved considerably since the early 1800s. The term 'oppressed' applies far more accurately to women at that moment in history than it does to those of us who live in the industrialized world today.

Dorothea Brooke, the main character in *Middlemarch*, is a principled woman born into the upper class who wishes to do something useful with her life—to leave a lasting, positive impression on the world. She marries a scholar much older than herself in the belief that lending him wifely assistance will be a noble undertaking. But his re-pudiation of her intellectual gifts leaves her trapped in a strained marriage, long before divorce was permissible. (Eliot herself scandalized society by living in sin with a man still technically married to someone else.)

Despite Eliot's obvious feminist sensibilities, she knows there are many different kinds of power. While her female characters are excluded from the political and economic spheres, they hold considerable sway in the domestic sphere. One of the least sympathetic male characters, who behaves ruthlessly in his public life, is described as having "unvaryingly cherished" his wife. After he's disgraced in the eyes of the community, it's her reaction he most fears, and we're told he awaits it "in anguish."[392]

The young doctor, Tertius Lydgate, is Dorothea's male counterpart in the novel. Through him, Eliot demonstrates that for all their formal rights, men were hardly all-powerful. Lydgate is a visionary, a man of science who hopes to make medical research breakthroughs. Just as Dorothea is mistaken about what marriage to the scholar will be like, Lydgate is mistaken about women.

Early in the book he consciously dismisses Dorothea because "she did not look at things from the proper femi-nine angle." He considers her "too earnest" and thinks it "troublesome to talk to such women" since, in his view, they "are always wanting reasons, yet they are too ignorant to understand the merits of any question."

Lydgate considers Rosamond Vincy, the mayor's attrac-tive daughter, more appealing. "She is grace itself," he thinks. "She is perfectly lovely and accomplished." But if he is more interested in looks than brains, and in docility rather than character, Rosamond is keenly aware of how her social status will be enhanced by marrying a man who wears stylish clothes and is able to speak French.

Within minutes of their first brief meeting (which takes place as a result of her contrivance), Rosamond begins fantasizing about the house she will live in when she marries Lydgate, and the visits she'll pay to his "high-bred relatives." Rather than feeling oppressed, Rosamond is used to men falling in love with her at first sight. She enjoys exciting jealousy among her suitors, and muses that it will be "especially delightful to enslave" a man of Lydgate's stature.

Later, when she discovers "that women, even after marriage, might make conquests and enslave men," she thinks to herself:

> How delightful to make captives from the throne of marriage with a husband as a crown-prince by your side—himself in fact a subject—while the captives look up forever hopeless, losing their rest probably, and if their appetite too, so much the better!

As the novel progresses, it becomes apparent that Rosamond's meekness is merely a facade. Beneath it lies the obstinacy of the self-absorbed. The young woman reminds her doting father, who opposes her marriage to Lydgate, that she never wavers once she's set her mind on something. She then proceeds to emotionally blackmail this community leader by suggesting she may take ill if he doesn't give her his blessing. Says Eliot's narrator:

> Mrs. Vincy's belief that Rosamond could manage her papa was well founded. Apart from his dinner and his coursing, Mr. Vincy, blustering as he was, had as little of his own way as if he had been a prime minister: the force of circumstances was easily too much for him, as it is for most pleasure-loving florid men; and the circumstance called Rosamond was particularly forcible by

means of that mild persistence which, as we know, enables a white soft living substance to make its way in spite of opposing rock.

Rosamond believes that men exist to indulge her whims. We're told she never thinks of money "except as something necessary which other people would always provide." Her idea of good housekeeping consists "simply in ordering the best of everything." She complains that Lydgate works too much after they're married, and then complains when he's unable to pay the bills.

Lydgate attempts to conceal money worries from her because she is pregnant, and yet Rosamond shows no concern for his medical opinion when she insists on going horseback riding with one of his cousins in order to be seen with the son of a baronet. Lydgate is described as "hurt" and "utterly confounded that she had risked herself on a strange horse" even before a repeat occurrence leads to a miscarriage.

Unlike his wife, Lydgate accepts blame, acknowledges his own foolishness, and feels guilty that he isn't able to keep Rosamond in the style to which she's accustomed. When he instructs an agent to attempt to sublet their pricey residence, she countermands the order behind his back. To his mortification, she also secretly writes to his relatives requesting financial assistance.

Lydgate begins to gamble and take opium, apprehensive about moving to smaller quarters with fewer amenities, since he knows Rosamond will be miserable. Gradually, he realizes he has joined his life to a woman who sees marriage as something less than a partnership. The narrator tells us that his "will was not a whit stronger" than Rosamond's. Regarding one matrimonial conflict, we read:

and again, she had touched him in a spot of keenest feeling by implying she had been deluded with a false vision of happiness in marrying him. *As to saying that he was master, it was not the fact.* [my italics]

A few pages later:

> He had begun to have an alarmed foresight of her irrevocable loss of love for him, and the consequent dreariness of their life...It would assuredly have been a vain boast in him to say that he was her master.

And then:

> When he left her to go out again, he told himself that it was ten times harder for her than for him: he had a life away from home, and constant appeals to his activity on behalf of others. He wished to excuse everything in her if he could—but it was inevitable that in that excusing mood he should think of her as if she were an animal of another and feebler species. Nevertheless *she had mastered him*. [my italics]

Lydgate's money problems eventually implicate him in an unsavoury affair and lead to a sullying of his good reputation—in itself, a crushing blow to this proud man. In an attempt to placate Rosamond, he resolves to leave town and abandon altogether his dream of conducting medical research. Having decided that he "must do as other men do, and think what will please the world and bring in money," he tells Dorothea that he'll attempt to somehow keep his "soul alive" in the process.

During this period, in which Lydgate feels Rosamond's silent reproach so acutely that he dreads even looking at her, she reassures herself that even he, the "most perverse of men, was always subdued in the long-run." In the novel's afterword we read that:

> Lydgate's hair never became white. He died when he was only fifty, leaving his wife and children provided for by a heavy insurance on his life. He had gained an excellent practice...but he always regarded himself as a failure: he had not done what he once meant to do.

This educated, upper class white male in a man's world, has his life destroyed by a woman. Rosamond is physically weaker than her husband, but it is her view of how he should behave that prevails, not his own. Whatever scientific contributions he might have made are reduced to dust beneath her delicately shod feet.

Lydgate's shattered dreams find their parallel in Dorothea. Following the death of her first husband, she remarries. In the afterword we read that she, too, failed to achieve her full potential:

> Many who knew her, thought it a pity that so substantive and rare a creature should have been absorbed into the life of another, and be only known in a certain circle as a wife and mother. But no one stated exactly what else that was in her power she ought rather to have done...

Other female characters have their options similarly constrained. One, an unmarried woman who lives with her mother, is described as being "nipped and subdued as single women are apt to be who spend their lives in uninterrupted subjection to their elders."

Power, who exercises it and how, are complex matters. The author of *Middlemarch* would no doubt consider preposterous the Canadian Violence Against Women Panel's declaration that "society has given the man the power over a woman from the point of earliest acquaintance."

She would likely consider the assertion, in one of the essays in *Women Respond to the Men's Movement*, that women have "no power" while men have "all the power all the time all over the world"[393] laughable.

Now let's fast forward to 1950s North America, just prior to the historical moment when women began questioning why they were expected to live only through their husbands and children. Margaret Atwood has described this as an era in which "condoms could not legally be displayed on pharmacy shelves, where we read Kotex ads to learn how to behave at proms, and always wore our gloves when we went out."

She says young women were told not to "neck on the first date" if they wanted boys to respect them and were advised: "Real women are bad at math. To be fulfilled you have to have a baby. If you lead them on you'll get what you deserve."[394]

This is the world we see in *Blue Sky*, the film for which Jessica Lange won her 1994 best actress Oscar. Compared with today, 1950s North America was formal and rigid. Carly Marshall, the narcissist played by Lange, has trouble fitting in. She too worries that, after her death, there'll be no trace of her left behind.

In this drama, Carly is a continuing source of embarrassment to Hank, her army major husband (played by Tommy Lee Jones). In the opening scene she goes swimming topless, causing a stir when she's spotted by her husband's colleagues. A superior officer then demands: "What the hell are you going to do? About your wife. She's a disgrace to the army and she's endangering your job." Hank is told the incident will be noted in his file "along with all the other" ones.

Soon afterward, Hank is transferred to a new base and Carly experiences a mini emotional breakdown at the thought of having to start all over again in a new community—without acknowledging that the frequent moves are connected to her own behaviour. On the first morning in their new home, Hank cooks breakfast for his two daughters, the eldest of whom insists Carly needs professional help. He responds by defending his wife, referring to her as "spirited" and "energetic" and saying that he made a decision, long ago, simply to love her.

When Carly becomes involved in an extramarital affair of which everyone becomes aware, her husband's endurance is sorely tested. Exhausted, demoralized, and betrayed once again, Hank takes off his glasses and presses his fingers to his eyes. His shoulders are slack, his face is strained. He is the picture of a beaten man, of a man who has struggled to conduct himself honourably, who has borne large and small humiliations with restraint, who has been a responsible parent to his children and treated his wife with compassion. But his well of inner resources has now run dry.

Blue Sky endeavours to provide us with a slice of real life, to render a reasonably accurate portrait of a fictional couple's relationship. This marriage wasn't typical of 1950s North America, but the script is so solid and the acting so believable it's difficult to dismiss it entirely as a Hollywood fabrication. The moment we're willing to admit that such a scenario is plausible is the moment we're forced to acknowledge that all men don't lord it over their wives. Patience, self-sacrifice, and forbearance are human qualities, not female ones.

In *Backlash*, Susan Faludi tells us that men take their family obligations extremely seriously:

> For twenty years, the Monitor's pollsters have asked its subjects to define masculinity. And for twenty years, the leading definition, ahead by a huge margin, has never changed. It isn't being a leader, athlete, lothario, decision maker, even just being "born male." It is simply this: being a "good provider for his family."

Faludi turns this against men by suggesting that it's "hard to imagine a force more directly threatening to fragile American manhood than the feminist drive for economic equality." But surely part of the reason being a good provider is so central to male identity is because this *matters to women*.[395]

In the 1994 film adaptation of Louisa May Alcott's novel, *Little Women*, the March daughters are at liberty to pursue writing and painting as young adults, but their male childhood friend, Laurie, is not. Since large amounts of money have been spent educating him, he is now expected to put his nose to the grindstone and make himself useful by becoming part of the family business. In one scene, after he graduates from Harvard, Jo March asks him whether his grandfather is "exceedingly proud." He replies, "Exceedingly bent on locking me up in one of his offices. Why is it Amy may paint china and you can scribble away, while I must 'manfully' set my music aside?"

Laurie is expected to become a breadwinner because that's what males do. But part two of the equation is that he won't be considered husband material otherwise. The adult Amy March, the youngest of the four sisters, declares that she has always known she wouldn't "marry a pauper," and considers accepting the hand of one of her suitors whom she doesn't love but whose sizable income makes him attractive. She tells Laurie that she despises his dissolute lifestyle: "You laze about, spending your family's money and courting women," she scolds, before urging him to make himself useful.

As a direct consequence, he resolves to settle into the job that has been waiting for him in order to prove himself worthy of her affection. Only afterward, does Amy agree to become his wife.

There's no need to depend on fiction to make the point that, for men, employment in the wider world is a prerequisite to marriage. Stephen Hawking is a world renowned theoretical physicist and author of the immensely successful book *A Brief History of Time*. In 1963, shortly after his 21st birthday, Hawking was diagnosed with the degenerative disease ALS, also known as Lou Gehrig's disease. He was advised that he probably had only a few years to live. In his words:

> There did not seem much point in working at my research because I didn't expect to live long enough to finish my Ph.D. However, as time went by, the disease seemed to slow down. I began to understand general relativity and make progress with my work. But what really made a difference was that I got engaged to a woman named Jane Wilde. This gave me something to live for, but *it also meant that I had to get a job if we were to get married.* [my italics][396]

Hawking is a brilliant intellect, but in this regard he was merely conforming to societal expectations.

Similarly, the American writer Kurt Vonnegut talks about how his own obligation to support his family meant that, for a number of years, he was unable to quit his "goddam nightmare job" at General Electric and devote himself to his craft. It was only after accumulating the equivalent of a year's salary in a bank account from selling short stories in the late 1940s that he was able to do so in good conscience. He relates this anecdote within the context of talking about his father, observing that it was only when his dad achieved the age of 65 that he admitted that being an architect had "been no fun at all." Writes Vonnegut:

> I now perceive his deception, so suddenly discontinued, as having been a high order of gallantry. While my two siblings and I were growing up, he gave us the illusion that our father was jauntily content with his professional past and excited about all the tough but amusing challenges still to come. The truth was that the Great Depression and then World War II, during which almost all building stopped, came close to gutting him as an architect. From the time he was forty-five until he was sixty-one he had almost no work. In prosperous times those would have been his best years, when his evident gifts, reputation, and maturity might have caused some imaginative client to feel that Father was entitled to reach, even in Indianapolis, for greatness or, if you will, for soul-deep fun.[397]

Vonnegut tells us his father spent much of his career taking jobs that wouldn't have caused a high school drafting class difficulty—because he needed the money to support his family. This man made the best of a bad situation with grace and dignity. Rather than allowing his professional disappointment to contaminate their young lives, he spent decades hiding the true state of affairs from his children.

(Vonnegut's mother doesn't appear to have been fulfilled by her domestic duties, either. Her says the poor woman was mentally ill and that, late at night "and always in the privacy of our own home, and never with guests present, she expressed hatred for Father as corrosive as hydrofluoric acid.")[398]

That men still face immense pressure to be breadwinners is illustrated by the answer Ann Landers gave to GROWING UNEASY in 1994. This letter writer told Ann she'd been living with a "very attractive, intelligent, charming, affable, humorous, loving" and thoughtful man (who was also good in bed) for almost a year, and intended to marry him. The couple were childless and planned to remain so. "Greg" was further described as being supportive of the woman and her career, as well as someone who shared "in the cooking and cleaning." But UNEASY was uncomfortable about the fact that while she herself earned an above-average wage, her partner was unemployed—partly because his profession was "saturated with qualified people" who couldn't find work, but partly, she suspected, because he lacked ambition.

"Is Greg a lazy parasite, exchanging sex and emotional security for an easy life?" she asked Ann. "Should I give him the boot and look for someone who can support me if I choose not to work?"

Ann told UNEASY that she was an "enabler" who had "made Greg so comfortable for so long that he sees no reason to try to support himself." She said the woman should insist Greg get "some kind of job—even part time—as a matter of self-respect." Ann made no comment about the fact that UNEASY thought she herself should have the option of choosing "not to work."

The number of avenues open to women have expanded in recent years, but men remain stuck in the past. Women think they should have the choice to work outside the home or not. Which means men are still expected to get up every morning and report for duty. In Warren Farrell's words:

Today, when the successful single woman meets the successful single man, they appear to be equals. But should they marry and consider children, she almost invariably considers three options:

Option #1: Work full time
Option #2: Mother full time
Option #3: Some combination of working and mothering

He considers three "slightly different" options:
Option #1: Work full time
Option #2: Work full time
Option #3: Work full time[399]

Calling her a "female chauvinist oink oink," Ann's male readers didn't hesitate to draw the advice columnist's attention to the double standard she'd applied in the case of UNEASY. "If women are now allowed to get *out* of the kitchen, why shouldn't men be allowed to get *in*?" (original italics) asked one of the letters she published. Ann responded by saying that the men had "made a pretty good case for themselves."[400]

When it comes to work, men are trapped in a 'damned if you do, damned if you don't' situation. On the one hand, they feel pressure to support their families, a feeling that often intensifies after the arrival of each child. On the other, they're criticized for working too much and paying too little attention to their families. Ironically, the better provider he is, the less time he's able to spend with his kids.

I remember my paternal grandfather as a quiet, gentle soul. My grandmother was a knitter, a quilter, a creative mind. She always had six projects on the go, and visiting her was an adventure. For his part, my grandfather would load us into his panel truck and take us to the store for a treat. Spending money on us was one of the ways he expressed his love. Earning it, even when that meant walking miles to and from his blue collar job in waist-deep snow, was how he showed his family of eight that he cared for them.

For many men, family life is about duty and responsibility. It's also mixed up with experiences that have nothing to do with expressions of their own power.

The women's movement has done a good job of articulating the idea that women who discover they're pregnant sometimes aren't prepared for motherhood. We've argued that parenting is too serious a matter to be embarked on by people who aren't committed to the task. We've said that every child should be a wanted child. Because it's the woman's body that goes wonky for nine months, we believe the final decision about whether or not to carry a pregnancy to term should be hers.

But where does this leave the man who's thrilled at the prospect of becoming a dad but discovers that she wants an abortion—which she then proceeds to have? Why has feminism chosen to deny the pain associated with these events? Why is there no recognition of the powerlessness of men who don't want kids but are told that it's her decision, his views don't count, and he's financially responsible for this new life for the next 20 years? Finally, where is the condemnation for women who, years later, demand retroactive support for a child whose existence they've kept a secret?

On three occasions in early 1995, Ann Landers published letters from individuals dealing with the latter scenario. The first was from a woman whose husband was contacted by someone he'd had a one-night stand with 14 years earlier. The child, whose paternity was confirmed by blood tests, was now 13.

The next letter was from the girlfriend of a man suddenly informed that a woman he'd gone out with briefly in 1973 had borne their son—who was now 21.

The last was from a man who, nine years previously, at the age of 18, had inadvertently impregnated a woman he'd been dating. He claimed that although he'd "ordered" her to have an abortion or put the child up for adoption, she'd refused. He now expressed outrage that while he's legally compelled to pay support, she refuses to work to support herself.[401]

I'm not suggesting that men should be able to veto an abortion—or force a woman to have one. But when feminists declare that a man unprepared to deal with such matters should have 'kept his dick in his pants,' my mind jumps back in time to the era of back alley abortions, of women hemorrhaging to death while being told they should have kept their legs crossed if they didn't want to get pregnant.

Even when both parties welcome the news of a pregnancy, becoming a father is intimidating and disruptive. For all our talk about men and power, few feel as though they're in control. In the rueful words of a cab driver I hired one evening, "Since she came, it's been 'baby this, baby that.' The house is upside down. Now everything revolves around the baby." This man's other remarks made it clear he was intensely proud of his first child, a 14-month-old daughter. But he was still adjusting to his new life. Should his marriage falter, once again he will feel anything but powerful—and old-fashioned, sexist notions about mothers and children may well work against him.

Some men aren't interested in their children after a marriage breakdown, but others have been full participants in their children's lives from the beginning. These guys attend childbirth classes, assist in the delivery room, get up for three a.m. feedings, pace the floor for hours with colicky babies, change diapers, and walk around with infant carriers strapped to their chests. Does feminism give these men the credit they're due?

Here's Marilyn French in *The War Against Women*:

Presenting themselves in a new role, as caring fathers, *an image built not on men's actual behavior but by media presentations* of ideal fathers, men increasingly seek custody of children after divorce or children they fathered outside marriage...If fathers wanted closeness with their

201

children, one would sympathize, but few men seeking custody are prepared to care for their children them-selves... [my italics]

French insists that men aren't so much interested in their children as they are in power struggles with the women in their lives. Based on the conclusions of Canadian feminist Susan Crean, published in a 1988 book about male cus-tody, French declares "that there is no evidence that men as a group are any more interested in or willing to deliver twenty-four-hour child care than they ever were."[402]

But it's individual males, not "men as a group," who seek custody of their children after a marriage breakdown. Individuals deserve to be judged on their own merits. Similarly, *Ms.* editor Letty Cottin Pogrebin tells us:

Today, in courtrooms and news stories, the fairy tale single daddy serves as a subliminal propaganda tool for "father's rights" advocates who battle for child custody in order to punish their ex-wives.[403]

Another feminist, writing in *Women Respond to the Men's Movement*, says:

once feminists began fighting for equal pay and for the right to abortion, the backlash was on. If women wanted the right to leave men or take men's jobs away from them, then men, and the women who support them, would simply repossess women's children.

She continues:

Divorcing fathers increasingly use the threat of a cus-tody battle as an economic bargaining chip. And it works. He gets the house, the car, and the boat; she gets the kids, and, if she's lucky, minimal child sup-port.[404]

These arguments are true some of the time. Some men *are* driven by anger, vengeance, and malice. They go to extreme lengths in an attempt to make the lives of their ex-wives miserable—including suing for custody of children they don't really love. But it's dishonest to suggest that only men behave this way.

Women also pursue custody for less than noble reasons. Peer pressure is one factor. There's still a widespread belief that no decent mother would 'abandon' her children. Greed is another: in Canada, the law requires that a grid be consulted. The amount of support is determined by the number of children and the salary earned. Each child is therefore worth hundreds of dollars per month to whichever parent is awarded primary custody. Lest we forget, lots of people are motivated by money. And we haven't even talked about *female* anger, revenge, malice, or mental illness.

One of the most heartbreaking testimonials I've heard came from a man whose wife is a chronic alcoholic barely capable of taking care of herself, never mind kids. Because she knows he cares about their two young children while having lost all patience with her, she's fighting him tooth and nail regarding custody. This has included making allegations of physical abuse against him which, at least until the matter is resolved in court, has resulted in his being able to see his children for only a few hours a week. This man is no 'fairy tale.' He's flesh and blood. He has been the primary caregiver and is genuinely afraid for his kids' safety during the time they spend alone with their mother.

Feminists claim that men frequently win court custody battles, but these figures—which range from 50 to 80 percent—are heavily skewed. Since everyone knows about the anti-male bias in family court, particularly in certain jurisdictions dominated by certain judges, lawyers typically advise men that unless they can prove the mother's a heroin addict or a prostitute, they might as well not waste their time trying to get custody. Other men are cautioned that, due to their lower chance of success, they should think carefully about such a course of action. Ugly custody battles can further traumatize the children and make an already strained adult relationship more difficult.

When men decide not to attempt to gain sole or joint custody of their children, feminism uses this as proof that they don't care about their kids. When they *do* go to court and win, feminists say men are trying to take 'women's' children away from them.

Another area in which men are emphatically not in positions of power involves post-divorce access and visiting rights. Women who complain about men who miss their support payments can turn to the state for assistance. Wages can be garnisheed. But there are no remedies for non-custodial fathers when mothers flagrantly violate court-ordered visitation. A feminist movement that views fathers as bad guys, that thinks men are always in positions of power, has nothing to say about the lives of millions of children who are being prevented from spending time with their dads.

Let us now circle back to the question of paid work. In a recent essay for *Playboy* magazine, feminist Betty Friedan writes about the frustration that her own bright, articulate mother experienced after quitting a newspaper job when she married at the age of 21 (the wives of businessmen weren't supposed to work outside the home in those days):

> Nothing [our father] did, nothing we, the children, did, was ever enough for her. And it got worse during the Depression when the business didn't make enough to feed her fantasies. We were drawn by our mother into a conspiracy against him, not to let him know if she spent money on a new outfit for herself or us. Besides, he worked late every night and all day Saturdays. On Sundays, he was really tired. Her mysterious, painful ailment (colitis, I believe) got better when his heart

disease required her to run the business. And so he died in his early 60s, and she lived until 90.

Friedan says her mother swam and played golf and tennis while the only exercise her father experienced came during the family's annual two-week vacation. She says this helps explain why her mother's health was sufficiently robust to survive all three of her husbands. Friedan, who suggests that her own upbringing wasn't unusual, reminds us that "there is more than one kind of power in any family, and women, kept from financial power, had to retaliate by denying and manipulating the power of love."[405]

The grass always looks greener on the other side. Before women flooded into the paid workforce, men performed most jobs. But that doesn't mean they were having a good time. There were good reasons why Friedan's mother was frustrated. But one of feminism's gravest mistakes has been to assume that men's experience was vastly better. If there were only two choices—a 90-year life span that included golf and tennis along with domestic drudgery, or a 60-year life span composed solely of work and worry—I know which one I'd pick.

Feminism compared the lives of women who felt trapped by domestic work not to all men—janitors, garbage collectors, taxi drivers, dishwashers and road crews —but to the men occupying the highest rungs of the ladder. It then concluded that women were being deprived of *power*.

But how much power did the average man really exercise on the job? Writes Warren Farrell:

Almost every woman had a primary role in the "female-dominated" family structure; only a small percentage of men had a primary role in the "male-dominated" governmental and religious structures. Many mothers were, in a sense, the chair of the board of a small company—their family...Conversely, most men were on their company's assembly line.

He adds:

> Historically, a husband spent the bulk of his day under
> the eye of his boss—his source of income; a wife did not
> spend the bulk of her day under the eye of her hus-
> band—her source of income. She had more control over
> her work life than he had over his.[406]

Participating in the paid work world doesn't automatically
translate into power, control, or satisfaction. Only a minority of individuals in our society appear to really enjoy
their work. Many would quit in an instant if they won a
lottery jackpot. But they get up every morning and report
for duty because, at the end of the week, they get a pay
cheque that puts food on the table.

Some of my feminist sisters will no doubt protest that
the economic clout that comes with earning your own
money shouldn't be underestimated. There is some truth
in this. But if, as David Thomas points out, one person
earns most of the money while the other one spends most
of it, "you do not have to be Karl Marx to conclude that the
second of those two" may not be exactly oppressed.

Research suggests that, when it comes to major as well
as minor household expenditures, women make most of
the decisions. Yes, there are male clotheshorses, as well as
men who spend large sums on what women derisively refer to as their 'toys'—golf clubs, power boats, and so forth.
But the average woman spends a great deal on her clothing, hair, and toiletries. It's more difficult to buy gifts for
men than for women because our society is used to pam-
pering women. You can give us perfume, bubble bath, cosmetics, jewellery, candies, chocolates, and flowers. Few of
these are considered appropriate for men.

Warren Farrell reports on a U.S. study in which "floor
space...offering male versus female items in shopping malls
and boutiques" was measured. The result: "seven times as
much floor space was devoted to female personal items as

to male personal items." Additionally, the most valuable, high-traffic space markets products for women.[407]

Some critics will retort that if women go to so much expense about their appearance it's only because males expect it. But this can only be partially true. If the woman in the 'Dear Abby' column who has exiled her spouse to the garage for fear of harming him gets her hair set and her nails manicured every week, it's difficult to argue that she's doing so to please her husband rather than to indulge herself. When Carly, in *Blue Sky*, causes her husband and children to nearly miss a plane while she gets a makeover at the hairdresser's, her own desire to appear glamorous is the overriding motivation—not her husband's expectations. In *Middlemarch*, Rosamond is concerned with bonnets, sashes, jewels, and other finery. Partly this is what's required in order to attract men, but she treats it as an art and a science because such matters really do consume her interest.

Which brings us back to the issue of sexual power. Like most things in life, it isn't constant—the balance can shift. If a car pulls up to the curb while I'm waiting alone at a bus stop at midnight and two young men lean out its windows and make suggestive comments, the fact that I've caught their eye because I'm a woman makes me feel at risk rather than powerful. But if it's broad daylight and I'm in an elevator with the same young men while struggling with a heavy box, after a few smiles in their direction they'll likely fall all over themselves trying to help me down the hall.

Despite feminist assertions that men control the sexual realm (due to the possibility that they might turn violent), the May/June 1995 issue of *Ms.* contains an account by 23-year-old Anastasia Higginbotham. She describes herself as having once been "patriarchy's wet dream." As she has matured, she says, she's:

> been transformed from masochist to feminist. The big hair, accompanied by moderately big breasts and a

207

dancer's ass bundled into a squeezy purple dress, attracted all sorts of attention. I could have brought my
high school to its knees on charges of sexual misconduct...In fact, I thrived on making guys hard and then
laughing in their faces at the obvious fact that they
could never have me. I thought I was god's gift to men
because I could play glam, sweetheart, and harlot all in
one shot. I had my pick [of young men]...[408]

Males are socialized to believe they aren't 'real men'
unless they've had intercourse. The more sex they have,
the better they're supposed to feel about themselves. In
other words, sexual success is closely tied to male self-
image in much the same way that a woman's weight af-
fects how she feels about herself.

If women are conditioned to dress in a certain manner
in order to attract men, males are also conditioned to respond to this stimuli. They are often quite powerless in
the face of women who 'thrive' on arousing them sexually
and then laughing at them. If America were the kind of
place many feminists would have us believe, a place where
men routinely seize what they want at women's expense,
it wouldn't have been so 'obvious' that Higginbotham was
sexually unavailable. Indeed, her high school experience
would have been dramatically different.

Let's try a thought experiment. Imagine that there's a
rare, addictive elixir. Imagine that women know that, by
consuming a small vial of this substance, we'll effortlessly
lose the extra ten pounds so many of us are always fret-
ting about. The only way we can acquire this elixir is directly from men. By some twist of fate, each of them is issued a supply of the stuff on reaching puberty. Females,
being conditioned to want this substance more than our
male counterparts do, are frequently on the watch for it
when we're hanging out with men. We often find ourselves
wondering whether we'll 'score.'

Some males, aware of how popular these vials make
them, wear one attached to their watchband. It amuses

them to observe the eyes of women—young and old, attractive and not so attractive, strangers and acquaintances—stray there. Sometimes, while in a bar, they remove the vial and nonchalantly hold it up to the light, twirling it around before tucking it away again.

Now imagine that a man and a woman retire to his apartment. The woman's mouth is dry and she's nervous because those vials have been haunting her dreams. Imagine that the pair sit on the sofa, while soft music plays in the background. The woman's fingers begin moving in the direction of the vial. But while she's trying to let him know she's interested, she doesn't want her desire to be too obvious. If it turns out she has misunderstood, if all he has in mind is a drink and small talk, she'd like to be able to withdraw graciously.

Her fingers move still closer and he doesn't protest. Finally, she makes contact. Seconds later, she loosens the strap and the vial slips free. Trembling, she holds it in her palm. The moment of truth has arrived. She needs his help, since the vial will shatter unless he himself removes the lid. She looks up, into his eyes. He's watching her, wondering what price she might be willing to pay.

Most of us would have no difficulty describing this as a situation in which the man, because he has something he knows the woman wants, is in a position of power. We'd say that he's calling the shots.

From men's perspective, female bodies are always on display. Men are surrounded by reminders of how much they want sex, and of how much they're expected to want it. They're also continually reminded of what failures they are if they aren't scoring often enough.

Imagine what wrecks women might be if everywhere we looked we saw men wearing vials on the street, men with vials on the television screen, on billboards, in subway ads, and in the pages of magazines at the dentist's office. No matter where we turn, we're reminded that there's something we urgently desire that depends on the co-operation of the opposite sex. We, too, might be tempted

209

to commit to a lifetime of financial support in exchange for a steady supply.

Feminism tells us that men are always in positions of power vis-à-vis women. An influential report prepared for the Canadian government agrees. But both art and real life challenge this view. George Eliot, our feminist foremother, didn't make the mistake of thinking that only one kind of power existed.

She knew that women wield immense power in the domestic sphere. She knew that paid work could be a form of servitude, and that the person who earns an income isn't necessarily the person who spends it. She also knew that, when men have children, their power is tempered by both vulnerability and responsibility.

If Eliot knew all of this 125 years ago, what's our excuse?

The desire to explore the limits of power and submission is not a *male* compulsion but a human one.[409]

    Erica Jong

7 - Our Secret Garden

The man, whose name is Warrick, is six-foot-three with broad shoulders and rippling muscles. He is naked except for a towel draped over his hips, and he is flat on his back on a bed. Iron cuffs attached to lengths of chain encircle his wrists and ankles.

Rowena, the woman, is young and slender, with waist-length blond hair. She stands over him and shakes her head when his eyes implore her to remove his gag. She strips the towel from him and tries to climb astride his body, but he struggles violently and she falls back. She tries again, and this time his resistance is so strenuous that the entire bed moves along the floor and his wrists and ankles become smeared with blood. "You stupid man," she says. "Why cause yourself pain over something you cannot prevent?"

She removes her clothing and tells him that, while he may fight her, it will do him no good. She begins to caress him and sweat breaks out on his brow as, despite the outrage he feels, his body begins to respond to her. The sight of her breasts swaying above him, the sound of her panting, and the feel of her hair on his skin all arouse him. He wages a bitter internal battle as she slides his erect penis into her vagina. He continues to struggle and strain. But all his willpower, all his conscious effort, isn't enough. Finally, she brings him to orgasm.

A servant is sent to minister to Warrick's injuries, to bathe him, feed him, and help him with his bodily functions while he remains chained. The next night his struggles start his wounds bleeding again as Rowena visits him three times, coaxing an ejaculation from him on each occasion. The following evening, she returns another three times. She examines him closely, remarks on his body, uses him. Despite the fury that burns in his eyes, he is powerless to stop her. Not once is he permitted to speak to her. Later, Rowena will recall how exhilarating it was to have him completely at her mercy.

On the fourth day, he is released, given a set of clothes and threatened with death should he ever show his face in the vicinity again. But the year is 1152, and Warrick, kidnapped from an inn by bumblers unaware of his identity, is an English lord who does return—with his army. He orders Rowena transported to his castle and locked in the dungeon. Before he leaves, he sets fire to the bed on which he had been confined and gathers up the chains.

After spending three weeks in the dungeon, Rowena is taken to Warrick's room. He threatens to beat her if she faints and informs her he intends to repay her in kind. After warning her never to interrupt when he's speaking to her, he orders her to strip. He assures her that, should he not find her sufficiently arousing, there's nothing stopping him from having as many as ten of his men rape her while he looks on. As she undresses, she watches him positioning the chains and pleads with him, promising not to resist. But to no avail. She lies down in the centre of the bed and he orders her to spread her legs. She's told to spread them wider, and he then chains each to a post. He secures her wrists and pushes a gag into her mouth.

Gradually her trepidation subsides as he begins to coax a sexual response from her. He caresses her gently, persistently. She begins to arch against him. His touch becomes rougher. When he enters her, her eyes fly open to see the triumph in his. "Now you know how it feels to have no control of a traitorous body," Warrick says to her. "You made me want this, despite my fury, so I have made you want it, despite your fear."[410] Soon she is screaming in orgasm. Afterward, she thinks it inconceivable that she found anything pleasurable in the experience.

Hours later, Warrick returns to the room where Rowena has remained bound and gagged. When she closes her eyes to block him out, he orders her to look at him. "Whenever you are in my presence, wench," he says, "you will look at me unless I tell you otherwise. Do not make me repeat it."[411] She is forced to do so as a servant feeds her and attends to her other needs, but she manages to look through him rather than at him. He punishes her by having intercourse with her again.

The next morning, he takes her before she is fully awake. Twice more he returns. The following day, it's the same. On the fourth, she is released from the chains, but Warrick has a reputation for exacting revenge in excess of the crimes committed against him. Rowena, who belongs to the upper class, is now dressed in the clothing of a servant. She is told that she is to refer to him as "my lord" and will be whipped if she fails to comply. She is now his personal attendant, required to clean his room, launder his clothes, and wait on him during meals in the dining hall.

She is ordered to prepare Warrick's bath and told to undress him. When she recoils against removing his lower garments, he threatens to chain her to the bed again, so she sinks to her knees as commanded, "'Tis quite satisfying, seeing you in that humbled position," he says. "Mayhap I will have you serve me at table just so."[412]

She is forced to wash and then dry him. "On your knees again," he says. "And take care, wench, that you do not miss a single drop of moisture. Do I catch a chill because of your negligence, I *will* beat you for it" (original italics). While she is performing these tasks, it becomes clear they are both sexually aroused. When she balks, he tells her it's his right to have sex with his servants "at any time, in any place."[413] He drags her to the bed and uses his superior strength to keep her there. Then he kisses and caresses her until, overcome with sexual hunger, she shames herself by obeying his command to beg him to take her.

Afterward, Warrick taunts her by reminding her of her capitulation and she thinks, "All the power was his. He had control over her body, control over her emotions, control over everything she did. She could not even get angry without his leave, for he knew well enough how to frighten the anger out of her."[414] He pulls her onto his lap in the dining hall and, in front of everyone, touches her intimately and then orders her to wait for him in his bed. He humiliates her by giving his daughters the fine gowns that had once belonged to her. He tells her she is stupid. Even when she comes to him willingly, he restrains her hands during love-making.

The above narrative isn't found in a pornographic video produced by misogynists and then rented from seedy triple-X outlets by male sex offenders. Nor has it been stopped at the border and examined by customs agents before being allowed into Canada, despite its blatant domination and submission theme. Rather, all of the above takes place in a romance novel written by a woman for other women. It appears in Johanna Lindsey's 1991 *Prisoner of My Desire*.

According to the inside back cover of *Surrender My Love* (a 1994 novel in which the heroine is fitted with specially fashioned shackles and tethered to a wall in the hero's bedroom), Lindsey is one of the "most successful authors of historical romance," with over 40 million copies in print.[415] Each of her more than two dozen books has been a U.S. national bestseller. A number of them incorporate similar themes. Her first, *Captive Bride* (originally published in 1977), is about a young woman who turns down a marriage proposal by an Arabian sheik she's just met, only to be kidnapped by him and brought to his isolated desert camp. Imprisoned within his tent, she's told, "You're mine now, Tina. The sooner you realize that, the better it will be for you." He informs her that she has missed her chance to marry him and will, instead, be his slave.[416] Despite her protests, he carries her to his bed. He pins her arms above her head and rips the clothing from her body. Then he lets her go, saying he will not rape her. But he promises that, when the time comes, her desire will match his. She tries to escape into the desert, but he chases after her. He threatens to tie her to the bed and says she deserves to be beaten. Laying her over the back of his horse, he smacks her bottom when she struggles.

Later, he takes her to the outdoor bathing pool and makes it clear that if she wishes to use it, she will have to disrobe in front of him. On another occasion, when she challenges his orders in the presence of others, he tells her: "I'm your master, and you belong to me. If you'd like me to find a whip and bare your back in public, I'll be happy to oblige you. Otherwise, return to my tent."[417] He brings her books but says she must kiss him if she wishes to read them. She complies and feels the stirrings of sexual desire. That night, she refuses to remove her clothing and so he does, forcibly. Gently, he kisses and caresses her, inserting his knee between her legs

The novel tells us: "Her mind cried out for him to stop, but her body demanded that he go on...She hated her body for betraying her, but she wanted him."[418] After receiving her consent, he takes her virginity. The next night, she fights him and he strips her again. He pins her to the bed and caresses her before she succumbs and asks him to make love to her.

Repeatedly, the sheik threatens to punish her for defiant behaviour. She physically struggles against him night after night until we're told that "her passions overcame her resistance and swept her away."[419] Elsewhere, he demands that she admit that she enjoys having sex with him, spanks her bare bottom, and angrily pushes her onto the floor:

His lips seared hers painfully, silencing her screams as he entered her viciously. Her mind was beyond reason

215

as her body accepted his like a wild animal, and the pain turned to violent waves of ecstatic pleasure.

We read that the sheik gets into the habit of having sex with her in the morning "before she awoke fully and knew what was happening."[420] When she is abducted by a rival tribe, she realizes that she is in love with her original captor.

In *Secret Fire*, published in 1987, the heroine is spotted on the street by a Russian prince visiting London in the 1840s. He instructs his servant to arrange for her to warm his bed that evening, but her lack of enthusiasm prompts the servant to pull her into a carriage and to administer a potent aphrodisiac. As it begins to work, she fails to understand what is happening. By the time the prince comes to her room, she is writhing on the bed.

He caresses her, bringing her to orgasm. During the brief respite, before her sexual tension builds again, she tries to pull away, but he pins her to the mattress. When he offers to make love to her, she refuses, so he waits patiently until she says, "I can't bear it anymore. Alexandrov, do what you will, please, anything—just do it now." She achieves orgasm after orgasm:

> As long as she obeyed his every command, he was there to soothe and relieve and give her hour after hour of the most incredible ecstasy, with his hands, his mouth, his body. All he asked in return was that she allow him to play with her, to caress her as he would.[421]

In the morning, the heroine is furious and insists that the servant's actions be brought to the attention of the authorities. In response, the prince takes her with him when he sails for Russia. She tries to jump overboard, but he stops her. Although the two are powerfully attracted to one another, she resists his further advances during the voyage, and the sexual tension builds.

She is taken to a country estate and humiliated before the servants when he drags her into the house and installs her in the bedroom adjoining his own. Despite his promise to never give her the aphrodisiac again, he orders it administered via her meal and then waits for her to be reduced to a state of sexual frenzy. Another passionate night follows, and she knows that she loves him. Part of her is "pleased that he could be so desperate to have her" that he would drug her.[422]

Not all romance novels are the same, of course. Within this genre of formula fiction, the variety is impressive. There are slim works that take place in contemporary, if frequently exotic, settings. There are thicker historical romances—often referred to as 'bodice rippers'—and futuristic romances involving alien planets and species. In comparison to Lindsey's books, the approach to sex in many of them is decidedly staid. But even acknowledging such variations, sex is a mainstay of much of the escapist fiction large numbers of women enjoy reading.

Sexual power struggles are frequently used to market these books. In Amanda Quick's 1994 *Mistress* (a *New York Times* bestseller), the preview inside the paperback edition has the hero trapping the heroine between his arms and a piece of sculpture while behaving in a sexually domineering manner.[423] The tantalizing tidbit at the front of Mary Lou Rich's 1993 *Bandit's Kiss* has the virginal heroine being undressed and caressed. When she protests, telling the hero he can't continue, he replies, "But I can."[424] The back cover of Karen Robards's 1985 *To Love a Man* (recently referred to as a 'classic' by *Romantic Times* magazine) reads, in part:

> Sam would make her his captive, his woman, taunting her, teasing her, treating her no better than a slave. He would take her when and where he chose, hurting her pride even as he healed her wounds. She would love him, hate him, fight him, need him...[425]

Other book covers declare: "She was his captive in the burning sands—at the mercy of his every desire," and: "He

217

took the proud vixen as his prisoner and swore she would serve."[426]

It's no exaggeration to say there's a whole sub-category of romance fiction in which male sexual dominance and female sexual submissiveness is a major theme. Titles such as *Sweet Silken Bondage, Captive Chains, No Choice But Surrender, Creole Captive, Passion's Prisoner, Bound by Ecstasy, Defiant Captive, Enslaved, Ravished,* and *Fires of Surrender* make this undeniable.

In Catherine Hart's 1993 *Silken Savage*, Tanya, the heroine, is kidnapped in a raid by Cheyenne warriors in the American Old West. On arrival at the Indian camp, a leather collar and leash are fitted around her neck. She is pushed from the horse and required to run beside it as a taunting crowd gathers to grab at her. A searing-hot brand is removed from the fire and applied to her thigh, permanently scarring her and marking her as the property of a warrior named Panther. During the night, she escapes, but he catches her and returns her to the teepee, where he beats her.

Tanya is led everywhere on the leash. With each passing night, Panther forces her into closer intimacy. At first he merely insists that their bodies touch. Then he begins caressing her before falling asleep. Kisses and whispers follow. Eventually, she begins to respond. On one occasion, he brings her to orgasm with his fingers.

The next morning, Tanya is filled with "self-loathing" but is unable to keep her eyes off Panther, who smiles to himself and decides that he has succeeded in ensuring that she will be "willing and eager."[427] That evening, he orders her to undress him and loosen his braids. He caresses her and, before commencing intercourse, makes her admit she wants him. Fifty pages and some time later, we read:

> She sensed Panther's need to master her and succumbed to him willingly. She made no protest when he locked her arms over her head and held them there,

218

nor when he spread her legs wide and anchored them with the weight of his own.[428]

It isn't uncommon for women to find rough sex enjoyable in these novels. *Allegheny Captive*, written by Caroline Bourne, includes a scene involving a drunk, emotionally distraught hero who ignores the heroine's struggles as he tears violently at her clothing and then has intercourse with her. We read:

> When, at last, glimmering lights filled her brain and her body in one delightful burst of energy, she forgot that his actions might be construed as rape. If he had done it again, oh so much more slowly, she would not have fought him, not even a little. His possession of her was the most erotic and wildly wonderful experience she had ever imagined...[429]

In *Slave of My Heart*, the hero encounters the heroine after she has run away from him. He accuses her of being a whore and attacks her from behind. Although the language isn't specific enough for the reader to be certain, the suggestion is that he sodomizes her. Furious and in pain, she feels her own desire awaken nonetheless.[430]

Even when the heroine is far from being an innocent, even when she doesn't need the hero to introduce her to the pleasures of the flesh, sexual jousting is a mainstay. This is the case in Susan Johnson's 1994 novel, *Pure Sin*. Flora and the hero, Adam, have intercourse within minutes of their first meeting—on page 12. But both protagonists are proud, obstinate, and short-tempered. Frustrated by his inability to win other skirmishes, and aware of how much Flora desires him, Adam strives to gain the upper hand in the sexual arena.

On one occasion, she arrives at his hotel room at two in the morning. He reclines in a chair and tells her to undress in front of him. She removes her blouse and he orders her to caress her breasts. He asks her whether or not she's wet and tells her to raise her skirt and insert her own fingers in order to prove it. We read that she does so "because she desperately wanted him and because she realized too she would have him only if she was obedient to his wishes." He asks her whether she's come to his room "to get fucked" and makes her answer.[431] He chastises her for having traversed the hallway in revealing clothing and asks her who else she's slept with since he's last seen her. When she says it's been 33 days and that she's had sex with no one else, he's pleased and tells her all she has to do is remove her skirt. Naked, while he remains fully clothed, she does as she's told and raises her foot, resting it near him on his chair. He looks at her open thighs and caresses her while she pleads with him to take her. He pulls her onto his lap and slides his penis into her but then holds her still. He makes her plead some more. He commands her to lift her breasts to his lips, telling her she isn't allowed to be too vocal in her response or she'll disturb the hotel guests in nearby rooms:

> "Now the other one," he said with that authority in his voice that intoxicated her libido, as if she had no control over her body, as if he possessed her, owned her, mind and soul. "You've been so quiet, you deserve a reward...
>
> "Bring it closer." He rested his head against the back of the chair and waited for her to lean forward to offer him the breast that always brought her to climax.[432]

Holding her hips immobile, Adam asks whether she is about to achieve an orgasm. "I asked you a question," he repeats. In the morning he tells her he thinks he'll keep her naked so she can "service" him any time.[433]

Where sex is concerned, contemporary feminist thinking often has much in common with old-fashioned mores. Pamphlets about date rape imply that, unlike men, women never aggressively pursue sex and don't get swept away by desire. In Katie Roiphe's words, this is "our grandmothers' assumption: men want sex, women don't."[434]

The feminist anti-pornography position is just another version of this. It says that while men crave raunchy, politically incorrect fornication, women prefer soft-focus, syrupy sweet, egalitarian love-making. While men find the idea of some kinds of violence sexually arousing, women don't. While men are titillated by the notion of dominating or being dominated in the bedroom, women aren't. While men think that pain can be pleasurable under certain circumstances, women don't.

In the words of the Canadian Panel on Violence Against Women, erotica (good) can be distinguished from pornography (bad) "by examining the issues of power." The report maintains that erotica "portrays or describes people in situations of mutual respect and pleasure," while porn "relies on the depiction of domination and unequal power relationships through the degradation and humiliation of human beings."[435]

According to the panel, pornography is one among many under-acknowledged "forms of violence" against women. It says that while "Canadian feminists have been working toward recognition of this strong link between pornography and violence," other people, such as "civil libertarians and some arts groups," equate anti-porn measures with censorship. The implication being that no feminists have concerns about censorship, and that one cannot be both a feminist and a civil libertarian at the same time.[436]

The anti-porn lobby has been so pervasive and adamant that much of the public believes a direct connection between porn and rape has been proven. That isn't the case.

If you put a group of young men in a room and show them videos containing violent sexual material, their adrenaline levels will increase and they will demonstrate a propensity to behave more aggressively than usual. But anything that causes higher adrenaline levels will produce the same result—including 20 minutes on an exercise bicycle, or watching violent material with no sexual content.

221

Unless we're prepared to ban exercise bicycles, jogging, and large numbers of mainstream films, there's no reason to scapegoat porn.[437]

Other people consider the fact that sexually explicit material has been found in the home of serial rapists—or that a few of these criminals have declared, in a new twist on 'the devil made me do it' defence, that porn caused their horrific behaviour—to be evidence of a link between crime and porn. But that overlooks the millions of people who use pornography and don't turn into rapists. It also ignores the fact that some criminals blame the Bible for inspiring their crimes. If we're going to hold porn responsible, there can be no reason not to indict the Holy Book as well.[438]

According to feminist anti-porn activists, there's only one way to interpret a photograph depicting a woman restrained and gagged. The possibility that it might be harmless sexual entertainment, produced and consumed by consenting adults who understand the difference between fantasy and coercion, doesn't even make it into the discussion. Instead, the image is considered a training manual for misogynists who, says the Violence Report, force their wives or girlfriends into similar poses once such ideas have been implanted in their heads.[439] (In *Only Words*, a collection of anti-porn lectures, MacKinnon says that permitting men to view porn is like telling a trained guard dog to "kill.")[440]

Anti-porn sentiment extends beyond feminist circles. In what is known as the Butler decision, the Supreme Court of Canada ruled in 1992 that pornographic materials that place women "in positions of subordination, servile submission or humiliation" violate "the principles of equality and dignity of all human beings." It further proclaimed that "Consent cannot save materials that otherwise contain degrading or dehumanizing scenes" since, in its opinion, "Sometimes the very appearance of consent makes the depicted acts even more degrading or dehumanizing."[441]

Referring to the findings of the controversial American Meese Commission investigation into pornography, the court said that since "a substantial body of opinion" considers this material to be dangerous, it isn't necessary to actually prove that this is the case. As a result, the depiction of certain sexual scenarios (in gay publications, men's magazines, and videos—but not in romance novels, apparently) is illegal in this country.

In order to come to such a decision, though, Canada's highest judicial body first had to arrive at a moralistic judgment. There's no law against tying up another consenting adult and having sex with them. There's no law against role-playing sexual fantasies in which one partner kisses the other's feet. Therefore, when the court called depictions of these perfectly lawful activities 'degrading' and 'dehumanizing,' it was making a statement about what kinds of sex it thinks are healthy and what it considers pathological—in the same way that some people still declare gay sex to be 'abnormal.'

Next, the court accepted the argument put forward by the feminist Legal Education Action Fund (Catherine MacKinnon was hired to co-author its brief) that this is an issue of *male* freedom of speech versus *female* safety.[442] In the name of promoting female equality, the court chose to believe that men and women are fundamentally different with respect to what turns us on—a profoundly sexist doctrine.

These views should give any thinking woman pause, because underlying them is the notion that no self-respecting female would have the slightest interest in sexual fantasies that involve power struggles. No healthy woman would fantasize about chaining a gorgeous man to the bed and having her way with him for 72 hours. It clearly can't conceive of any woman in her right mind day-dreaming about being kidnapped by a tall, dark, and handsome stranger who finds her so alluring he can't keep his hands off her, who is so overcome by desire that he rips the clothes from

223

her body, pins her down, and drives her wild with sexual pleasure.

Not long ago, 'pure' women—the sort that men brought home to their mothers—were expected to view sex as an unpleasant duty. Those who acknowledged their own libidos were considered aberrant. In 1858, for example, a British surgeon named Isaac Baker Brown introduced clitoridectomies as a 'cure' for female masturbation.[443]

Today, women are being told—by mainstream feminism and the Supreme Court of Canada—that 'good' girls aren't interested in sexual fantasies that involve domination, submission, or bondage. We're told that only men (violent, nasty ones) get turned on by such things. We're told that we shouldn't think these sorts of thoughts. If our sexuality isn't as strait-laced as the court assumes it to be, we're filthy, perverted, and abnormal.

But the truth is that women do find porn—kinky or otherwise—arousing. In 1987, *Time* magazine estimated that women were renting as much as 40 percent of X-rated videos.[444] A British women's magazine readership poll published in 1993 found that 83 percent of women acknowledged being turned-on by porn, while a joint *Details* and *Mademoiselle* readership survey that same year determined that 21 percent of female respondents enjoyed explicit videotapes, and that one in four had been tied up during sex.[445]

No one remotely familiar with the romance fiction I've described above can deny that plenty of women are interested in sexual fantasy material that involves overt or implied bondage. Despite what anti-porn feminists would like to believe, many women are also aroused by scenarios in which females are kidnapped and threatened with rape.

Let us be clear about this: *female* consumers are the reason the $855-million (U.S.) per year romance industry exists.[446] While men purchase most of the material we normally think of when we talk about pornography (*Playboy*, *Penthouse*, explicit videos), and while we may quibble over who reads other types of erotic literature, there's no question that women buy the vast majority of romance

novels. If domination and submission held no allure whatsoever for women, if every last one of us was interested
solely in unmistakably consensual sexual fantasies, the
kinds of novels I've described wouldn't be readily available
in every general interest bookstore.

Formula fiction publishers publish what sells. Although
the writing is often more than competent, no one is pretending these are literary masterpieces. Romance novels
are a commodity, and commodities that have no appeal in
the marketplace are pushed aside by those that do. Whatever else one might say about this genre, readers have a
great deal of choice with respect to what kinds of books
they buy and which authors they choose to support or
avoid. How women have been exercising these choices tells
us something important about female sexuality—if only
we were honest enough to admit it.

In a 1991 article published in *Ms.*, Gloria Steinem describes a typical scene in a movie, involving the hero (who
possesses an air of authority) and the heroine (who's beautiful):

> At first, she resists. He uses just enough strength to be
> a real man, but not quite enough to be a bad guy. She
> guards her virginity—or in a modern movie, the psy-
> chic virginity of her independence—with words, with
> the language of her body arching away, with her fists
> pushing against him.
>   Then he kisses her—and suddenly, everything changes.
> Her body softens, her fists unclench. The camera focuses
> on the ritual image: her hands sliding around his neck
> in total surrender.[447]

Steinem tells us that, as "a little girl watching versions of
this scene in Saturday matinees," she remembers feeling
"betrayed." She says she was left wondering why the heroine was "giving in to a man who behaved like a bully." Initially, she assumed that these "dominant/submissive
scenes" were an accurate reflection of adult reality. Later,

she says, she came to realize that "even a little aggression was a sexual turnoff," but she still assumed that most women disagreed. She writes:

> Only when I was past 30 and feminism had arrived in my life did I finally stop believing movie dialogue and listen to what real women said. I discovered that most of them felt endangered by domination, as I did; that the few who found it sexual often had grown up with attention, love, sex, and violence so intertwined that they believed you couldn't get one without the others.[448]

This is Steinem's rendition of the 'healthy women aren't interested in sexual domination fantasies' argument. These movie scenes don't work for her and many other women. Big deal. The problem is that she then she declares her own response to be normal and implies that women who *are* aroused by such scenes come from abusive backgrounds. According to Steinem, these "resistance to surrender" scenes are *male* fantasies, which serve to justify real-life violence against girls and women. She spends the remainder of the article linking childhood sexual abuse to former Hollywood sex goddesses, and the people who exploited them during their careers.

Steinem, who thinks it's OK to drug real-life women until they admit to sexual invasions that may or may not have happened, refuses to acknowledge the all-important distinction between fantasy and reality. Hollywood is in the business of producing escapist entertainment. It's understandable that, as a child, Steinem failed to appreciate that a heroine who melts after being kissed by the hero is acknowledging the power of sexual passion, of lust.

One might also observe that the unspoken rule in women's fiction is: context, context, context. In *Heart's Surrender*, a 1994 novel by Kathleen Morgan, Rissa is among a group of women captured by a small band of Cat People, an alien (but still humanoid) species living on a fictional planet.

Rissa is selected as a mate for the leader who, early in the novel, thinks:

> As furious as Rissa could make him, he knew he couldn't raise a hand against her. Cat Men never struck their females. The few that ever did were severely punished, their mates given to another. And now that females, in their scarcity, were an even more precious resource, no one could dare be permitted to harm one. Even one such as Rissa, who dearly needed a lesson in respect, not to mention obedience.[449]

Although male sexual dominance and female sexual submission is an unmistakable theme, the threat of Rissa suffering vicious, ugly violence at the hands of the hero is explicitly ruled out early on. It's the *suggestion* of violence that appeals to readers.

As this story progresses it becomes evident that the hero, despite his aggressive posturing, is not only strong and handsome but honourable and kind. Rissa is eventually reunited with her father (whom she hasn't seen since she was a child), only to find that he treats her with less affection and respect than her 'savage' Cat Man lover. The fact that her kidnapper ends up looking good by comparison gives Rissa permission to love him unashamedly—just as the often convoluted plot lines in other novels give female readers permission to fantasize about things they know shouldn't appeal to them. In real life we're well aware that we're more likely to be abducted by a physically unappealing sicko than by a heart-throb who turns out to be a well-balanced, decent guy.

Again and again, authors signal to readers that only certain kinds of violence, in certain situations, are being eroticized. In Heather Graham's 1989 *A Pirate's Pleasure*, set in the early 1700s, Skye's ship is boarded by pirates. An accomplished swordswoman, she kills one of the men who tries to abduct her, before the leader—described as "a small, sinewy man" with an "evil leer" and "yellowed, rotting teeth"—

gives instructions that she isn't to be harmed. "If she's as feisty beneath the covers, I want her alive!" he says.

Since such a scenario veers too close to a real rape situation, the ship is promptly rammed by another, under the command of a different pirate. Known as the Silver Hawk, he's dressed stylishly, is tall, and "whipcord lean and hard-muscled." It is Hawk who, after besting her with a sword, plants one "foot on either side of Skye, catching the tattered remnants of her once-beautiful gown and strands of her golden hair beneath his boots" and takes her prisoner.

Despite his overbearing manner, sexually charged taunting, inappropriate caresses, and the fact that he forcibly undresses her, Hawk doesn't rape her—even though we have no doubt the first pirate would have done so. When they finally have sex, on page 159, she runs into his arms and invites it.[450]

Hawk, like other heroes in this genre, is beyond exceptional. In addition to exuding an animal magnetism, he is smart, self-assured, kind, rich, powerful, and titled. Just as very few women possess the perfect bodies one finds in magazine centrefolds aimed primarily at the male market, few men walking the earth can possibly compete with the fantasy males in such romances. Most real men aren't independently wealthy, and we all know that brains and brawn don't necessarily come in the same package.

In *Beloved Bondage*, a 1993 book by Katharine Kincaid set in ancient Rome, the hero is a slave who is purchased by the female protagonist and told that he must be "submissive and obedient." He has "the body of a giant" and is "truly the most magnificent male specimen" she's ever seen. Though neither rich nor powerful when she first meets him, he is loyal and trustworthy. Significantly, before she orders him to take off his clothes and have sex with her, she first assesses the quality of his mind. They discuss politics and philosophy and we read that, as "they debated back and forth, she could not remember ever having been so mentally stimulated, so excited."[451]

What the men in all these novels have going for them is their skill in bed. They are irresistible because they have the ability to both awaken and satisfy a heroine's deepest longings. These books are about female desire as a powerful force in its own right, powerful enough to overcome fear and shatter social convention. It doesn't matter that she's there against her will, that he's insufferably arrogant, or that he's using sex as a weapon in a power struggle between them. The lust she feels is so overwhelming, sex with him is so good, that thinking has been replaced by feeling. In one novel, we read:

> he knew how to make love. He knew how to move: how fast; how deep, how slow; how hard. He knew how to kiss a woman's mouth and the tender warmth behind her ear; how to suckle her nipples and draw his tongue lightly over the curve of her breast or the pouty fullness of her lips. He knew when to lift her hips to meet his plunging invasion, when to be gentle and when not to be. He understood the delicate balance between violence and pleasure, between harshness and tenderness. He was accomplished at bringing a woman to climax simply by caressing her or talking to her. He was very good.[452]

The world of the romance novel is a place where female readers are freed from the pressures and expectations of society, religion, and family. It's a place where disapproval and responsibility fall away as female characters abandon themselves to lust. This world is attractive precisely because it conflicts so profoundly with the real one, in which dirty diapers, financial worries, and indifferent sex are more common experiences.

In this world people are every bit as glamorous as the ones who inhabit Hollywood movies and the pages of fashion magazines. These are fantasies not only about meeting handsome princes but (often) about being breathtakingly beautiful as well. In *The Beauty Myth*, Naomi Wolf argues that society exerts great pressure on women to expend large amounts of time, energy, and money on their appearance.

In romance novels, readers get to fantasize about what it would be like to be so attractive that men view you as a 'prize' to be sought after, fought over, and worth breaking laws to get their hands on. Readers experience, vicariously, the thrill of being so desirable that otherwise emotionally distant heroes astonish long-time friends with their obsession for you, their clouded judgment, their loss of self-control while in your presence. The notion that a man as perfect as these heroes are would have to struggle to keep his sexual hunger in check whenever he looks at you is highly gratifying. Why wouldn't such fantasies be appealing?

I am hardly the first person to observe that a fantasy situation in which a woman is, to some degree, forced into having sex (with the right man) has the allure of absolving her of responsibility. Many women still associate sex with worry about pregnancy and bad reputations. These fantasies push all of that aside. If a woman can reply to those whispers in her head: "It's not my fault, I tried to resist, but there was nothing I could do," she's freed to play the wanton.

Being the child of two avid readers, I consumed both romance novels and westerns from an early age. I can attest that these books have become significantly kinkier over time. The heroines in these novels have always been spirited, courageous, resourceful, smart, articulate, and headstrong—in other words, anything but submissive outside the bedroom. They often challenge the authority figures in their life and, in the numerous novels set in the Old West, frequently stand up to anti-Indian racial prejudice. The increased emphasis on female sexual satisfaction is a more recent development.

It's one thing to suggest, as old Hollywood movies do, that a mere kiss can transform resistance into surrender. It's another matter altogether to introduce chains and gags, repeated sexual encounters, and extended flesh-on-flesh seductions. In earlier years, women weren't really supposed to want sex, but they would respond to 'the right

230

man.' Here, women end up wanting sex badly enough to beg men for it—even men with whom they are angry.

A woman who pleads for sex is one who acknowledges she's capable of feeling desire as powerfully as any man. We aren't overly surprised when the chained Warrick responds to Rowena's caresses. Conventional wisdom tells us that men—particularly young, virile ones—always want sex. The fact that Warrick is able, in turn, to arouse Rowena so completely that nothing else matters represents a profound repudiation of long-standing sexual double standards. In these books, female desire is a robust, dizzying force—too potent to be fenced in and parcelled out by even the most determined of heroines.

Considering that thousands of women have told Ann Landers they prefer hugging and kissing to intercourse, and that nearly four out of ten Canadian women prefer chocolate to sex, many people's sexual experiences appear to be less than mind-blowing.[453] Women's formula fiction, by featuring sexual dynamos who typically spend a great deal of time ensuring that the heroine experiences absolute bliss, tells us something important.

Many women no doubt find such fiction unappealing. But the fact that so many others enjoy it makes it impossible to claim that fantasies involving dominance, submission, bondage, humiliation, and rape are the products of sick male minds.

Romance novels are an important element of 'female culture,' and their contents have remained a secret-that-must-not-be-revealed for far too long. Women are in no position to be casting stones at male porn for featuring unrealistic objects of desire, or for mixing sex with issues of power. Anti-porn feminists have never acknowledged that these novels contain huge amounts of politically incorrect sex.

Feminists further accuse male porn of fanning racism. That some male consumers—who may or may not be white—have an interest in sexual fantasy material featuring women who aren't white is considered evidence of racial bigotry.

Asserts the Canadian Panel on Violence Against Women report:

> There is very little published material on the role of racism in pornography, or on the links between pornography and racism. Yet in magazines and videos, women of color are often featured as "exotic." Mainstream men's magazines such as *Playboy* and *Penthouse* frequently publish photo features which degrade women of colour and feed and build upon ideas perhaps already existing in the mind of the viewer.[454]

As vaguely worded as it is, this statement is more than sufficient to telegraph the feminist 'party line' regarding porn and race, to make it clear that non-white models are a bad thing.

This is a case of 'damned if you do and damned if you don't.' If male porn featured only white women, would feminists not be criticizing it for considering only white women sexy? As has already been mentioned, there's no shortage of 'exotic' heroes in romance fiction. Relationships between white women and aboriginal men are so common there's a Reviewers' Choice Award for Best Indian Series. Some heroes are 'half-breeds,' whose native heritage is said to be responsible for their tall, dark, and handsome appearance, their mysteriousness, as well as the fact that they're considered 'untamed' and a little dangerous. In futuristic romance novels, heroes belonging to other species are considered appealing because they're believed to be more sexually skilled than mere human males.

In addition to the evidence available in the romance section of your bookstore, there's another reason to reject the idea that women have no interest in anything other than the vanilla sex most of us imagine our parents having. For decades, landmark erotic fiction has been authored by women.

Story of O, which first appeared in France in 1954, was written by journalist Dominique Aury under the pseudonym Pauline Reage.[455] It's a fictional account of a woman who becomes a sex slave and is frequently whipped, humiliated, and abused by (mostly) male lovers and strangers. Rather than rebelling against such treatment, 0 revels in it, striving to be utterly submissive.

Elizabeth McNeill's *9 1/2 Weeks: A Memoir of a Love Affair* appeared in 1978. We're told that McNeill is a pseudonym for the "New York career woman" who experienced these events. The book begins: "The first time we were in bed together he held my hands pinned down above my head. I liked it. I liked him."

The intense, obsessive, extreme relationship that follows includes blindfolding, bondage, spectacular sex, beatings, and public humiliation—all of which end when she suffers a mental breakdown. The book remains popular and has engendered an even more widely known movie.

But it is perhaps the *Beauty* trilogy, by American author Anne Rice, first published under the pseudonym A.N. Roquelaure between 1983 and 1985, that demonstrates most clearly that the female erotic imagination is as varied as the male one. The first book, *The Claiming of Sleeping Beauty*, is based roughly on the fairy tale. The entire castle has been asleep for 100 years. The book begins with the prince taking 15-year-old Beauty's virginity prior to kissing her awake.

What follows is a novel of "tenderness and cruelty," in which Beauty is one of a number of young men and women required to complete a term of sexual servitude in the kingdom of a powerful queen. Tormented by female as well as male masters, the slaves are routinely slapped, spanked, paddled, and lashed in these novels, which feature both heterosexual and homosexual sex. They are required to perform demeaning tasks and are subjected to ritual humiliations.

All of these books have been wild bestsellers.

Women have been dealt a full share of all those qualities that make us human—the ones we are proudest of as well as those that most disturb us. That there are people—both male and female—who are left stone cold by the above described sexual material is beyond dispute. Noting the enormous variety of sexual responses among individuals, anti-censorship feminist Carole Vance has formulated what she calls her "One-Third Rule." She says: "show any personally favored erotic image to a group of women, and one-third will find it disgusting, one-third will find it ridiculous, and one-third will find it hot."[456]

Among those who are turned on by porn, there is infinite variety as well. Many people are titillated by specific elements and repulsed by others. Some individuals are so discomfited by their positive response that they're barely able to admit to it. Others happily imagine, read about, and watch videos of dominance and submission, but stop there. Some enjoy play-acting these scenarios with consenting adult partners, while others push things further by participating in activities that approximate the real thing—as the author of *9 1/2 Weeks* did.

A minority of individuals step over the line into illegality, forcing unwilling sexual partners or children into taking part. It is at this point that such behaviour becomes morally objectionable, that the term 'violence' becomes appropriate.

Although raised as a Roman Catholic, I abandoned the Church during my teen years because I wasn't prepared to accept its view that I should feel guilty about impure thoughts as well as actual deeds. There is a difference between thinking about something and actually doing it. There is a difference between fantasy, play, pretence, and the real thing.

In the words of one of the men interviewed by Wendy Dennis for *Hot and Bothered: Sex and Love in the Nineties*:

I find the idea of overpowering a woman sexually and taking her against her will extremely erotic. That's rape, and I would never dream of acting on that desire in reality because rape is vicious and horrible. There's a difference, though, between having an erotic desire and acting on it. A fantasy is a pretend story...[457]

Dennis begins the first chapter of her book with the following: "I won't divulge *all* the dirty details of my sexual fantasies here, just a few choice tidbits. I will confess up front, however, that they're not even marginally politically correct" (original italics).

She goes on to explain that, over the years, she's had difficulty reconciling the content of her submissive fantasies with the modern, assertive woman she knows herself to be. "In the juiciest variations, I willingly submit while Mongol hordes of broad-shouldered, masterful, slavering men do unspeakable things to my body." After interviewing hundreds of people in cities across the United States and Canada, Dennis reports that what we humans find sexually arousing runs the gamut:

> what's "interesting" to some is conventional beyond words to others. If I tell you, for instance, that some couples revitalize their sex lives by lighting candles in the bedroom and taking baths together, some of you are going to think that's baby stuff. If I tell you that some couples watch porn regularly, or make their own dirty movies, or make dirty movies with other couples and watch them together, some of you are going to say that's disgusting while others will say, "Yeah, tried that...what else have you got?[458]

When Dennis asked people specifically about their sexual fantasies, she found no less variety:

> I heard female fantasies that involved a woman masturbating in a roomful of guys, being tenderly caressed by two adoring men, being the only woman on a plane hijacked by Iranian terrorists and being savagely "taken"

by them in the cockpit, having her pussy licked by a German shepherd, seducing an uninitiated teenage boy who was hired to clean out the garage, servicing a hundred guys in a hotel room, all of them eating beer and pretzels and waiting for their turn...[459]

"I assure you," she hastens to add, that the people "having these fantasies are solid citizens and contributing, productive members of society."

As a rebellious teen, I was also disinclined to feel guilty about being sexually active before I was married just because the Catholic Church said I should. (The Church, incidentally, continues to view masturbation as a sin.) Many things in this world are unjust or otherwise unacceptable. But assuming that people take precautions against disease and are responsible about birth control, in my opinion sex isn't one of them.

It's amazing how easily we can be led to believe that sexually explicit materials are the problem—that if we just regulate it tightly enough, if we force *Penthouse* to black out portions of its comic strips and lines of text in lewd limericks (this happens routinely now, prior to its importation, at the behest of Canada Customs),[460] we're behaving sensibly.

Anti-porn feminists have been so successful because, while we are a sexually permissive culture in many ways, many people still view sex as shameful and filthy. Feminism has tapped into these sentiments big time.

That this is the case becomes evident when one considers what feminists haven't attempted to demonize: alcohol. Diana Russell, one of the violence-against-women researchers whose work is frequently cited by feminists, admits that alcohol is a factor in a significant percentage of rapes and wife assaults.[461] Linda Fairstein, a Manhattan sex-crimes prosecutor and the author of a recent book about sexual violence, estimates that alcohol plays a role in up to 70 percent of date rapes.[462] Even though alcohol turns up more often in such research than does porn,

236

feminists haven't mounted a large-scale campaign against drinking. They haven't produced emotionally manipulative documentaries such as the National Film Board of Canada's *Not a Love Story*, or travelled from campus to campus talking about how alcohol's real purpose is the subjugation and degradation of half the population.

History teaches us about the Prohibition era and how futile it was to try to outlaw a product that millions of ordinary, otherwise law-abiding citizens want to consume. Attempting to restrict alcohol merely enriched the coffers of organized crime. Most people who consume alcohol don't metamorphose into rapists.

That feminists have insisted porn, rather than imbibing, is a violence-against-women issue demonstrates a willingness, on the part of these activists, to play on people's deep-seated guilt and shame about sex in order to advance their political agenda. In a revealing moment, MacKinnon, speaking at a conference in 1987, said of feminists such as herself:

> To change the norm, we looked for a vulnerable place in the system. We looked for something that could be made to work for us, something we could use. We took whatever we could get our hands on, and when it wasn't there, we invented. We invented a sex equality law against pornography on women's terms.[463]

The effectiveness of the feminist anti-porn campaign reveals how vulnerable our fundamental freedoms are when pitted against ideological fervour. In 1986, the city of Minneapolis temporarily enacted an anti-porn ordinance co-written by MacKinnon and radical feminist Andrea Dworkin. The ordinance contained no exemption for works having artistic merit, even though this is a usual feature of anti-obscenity laws.

MacKinnon has remarked that if "a woman is subjected, why should it matter that the work has other value?" For her part, Dworkin has declared: "It's very hard to look at a picture of a woman's body and not see it with the perception that her body is being exploited."[464] As Nadine Strossen warns in her impressive book, *Defending Pornography*:

> If the procensorship feminists had their way, pornography would be equally unattainable for women and men, for gays and straights. Those concerned about the rights of lesbians, gays, and bisexuals should not delude themselves that the feminist antipornography juggernaut would not ride roughshod over their preferred sexual materials along with everyone else's.[465]

In other words, a world run by anti-porn feminists would be one in which women's magazines, women's romance novels, and the book you are currently reading would all be banned. The Minneapolis ordinance prohibited the exhibition of women's body parts such as "breasts and buttocks"—leaving exercise videos and feminist works such as *Our Bodies, Ourselves* (whose authors campaigned against the ordinance)[466] vulnerable to suppression. Laws of this nature have the potential to cripple much television and film, gut libraries, and ransack art galleries. How many paintings by the Old Masters would receive the Feminist Purity stamp of approval?

This sounds an awful lot like a totalitarian state, in which—in the words of Isaiah Berlin—people whose "eyes are fixed upon some ultimate golden future" sacrifice much of what their fellow citizens hold dear in order to advance their brand of fanaticism.

During the years I marched and picketed for abortion access, one of the more enduring slogans was the one that said: *Keep your laws off my body.* The idea was that the decision about whether or not to carry a pregnancy to term was a personal, individual matter. I still believe that (barring exceptional circumstances, such as a considerably advanced pregnancy) neither the church nor the state has any business interfering with women's difficult choices in this regard.

I consider the issue of pornography to be a similarly personal, individual matter. I don't think it's any of my concern what kind of sexually explicit material my neighbour consumes. According to the 'One-Third Rule,' there's a reasonable chance he or she may have qualms about by what I'm reading. We need to keep laws off our fantasies as well as off our art.

Instead, we should commit ourselves to loudly acknowledging the difference between pretence and reality, between play and the real thing. We should ensure that our children understand that the stunts they see on television aren't humanly possible, that movie stars require special lighting and airbrushing to look the way they do, that physical violence is rarely appropriate, and that other people should be treated with respect both in and out of the bedroom.

Porn is a challenge for many couples. Large numbers of women say their self-confidence is undermined by the knowledge that their mates are ogling the flawless bodies that appear in men's magazines.

Everyone has a right to decide what they will and won't tolerate in their own homes. But a woman tempted to censor her spouse's fantasy life might ask herself how she'd respond if her husband demanded that she stop reading romance novels. She might consider how she'd react if he asked her not to bring home any more interior decorating magazines, since he feels inadequate knowing she's daydreaming about houses and furniture that are beyond their financial reach.

In the words of Christie Hefner, the daughter of Hugh Hefner and now the CEO of Playboy Enterprises Inc., "Men are very visual in their sexual lives. That doesn't make them bad, it just makes them different" from many women.[467]

Here, as elsewhere, tolerance and flexibility may be the best policy.

How brittle, fragile and aggrieved we have become.[468]
Globe and Mail (editorial)

8 - Sex, Lies and Court Transcripts

In the heart of Toronto, in office space leased by the Ontario government, in the files of an official body are gathered a selection of pornographic magazines bearing titles such as *Couples in Heat*, *D-Cup*, *Hot Shots*, and *Tight Cheeks*. They have been purchased with taxpayers' money, photographed, and duly examined—in an effort to force three mom-and-pop convenience stores to stop selling them.

In January 1988, teacher Pat Findlay and psychologist Marty McKay approached the operators of three stores in their Toronto neighbourhood and asked them to discontinue the sale of pornography. According to documents filed by the two women, one of the owners refused their request, the second "became very defensive and hostile and refused," while the third "became very hostile and started shouting at us, advising us that the magazines were there for men to buy and were none of our business."

Undaunted, the women returned two weeks later. On this occasion, the owner of Mike's Smoke and Gifts again declined to listen to them, the cashier at Jug Mart picked up the phone and began to call the police (prompting the women to leave since "his manner was threatening and he was not willing to hear our complaint"), while the person behind the counter at Four Star Variety "again became hostile and shouted." Findlay and McKay say they followed up by writing to each of the stores in question, once again asking them to step selling such material.[469]

These women have every right to express negative opinions about pornography. They have every right to

lobby their elected representatives and to attempt to per-
suade others to share their views. They were entitled to
communicate their opinions to the businesses in question
and, having been unsuccessful at convincing them to adopt
another course of action, had the right to do their shopping elsewhere.

For their part, the stores were selling perfectly legal
publications, many of which would have been inspected by
Canada Customs prior to being allowed into the country.
They were in compliance with a municipal by-law that requires adult magazines to be displayed five feet above the
floor behind barriers that reveal little more than the publications' titles.[470] Having been informed that two of their
customers found such magazines offensive, the proprietors
had a choice: either act on these concerns or disregard
them. They were well within their own rights to choose
the latter.

But matters didn't stop there. The women then filed formal complaints with the Ontario Human Rights Commission, alleging that they were being discriminated against on
the basis of their sex. Findlay and McKay contended that
the mere presence of such publications creates "an environment which is hostile to and discriminates against women."
They claimed that, "because of their stereotypical and demeaning portrayal of women, the display and sale of these
magazines creates a negative environment for [us] as well
as for other women."[471]

McKay would later tell the media that porn makes her
feel like a second-class citizen, that she symbolically identifies with the models in these magazines, and she doesn't
think she should have to walk by such publications when
coming in for a loaf of bread. Findlay would express frustration that, after having been informed that the magazines were 'harmful,' the store owners persisted in selling
them anyway.[472]

This matter has consumed inordinate amounts of time
and money. Human rights officers have visited the stores
and photographed the magazine racks. They have pur-

chased and examined copies of these publications. Bylaw enforcement personnel have been interviewed. Two different investigative reports have been written and distributed.[473] A number of legal opinions have been solicited.

In January 1993—five years after this saga first began—a relatively rare, three-person board of inquiry was appointed to preside over a human rights hearing that was expected to stretch on for weeks. The store owners, all of Korean extraction, who work long hours at their family-run businesses, were advised that if they or their lawyers failed to show up for the proceedings they would "not be entitled to any further notice" of what transpired.[474]

Press releases were issued and newspaper ads were purchased informing the public of the inquiry.[475] In response, nearly three dozen groups and individuals applied for intervenor status, including feminist anti-porn organizations, the Canadian Civil Liberties Association, and Canadians for Decency. A judge was interrupted during a party one evening by lawyers seeking a ruling on whether the board was within its rights to ban the publication of Findlay and McKay's names in the media (he decided they were not entitled to anonymity.)[476] The total cost to taxpayers is estimated to be in excess of half a million dollars. How much the store owners, as well as a periodical distributors' group that came to the defence of one of them, have been obliged to spend on legal fees remains unknown.

In October 1994, the board of inquiry decided it couldn't continue hearing the case, but only because of a technicality. By not attempting to negotiate a settlement between the parties prior to turning the matter over to the board, the Human Rights Commission was found to have violated its own guidelines. Significantly, the board unanimously rejected preliminary arguments that the Commission was overstepping its mandate by taking such complaints seriously in the first place.[477]

The Ontario Human Rights Code was established to give people who are denied employment, accommodation, or goods and services as a result of their race, creed, gender, marital status, disability, and so forth somewhere to turn. As one of the board members has conceded, this case isn't your run-of-the-mill human rights matter. It represents an attempt to "expand the existing jurisprudence to include the concept of a 'poisoned or hostile environment' in the provision of services." It is "based on a ground not specifically set out in the Code."[478]

In other words, the selling of pornographic magazines in corner stores isn't on the list of behaviours that the Code clearly and expressly forbids. Nor is this a situation in which such behaviour has already been found to be a legitimate human rights issue. Rather, this is a test case, in which people are trying to use mechanisms that were intended to address concrete instances of harassment and discrimination to determine where goods can be bought and sold. This is also a case that has received large amounts of attention at the same time that other, more obviously appropriate human rights complaints, continue to be backlogged at the Commission.[479]

The fact that these complaints have been treated with such gravity provides an indication of the thoroughness with which feminist thought has permeated the highest levels of our society. It also demonstrates how well-intentioned activists can end up making the world less just rather than more so.

In this instance, three convenience stores out of an estimated 4,500 retailers of adult material in the province were singled out for a stressful, time-consuming, and potentially expensive legal ordeal—simply because they're located near the Findlay and McKay residences. (A report prepared by the Commission found that there were other stores in the area that didn't stock porn, which these women could have frequented instead. The *Toronto Sun* noted that a retailer across the street from one of the three stores "opens earlier, stays open later and sells no skin magazines at all.")[480]

Once these women filed their complaints, the vast resources and intimidating authority of the state were arrayed against small, law-abiding businesses. At the time of this writing, nearly eight years after their filing, the nightmare continues. The Human Rights Commission, having been unsuccessful in mediating a settlement between the complainants and Four Star Variety, is considering whether to call a second board of inquiry.

As of March 1995, McKay said she'd be satisfied if Four Star restricted its sale of pornographic magazines to no more than three titles. Findlay insisted that such publications shouldn't be displayed at all, but kept "under the counter" so that patrons had to ask for them. Four Star rejected these terms, since such restrictions wouldn't apply to its competitors and afforded no protection against someone filing a future Human Rights complaint over the few remaining publications. The other two stores have come to some arrangement with the women, but the Human Rights Commission has declined to release details.[481]

Responding on behalf of his parents, the co-owners of Four Star Variety, Peter Kwon calls Findlay and McKay's paperwork one-sided. He alleges that the women went behind the counter without permission, "aggressively seeking the store's vendor permit," behaved rudely, and tried to intimidate his mother by threatening to call the police.

He says he believes Findlay and McKay are "on a crusade to decide what society should or should not read," something he finds disturbing in a democratic country.[482] While Findlay and McKay weren't required to hire lawyers when they filed their complaint and ran no risk of being hit with a $10,000 fine should the decision go against them, the same cannot be said for the store owners.[483]

What conclusions are those of us who believe there's more than one kind of injustice in the world supposed to draw here? First, two established, middle class women choose to make a statement about pornography not to a large milk-store chain but to the working-class proprietors of family-run businesses. That the sale of this material might determine whether or not these people earn an adequate living appears never to have crossed their minds. Next, these women took steps to subject the store owners, some of whom have a limited command of the English language, to a bureaucratic ordeal that has stretched on for the better part of a decade. Moreover, they have had the audacity to insist that they themselves have a "right to privacy," that the media shouldn't be allowed to report their names.

In 1993, a Commission lawyer told the board that "the claimants feel that they at this point are on trial for having voiced a complaint." Findlay "and her children and husband have been shouted out of one of the stores," he says, and "feels that publication of her name may increase this kind of treatment." Reva Landau, acting on behalf of McKay, said of the psychologist:

> my client is in a profession where she deals with other people, and the other people she deals with might react very negatively to the knowledge that she had been involved in this kind of case. I do not mean that they will take away their business and she will suffer financially, I mean it would create a very unpleasant atmosphere.[484]

Who says taking a political stand should be a 'pleasant' experience, insulated from all risk, consequence, or inconvenience? Changing people's attitudes, or the direction of public policy, shouldn't be easy. Demonstrating against capital punishment or nuclear weapons often isn't pleasant either—especially when one is confronted by equally passionate protesters on the other side of the debate. But surely this is the price one pays for having moral convictions.

Findlay and McKay seem to he saying that while they believe pornography is harmful to women, they should be able to protest it without disturbing the calm of their own lives. These women deserve to be protected from criminal

245

behaviour like everyone else. But why should they be shielded from the opinions of fellow citizens who disagree with them, or who think their behaviour is shameful? Why should they think they're entitled to a 'pleasant' life when they deliberately set into motion a series of events that have caused other people a great deal of anxiety and grief?

Surely there were other ways Findlay and McKay could have protested against pornography. Surely these mom-and-pop stores have a right to earn a modest living in the same manner that those across town do without being persecuted by governmental bodies that can afford to view the entire matter as an intellectual exercise. Surely the discomfort two women feel while being exposed to little more than the titles of such magazines during the few minutes they're in a store they needn't be shopping at anyway should be balanced against the views of numerous other customers who regularly purchase porn there.

(Incidentally, in Ontario a human rights board of inquiry doesn't enjoy the same far-reaching authority as a court. Any ruling it makes applies only to the specific store against which a complaint has been filed. Therefore, in order to enforce a ban on porn in *all* corner stores in the province, a complaint against each of the thousands of individual stores would have to be filed with, and investigated by, the Human Rights Commission. It's difficult to imagine a more inefficient, costly, and ungainly mechanism than the one Findlay and McKay chose to make use of in their campaign against porn.)

But just as Findlay and McKay think they have a right to a pleasant existence while they make other people's lives miserable, underlying their assertion that the mere presence of porn creates a 'hostile' and 'negative' environment is the idea that women have a right to go through life without ever being offended, insulted, or uncomfortable. Says who?

The first investigator's report prepared by the Commission observed that some of the adult material being stocked by these stores was in "bad taste," and added: "Although many women have come to ignore the magazines in question, those women who acknowledge or examine them, will *probably feel insulted* by at least some of them" (my italics). In a newspaper opinion column, Landau (McKay's representative at the hearing) has written:

> The argument is over which is more important: the right of men to have quick access in residential neighborhoods to magazines that degrade women or the right of women to buy milk for themselves or their families in the "convenience store" most "convenient" to them without being *insulted*. Men are not *insulted* when they buy milk: Why should women be? [my italics][485]

Let's take this one step at a time. First of all, being in bad taste—or offensive—isn't the same thing as being discriminatory. Second, many women are genuinely offended by the pornographic material available at their corner store. So, too, are many men. But this matter doesn't break down neatly along gender lines. Some of us are offended and insulted by Findlay and McKay's arrogance in claiming that they speak for all women.

Third, who says men aren't insulted by copies of *Playgirl* when they buy milk at these stores—a publication whose presence on these very same shelves both the complainants and the human rights investigators managed to avoid even mentioning?

Fourth, why should adult magazines be the only items a person might find disturbing? Do vegetarians get to argue that luncheon meat in convenience store coolers creates a hostile shopping environment? Do people trying to stop smoking, or who are struggling with compulsive gambling, get to argue that they shouldn't be exposed to tobacco and lottery tickets whenever they drop by for a soda? Do diabetics get to claim that a large percentage of the items available in your typical corner store are a health hazard (forget poisoned 'atmosphere') to them and therefore should be removed? Surely it's obvious where we'll end up once we start down this path.

Fifth, if these publications are offensive "because of their stereotypical and demeaning depiction of women," why did Findlay and McKay restrict their complaint to sex magazines? I could show you covers of *Cosmopolitan* that are equally stereotypical in their portrayal of women. If we're talking about the casual exposure one gets to such material when lining up at the cash register, why is a copy of *Penthouse* that's mostly hidden behind a barrier worse than the cover of *People* featuring Hollywood actresses falling out of their dresses? (To its credit, the second report prepared by the Human Rights Commission acknowledges this point.)[486]

Finally, if the Human Rights Commission is required to respond every time someone feels offended, why not look beyond the corner store? If I were to file a complaint every time I feel something insults my intelligence, the government would be spending a lot of time investigating television laundry detergent advertising.

We all know it's impossible to please everyone. Since even my closest friends are sometimes appalled by material I consider harmless or even hysterically funny, how much is going to be left over after we all register our gripes with the authorities? This book will undoubtedly offend some people. Should it be kept out of stores and libraries so as not to contribute to a 'negative' and 'hostile' environment for establishment feminists?

Let's backtrack for a minute to the issue of sex, to the fact that the only magazines Findlay and McKay complained about were publications that, whatever else one might think of them, are honest enough to admit they're about sex. Unlike *Cosmopolitan*, or *Sports Illustrated*'s swimsuit issues, these magazines aren't coy about the fact that they regard female bodies as sex objects. What appears to have offended Findlay and McKay, then, wasn't so much sexism on the magazine rack but sex itself. They didn't zero in on all kinds of stereotypical portrayals of women, only those appearing in sex magazines. And even then, they didn't target all sex magazines, only those aimed at a male audience.

Hiding behind the issue of how women as a group presumably feel about porn in convenience stores, we find something else: feminist hostility toward male sexuality. In fact, we've arrived right back at Catharine MacKinnon and Andrea Dworkin. In certain circles, these extremists are considered heroes for their anti-porn efforts.

Dworkin says that women who enjoy sex with men are

collaborators, more base in their collaboration than other collaborators have ever been, experiencing pleasure in their own inferiority, calling intercourse freedom.[487]

Her book, *Pornography: Men Possessing Women*, describes Caesarean sections in the following manner:

Modern childbirth...comes from the metaphysics of male sexual domination; she is a whore, there to be used, the uterus of the whore entered directly by the new rapist, the surgeon, the vagina saved to serve the husband.[488]

In 1991, the Canadian Mental Health Association sponsored a conference titled *Women in a Violent Society*. It was attended by 1,200 delegates including prosecutors, defence lawyers, and social workers. Invited to be a keynote speaker, Dworkin received a standing ovation when she *entered* the hall in Banff, Alberta.

On that occasion, her controversial suggestion was that battered wives should kill their abusers since governments and the courts don't seem to be responding effectively. Michele Landsberg, the Canadian feminist newspaper columnist who used to be one of my heroes, commented on that occasion:

In case you haven't read Dworkin, and have accepted the male descriptions of her as crazed and dangerous, she is indeed a radical theorist. Her searing analyses of sex, porn and violence are deeply disturbing and brilliantly argued.

You don't have to agree with all her conclusions to be galvanized by her.[489]

Nor do I need to be male to be alarmed by the fact that people in positions of power, who make decisions about the lives of other human beings in their capacity as lawyers and social workers, are prepared to give a lunatic like this a standing ovation.

Landsberg insists it isn't necessary to agree with everything Dworkin says. This sounds all very tolerant and admirable. But as we've seen, feminist tolerance is highly selective. Any movement that excuses Dworkin's anti-male tirades while denouncing Madonna and Camille Paglia is a movement more interested in covering up for its friends than in moral consistency.

Prior to becoming an anti-porn activist, MacKinnon made history as a sexual harassment lawyer.[490] The terms 'poisoned environment' and 'hostile environment' employed in the corner store human rights case derive from sexual harassment theory.

There are, of course, legitimate cases of sexual harassment. But feminism has pushed this idea to such an extreme that virtually anything that makes a woman feel 'uncomfortable' is said to be intolerable discrimination that the authorities must step in and do something about.

These days, charges of sexual harassment aren't limited to instances in which a person is threatened with retribution in an employment situation for rebuffing sexual advances - or to instances in which people persistently make inappropriate sexual remarks long after they've been told these remarks are unwelcome. Rather, hostile environments are said to be created by photos of wives dressed in bathing suits displayed on men's desks. In 1993, a graduate teaching assistant at the University of Nebraska was compelled to remove such a photo.[491]

Sexual harassment has been alleged when professors discuss nude images in photography courses. In 1993, fine arts professor Don Evans was charged with sexual harassment at Tennessee's Vanderbilt University when a female student complained about his use of such images. The institution has since instructed all professors to warn students about sexually explicit material at the beginning of each course.[492]

Sexual harassment has been deemed to occur when professors use examples from the Talmud, the Jewish law book, in class. In 1994, a female student complained about a professor who referred to the story of a man who fell off a roof, landed on a woman, and inadvertently had intercourse with her. Although the professor had used this example for 30 years when discussing moral issues such as guilt and responsibility, the Chicago Theological Seminary that employed him responded to the complaint by formally reprimanding him. A memo was sent to every student and faculty member, informing them that he had engaged in sexual harassment.[493]

These days, sexual harassment takes place when children call each other names and tease one another about body development in schoolyards. During the 1991-92 school year more than 1,000 elementary school kids were suspended or expelled under Minneapolis's Hostile Environment Sexual Harassment Program.[494]

Sexual harassment happens when professors and students feel 'uncomfortable' about reproductions of famous paintings in their classrooms. Pennsylvania State University agreed to remove Francisco de Goya's *The Nude Maja* in 1992, after an English professor complained that she and some of her female students were embarrassed by the fact that it hung at the front of her classroom. The professor refused the institution's offer to relocate the class, and was only satisfied when the painting was banished from campus altogether.[495]

Sexual harassment is alleged when customers read *Playboy* in diners. In 1991, a California waitress refused to serve a journalist who was doing so. In her view, his behaviour amounted to sexual harassment in the workplace. As Nadine Strossen, the president of the American Civil Liberties Union, asks in her book, *Defending Pornography*:

> Suppose a customer had been reading a newsletter from the National Organization for Women or from Planned Parenthood, and the waitress was a Catholic who believed that abortion is murder. Should she be permitted to deny service to the customer on the ground that this reading material constituted religious harassment...[496]

Guidelines enacted to ensure that everyone has the right to be served in a restaurant regardless of their gender or the colour of their skin are now being manipulated by people who want to use their own rights as an excuse to trample on the rights of others. Rather than ensuring that we all have as many options and opportunities as possible, rather than pursuing "a climate of understanding and mutual respect" (as is the stated intention of Ontario's Human Rights Code), the complainants in such cases insist their right to feel 'comfortable' supersedes other people's rights to free expression.

What sorts of messages are being sent by and to women in these cases? Let me give you another example. I have a friend who is attractive, athletic, blond, and friendly—in essence, many men's dream girl. A couple of years ago she attended a staff meeting at the government-run institution in which she works. A fellow (male) employee she'd never spoken to before asked her whether she "was as nice as she looked."

Afterward, my friend was approached by another (male) staff member who suggested she consider filing a sexual harassment complaint based on this single comment. Being a feminist with a sense of perspective, my friend laughed out loud and that was the end of the matter. But it might not have been. Had she responded differently, a great deal of official attention and a large stack of paper-work might have been devoted to investigating a remark that was a long way from being a misogynous diatribe on the one hand or an overtly sexual threat on the other. But there she was, being urged by a male co-worker to con-sider herself grievously wounded.

What view of male sexuality are women being encour-aged to adopt when the definition of sexual harassment expands so absurdly? What message are we telegraphing to young girls when feminists refer to boys who try to lift up skirts in the school yard as "gender terrorists"?[497] Is this how we produce strong, capable women equipped to overcome life's obstacles? Or is it how we end up with pampered, helpless whiners?

How can people such as Findlay and McKay think they're doing women a favour by suggesting that our sensibilities are so delicate that society needs to shield us from porn in convenience stores? Feminism has spent decades trying to lay to rest the Shrinking Violet and Nervous Nellie stereo-types. We don't need women reviving them again.

To quote the U.S. group, Feminists for Free Expres-sion, concerning a similar matter:

> It is ironic that just as women are finally making in-roads into such male-exclusive venues as handling a skyscraper construction crane, a hostile corporate take-over attempt, and an Air Force fighter plane, we are being told we cannot handle dirty pictures, and cer-tainly that we would never enjoy them.[498]

Paglia has a point when she says that what troubles her about the "'hostile workplace' category of sexual harass-ment policy is that women are being returned to their old status of delicate flowers who must be protected from as-sault by male lechers."[499] When Katie Roiphe talks about the images of "men as hunters and women as hunted," she's touching on the same subject.

253

Concerning the Minnesota mother who initiated sex harassment charges against boys on her seven-year-old daughter's school bus, Roiphe observes: "The idea of boys as a sexual threat, girls as vulnerable, now takes root early and stubbornly. These are not the facts of life they are learning, but a way of interpreting them."[500]

In our urgency to ensure female safety, we've lost the ability to make intelligent distinctions. The feminist 'continuum theory'—which maintains that remarks about a woman's appearance are connected to violent rape[501]—is massively responsible. Being *connected* to something is not, of course, the same thing as being *as bad as*. As John Fekete has noted, steam and ice "may both be composed of water molecules in a continuum of transformations, but if we lose the distinction between hot and cold" we're likely to either drown or get burned.[502] When people declare that there should be 'zero tolerance' for any kind of suspect behaviour (as the Canadian Violence Panel does),[503] our society loses the ability to function.

The tendency to interpret sexual harassment so broadly that *anything* that makes women uncomfortable becomes an offence is echoed by our current approach to rape. In 1993, I attended a Toronto court case in which three 13-year-old boys (whose names cannot be published under Canada's Young Offenders Act) were accused of sexual assault. This term encompasses offences up to and including brutal violence and penetration. On at least one of their trial dates, court documents indicated that this was a case of 'gang rape.'

In reality, one of the two female complainants—who were both schoolmates of the accused—alleged that one of the boys had touched her breasts while a number of the young people had been roughhousing. The other complainant alleged that, on a separate occasion, a second boy had grabbed her arm in the school hallway so that the third could try to kiss her (everyone agreed he didn't succeed).

After the girls mentioned these incidents to a teacher, they were brought to the attention of the school principal, who advised the girls' parents to report them to the police. Charges were laid. The girls received moral support from their elementary school teachers, some of whom apparently behaved less than warmly toward the boys. Before the matter wound its way through the court system, the young people graduated from elementary school and began high school, where the social stigma associated with the charges followed the boys. One of the girls complained that the presence of an accused in one of her classes made her uncomfortable. In the interests of treating victims of sexual assault sympathetically, the boy was required to take another course.

Eventually, after five adolescents and five sets of parents had shown up a handful of times in court over a period of months, after the police officer who had laid the charges had spent many hours in court as well, after the young people had all testified, after three legal aid lawyers had made their arguments, the boys were acquitted of all charges by a judge still capable of telling the difference between normal adolescent behaviour and rape.

This costly affair could have been avoided had the teacher, the principal, the girls' parents, the police officer, or the prosecutor exercised some common sense. But none of them did. These grown adults were blinded by zero-tolerance thinking. None of them was willing to risk being accused of not taking 'sexual assault' seriously. Parents of the boys insist matters could have been resolved if they'd merely been contacted by the school, and the boys had been given an opportunity to apologize. Two of the three defence lawyers claim they suggested to the female prosecutor on several occasions that the boys be allowed to sign peace bonds. This would have brought matters to a speedy conclusion. Independently of one another, however, they told me she'd responded by declaring the young males to be 'rapists in training.'

It's unclear what kinds of attitudes about sex, women, and rape these three young men will take with them into adulthood. Perhaps the fact that they were acquitted will, with time, blunt their bitterness and confusion. But should any of them be accused of such an offence again, this matter could return to haunt them.

Conversely, if either of these two young women—who were encouraged by the adults around them and by the kid-glove treatment they received in the courtroom to consider themselves rape victims—should ever be genuinely assaulted, they're going to start with a black mark against them. In the eyes of some people, they've already 'cried wolf' once.

Surely we can do better than this. Surely the puritanical, reactionary nature of zero-tolerance thinking is obvious. Zero tolerance was Ronald Reagan's response to illicit drugs. During the 1980s, the United States increased spending on anti-drug measures by 1,300 percent. Over a 12-year period (1982-94), the number of people incarcerated in U.S. prisons doubled.[504] Despite this, the authorities aren't any closer to stamping out illegal substances now than they were in the 1970s. All this coercive state power might have inspired fear but there's little evidence it has changed people's attitudes and beliefs.

Zero tolerance says that everyone who smokes marijuana ends up becoming a heroin addict, that people who start off drinking beer will become alcoholics. It's an approach to the world that is absolute, inflexible, and unforgiving. Yet we're tilting ever more in that direction.

When Ohio's Antioch College introduced a sexual offence policy in 1992 that requires students to ask for express verbal consent before kissing someone, and again before proceeding to the next "level of sexual intimacy," a number of U.S. commentators reacted with ridicule and scorn.[505] Little did they realize that federal sexual assault legislation passed that same year in Canada (after the Justice Department had consulted with Catharine MacKinnon) has enshrined similar ideas into this country's Criminal Code.[506]

Dubbed the 'no means no' law, this legislation was hailed by feminists but criticized by lawyers, who argued that it's inappropriate to use criminal sanctions to bring about changes in sexual etiquette. In the words of one spokesperson for the Canadian Bar Association, "I'm not sure that we want to put people into jail to educate them."[507] The following passage, taken from a May 1995 front page article in Canada's national newspaper, describes matters three years after this law came into force:

> Crown lawyer [prosecutor] Marc Garson likes to tell university students the story of a young man and a woman who were kissing when the man stuck his hand under the woman's shirt and touched her breast.
>
> The woman pushed his hand away and the two even-tually parted without further incident. But the woman, a high-school student, told her parents. They reported the man to the police, who charged the man with sexual assault under Canada's no-means-no law of 1992.
>
> "The defence lawyer was saying, 'This is a joke,'" Mr. Garson, an assistant Crown attorney in Sudbury, told 50 employees of Ontario university residences at a conference this week...
>
> But there was no laughter when the man was con-victed and put on probation.

The news story continues:

> The law means much more than no means no: Even without a formal no, tears or physical resistance, a sexual act may be considered an assault. It's up to those who ini-tiate the acts to show that they took reasonable steps to determine whether the other person consented.[508]

Despite the prominence given to this story, there has been little public outcry. Few people seem to care that young men are being burdened with criminal records, are facing life with the label of 'convicted rapist' hanging around their necks, for doing things no sane person could view as sex-ual assault. Garson, who's only 32 himself, isn't perturbed by this state of affairs. On the contrary, he told the news-paper, "The government [has done] a tremendous job of finally offering protection to women."

But at what cost? And how could we have possibly arrived at this point? How can we be living in a society in which governments fund pamphlets that advise young men that if they've ever convinced a woman to have intercourse with them by "begging," then they have "had sex through pressure, coercion or force" and that this is against the law?[509] It all might be outrageously funny if real people's lives and reputations weren't at stake.

Rape is a serious matter. It's one that I, as a long-time advocate of female self-defence courses, consider an important feminist issue. But laws that transform minor sexual missteps into criminal offences are unjust. Laws that assume that sexual interaction can be sanitized of all ambiguity, misunderstanding, confusion, or unpleasantness are foolish. Laws that take it for granted that men are more likely to be brutes than awkward, vulnerable, imperfect human beings are morally objectionable.

But such laws are the logical consequence of much feminist thinking. In 1988, the *Ms.* Foundation published a book titled *I Never Called It Rape: The Ms. Report on Recognizing, Fighting and Surviving Date and Acquaintance Rape*. Based on the results of a study involving more than 6,000 male and female undergraduates on 32 U.S. college campuses, the book claims that one in four female respondents had had "an experience that met the legal definition of rape or attempted rape."[510] This number has since been quoted *ad nauseam* by people who suggest we are in the midst of a date rape epidemic. But certain facts don't get reported. According to the book:

> "Only 27 percent of the women whose sexual assault met the legal definition of rape thought of themselves as rape victims." (page 26)

"42 percent of the women who were raped said they had sex again with the men who assaulted them." (page 63)

In other words, researchers specifically ask 3,187 young women whether they've ever been raped. A small minority of them—less than 3 percent—say 'yes.' The researchers then reply, *Ah, but we're smarter than you. What you think happened doesn't count. We weren't there, but we know what actually took place. Based on other information you've provided, we've decided that four times as many of you – 10.3 percent – are rape victims.*

If I punch my brother in the shoulder the next time I see him, I will technically commit an assault that fits the legal definition of that offence. Theoretically, I *could* be charged and convicted. But a world in which strictly legal definitions are applied to everyday life is a world in which we all end up behind bars. In a 1991 letter to the editor of the *Wall Street Journal*, Mary Koss, the study's primary researcher, tried to explain the incredible idea that these purported rape victims had had sex with their rapist again:

The observation that 42% of the women had sex again with the man who perpetrated the rape requires explanation. The rape victims in the national study were young, sexually inexperienced women; almost half were virgins at the time of the assault. Thus they lacked familiarity with what consensual intercourse should be like. Even though most of them said "no" repeatedly, tried to reason with the offender, and physically struggled, many victims reacted to the first rape with self-blame and thought that if they tried harder to be clear they could influence the man's behavior. Only after the second rape did they realize that the problem was the man, not themselves. Afterward, 87% of the victims ended the relationship with the man who raped them.[511]

Many of the men under discussion may have exceeded the bounds of civilized behaviour. But it's worth observing

259

that Koss's explanation invokes a flagrant double standard. She asks us to believe that these young women were so sexually inexperienced, so lacking in adequate information about what "consensual intercourse should be like," that they didn't even recognize rape when it happened to them. If that's the case, why can't the presumably young, sexually inexperienced men with whom they were having relations be assumed to be equally ignorant? If a woman can be raped and not realize it, why can a man not commit rape without realizing it? If this is what's actually going on, why characterize these men as criminals rather than ill-informed young people in desperate need of education? Criminals they become, however, when women who 'never called it rape' begin doing so at *Ms.*'s urging.

A further illustration of the way our definitions of sexual assault have been stretched almost beyond recognition was provided by the lap-dancing controversy that raged in Toronto during the summer of 1995. While strip clubs featuring female dancers used to have 'no touching' policies enforced by bouncers, in recent years the market has changed. The clientele of such establishments apparently lost interest in stage shows and table dancers once they were offered the option of having performers dance literally on their laps—the nominal price per song seemingly negotiable according to what the customer was willing to pay for the privilege of touching.

Women who were willing to remove their clothes for a living but who drew the line at strange men groping them were understandably agitated. They took their complaints to the media and soon municipal politicians jumped into the fray, eventually passing a bylaw banning lap-dancing.

Whether or not you believe it's appropriate to legislate sexual behaviour between consenting adults is a separate issue. For the purposes of this discussion, what's significant is that Jack Layton, one of the municipal councillors opposed to lap-dancing—and a long-time campaigner against male violence—publicly declared that dancers who were unhappy about doing such work were being *sexually assaulted*.[512]

According to this argument, it didn't matter that these women were showing up for work of their own accord rather than finding another job. It didn't matter that they were approaching customers, performing certain services, and accepting money in exchange. It didn't matter that they were spending that money and, the next day, returning to work again.

Rather than being viewed as adults who had made conscious, if difficult, decisions about whether or not to abandon the lucrative sex industry when their job description changed, male politicians on white horses were insisting these women were damsels in distress who were being raped.

It does no one any good to trivialize real rape in this manner. We live at a time in which complex matters are perversely over-simplified. Intelligent discussion is replaced by slogans and sound bites. The real world gets reduced to a comic book containing clear-cut heroines and malicious villains.

Among feminism's most ubiquitous slogans is the one that declares: 'No means no.' If only this were the case. In 1990, Paglia raised hackles when she asserted that contemporary feminism

> has shut itself off from [Freud's] ideas of ambiguity, contradiction, conflict, ambivalence. Its simplistic psychology is illustrated by the new cliché of the date-rape furor: "'No' always means 'no.'" Will we ever graduate from the Girl Scouts? "No" has always been, and always will be, part of the dangerous, alluring courtship ritual of sex and seduction...[513]

In Vancouver, a judge found himself picketed by angry feminists in 1991 when he observed, in the context of acquitting a man of sexual assault, that "at times 'no' may mean 'maybe' or 'wait awhile.'"[514]

This is considered heresy by the women's movement. In a chapter addressed to men, *I Never Called It Rape* tells us:

"No" means "no." Forget all the times your friends told you that all women say "no" when they mean "yes." It's not true. When a woman says "no" that means "no." Stop. She does not want to go further. Do not try to cajole her or argue with her. And do not ignore her...

If a woman says "no" and really means "yes, but you have to convince me," then you don't want to be with her anyway. She's playing a game and it's a game that nobody wins. Forget about "losing an opportunity." Just walk away.[515]

The book deserves credit for its willingness to include this last paragraph. And, in fairness, the chapter addressed specifically to women tells them that they must clearly communicate with their sexual partners since "most men are not psychic." It further advises them: "When you say 'no,' be sure that you mean 'no.'"[516] While pamphlets about date rape routinely tell men it's a "myth that women say 'no' when they really mean 'yes,'" I've yet to see one that urges women to speak up about flaky female behaviour that contributes to such beliefs.[517]

Let there be no mistake. Any man who doesn't take 'no' for an answer is playing with fire and shouldn't be surprised to find himself hauled into court. But few people living in the real world can deny that human beings don't always say what's exactly on their minds. Because they're often in a position of power when it comes to sex, many women expect the guy to work for it. This can take the form of requiring him to say the things she wants to hear—such as telling her she's attractive, that he's missed her, that he loves her, that she turns him on, that he really really needs her, and so forth.

People do change their minds. If a woman is entitled to withdraw her 'yes,' to back out of a sexual situation that's suddenly become too weird, why can't she also do the opposite? When this happens, the man who has stuck around learns that, feminist dogma to the contrary, 'no' can, in fact, mean 'we'll see.'

Do women lie about being raped? *I Never Called It Rape* tells us:

> In acquaintance rapes, it is especially likely that myths about rape and the continuing belief that women lie about rape to "punish" men for broken relationships or [to] win attention for themselves greatly influence police decisions to declare some cases "unfounded." Although better education about rape is changing these attitudes, old ideas still die hard.[518]

In 1991, Michele Landsberg declared in one of her *Toronto Star* columns that women "don't falsely report rape, precisely because the courts are so relentlessly biased and the trial process so grueling."[519] If only this were true.

Two of my female friends are criminal lawyers practising in downtown Toronto. They're also feminists who have no sympathy for real rapists. Yet they both routinely represent clients who are falsely accused of sexual assault by girlfriends trying to get back at them after relationships end.

Similarly, Rikki Klieman is a U.S. attorney who prosecuted rape and other sex crimes during the 1970s. In 1983, *Time* magazine named her one of the country's top five female trial lawyers. Currently, she spends much of her professional life defending men she feels have been falsely accused of rape.[520]

No amount of official feminist naysaying changes the fact that these women have encountered false rape allegations firsthand. They know such cases exist. The rest of us can bury our heads in the sand, or we can acknowledge that the real world isn't the way we'd like it to be.

According to Statistics Canada, 14 percent of sexual assault complaints in this country are classified as unfounded by police.[521] That's one in seven. How many of the allegations that make it to court end in acquittal—not because the justice system is sexist but because it seems clear the complainant is lying—is unknown. Incidentally, only eight percent (one in 12) of non-sexual assaults are classed as unfounded by the police, thus contradicting the claim that there's no difference between the rate of false allegations associated with sexual assault versus other kinds of crime.

In 1994, researcher Eugene Kanin published the results of a study of false rape allegations reported to a single police agency in a small mid-western U.S. community between 1978 and 1987. He cautions that his study involves only 45 cases and so cannot be accurately extrapolated to other populations. (He also notes, however, that "nothing peculiar exists about this city's population composition to suggest that an unusual incidence or patterning of false rape allegations would occur.")

Over this nine-year period, a full 41 percent of the forcible rapes reported to police were classified as false after each of these complainants later admitted she'd lied. Luckily for the men involved: "These women were not inclined to put up a steadfast defense of their victimization, let alone pursue it into the courtroom. Recantation overwhelmingly came early and relatively easily." To quote the report:

> We know that false convictions occur, but this study only tells us that these false accusers were weeded out during the early stages of investigation. However encouraging this result may be, we cannot claim that false charging does not incur suffering for the accused. Merely to be a rape suspect, even for a day or two, translates into psychological and social trauma.[522]

Kanin found that over half of these women lied about being raped because they needed "to provide a plausible explanation for some suddenly foreseen, unfortunate consequence of a consensual encounter, usually sexual, with a male acquaintance." For example, the wife of a man who'd had a vasectomy was worried that she might become pregnant by her lover when his condom broke, and therefore fabricated a tale of being raped.

A further 27 percent of the complainants brought false rape charges out of revenge—because they were rejected by men, either initially or afterwards. Another 18 percent made up stories about being raped in order to get attention.[523] These findings suggest that when feminism insists that women never lie about rape it's merely trying to replace old patriarchal stereotypes ('a woman can run faster with her skirt up than a man can with his trousers down') with equally flawed feminist ones. This isn't progress.

I fervently believe we should strive for a world in which women are able to live their lives without being sexually harassed by their supervisors, bosses, superintendents, and professors. I believe women should live free of the threat and fear of sexual assault—from strangers, acquaintances, relatives, roommates, dates, and spouses. But I also believe women are more capable of standing on their own two feet than contemporary feminism gives them credit for.

It disturbs me that female self-defence training as a regular part of high school physical education programs is such a hard sell among, of all people, feminists. Feminism seems to take the approach that it's everyone else's responsibility—men, business, government—to fix things, to protect us.

In 1992, one of my newspaper columns pointed out that while a recent federal government report had advocated media literacy training in schools in order to combat violence against women, it made no mention of self-defence instruction. In response, a letter to the editor declared that women "are fed up with being blamed for being attacked." Its female author said this was what I was doing by arguing that women "are responsible for the prevention of violence perpetrated against" them - not quite what I'd said.[524]

I don't think women should be encouraging each other to run to the authorities every time we see or hear something that offends us. I think we should learn to tell the difference between real cases of sexual violence and run-of-the-mill, oafish behaviour. If the choice is between the dainty, spineless creatures that much of contemporary feminism suggests women are and the assertive self-reliance advocated by dissident feminists, well, there's just no contest. Writes Roiphe:

> Instead of learning that men have no right to do these terrible things to us, we should be learning to deal with individuals with strength and confidence. If someone bothers us, we should be able to put him in his place without crying into our pillow or screaming for help or counseling. If someone stares at us, or talks dirty, or charges neutral conversation with sexual innuendo, we should not be pushed to the verge of a nervous break-down.[525]

Adds Paglia:

> A male student makes a vulgar remark about your breasts? Don't slink off to whimper and simper with other campus shrinking violets. Deal with it. On the spot. Say, "Shut up; you jerk! And crawl back to the barnyard where you belong!" In general, women who project this take-charge attitude toward life get harassed less often.[526]

We need to take a hard look at where establishment feminism is now leading us. This task can't be left in the hands of experts or academics. This isn't a debate about obscure, arcane points of law. These issues matter to flesh-and-blood people in the flesh-and-blood world.

The women's movement has been responsible for much positive, reasonable, sensible change. But shoddy feminist thinking is now adversely affecting real human lives. Women, as well as men, are being accused of cannibalism by daughters who—with the aid of feminist therapists—have come to believe they were ritually abused while still in diapers.

Women, as well as men, are having their reputations smeared by feminists who cavalierly call those with whom they disagree traitors, attention-seekers, anti-feminists, racists, homophobes, and Holocaust deniers.

Women, as well as men, are affected when young males commit suicide at alarming rates. Every male corpse was once some woman's son.

Women, as well as men, are affected when our society encourages females to see themselves as victims-waiting-to-happen.

Women, as well as men, lose when frank discussions about female sexuality are discouraged.

Women, as well as men, have their lives turned upside down when a family member is charged with sexual assault for trying to kiss someone.

Mainstream North American feminism has gone badly off the rails. It's time that honest, decent people started saying so.

We have fallen into the belief that morality can be ascribed to groups...but no one is a better person simply by virtue of belonging to a group. Groups are essentially imaginary. Souls are real, and they can be saved, or lost, only one at a time.[527]
    Louis Menand

The Western world is full of people who've been through this experience of being, when young, a member of a group of raving bigots and lunatics, and have emerged from it.[528]
    Doris Lessing

Epilogue: Approaching Tomorrow

When my mother was 12 years old, Canada got its first female cabinet minister. As a teenager, she'd never heard of rape crisis centres or battered women's shelters. They didn't exist. If she'd gone to university she would have encountered professors who felt free to tell overtly sexist jokes in class, and who declared certain essay topics 'too difficult' for female students to attempt.[529]

During job interviews, she'd have been advised that since she wasn't a male with a family to support, she had less chance of being hired. Had she been an airline stewardess, she would have been expected to resign at age 32, since youth was a necessary employment qualification. In 1969, when Canada's Criminal Code was amended so that disseminating information about birth control was no longer illegal, my mother was 24 years old and had already borne two children.

When I was 15, Air Canada hired its first female pilot. Four years later, the Supreme Court acquired its first woman judge.[530] The idea that women are men's intellectual and political equals is an incredibly recent one. Within the lifetimes of people who are currently in their eighties, women won not only the vote but everything else that came afterwards. Seen against a backdrop of thousands of years of human history, the past century has been astonishing. It's time we acknowledged that that century is also a testament to the goodwill of men.

In the face of feminism's current anger and extremism, it's easy to forget that it was male politicians, elected solely by male voters, who extended the franchise to women. If most men had viewed their wives and daughters as hopelessly inferior beings, if most had considered females to be merely sex objects and baby machines, if most had been unwilling to share political power, we'd be living in a radically different world.

It might well be one in which birth control would still be illegal. Where women, rather than being professors, judges, politicians, and doctors, would be treated the way they often are in historical romance novels—as domestic possessions expected to be "constantly and immediately [sexually] accessible."[531]

It's time we asked a few obvious questions. If men are primarily violent brutes who believe they have a right to hurt and control women, why aren't we still considered their legal property? Why aren't we confined to our homes by law? If men are waging an "unremitting war" against women why did male-dominated legislatures outlaw wife battering?

Let's get a grip. When males conduct real wars, they kill hundreds of thousands of their opponents in shockingly short periods of time. Despite the very real sadism and violence of a small minority of men, most men don't spend their lives jealously guarding their male privilege.

The concepts of equality, justice, reason, and fair play were all invented by male-dominated societies. Those ideas inspired men to bestow voting and other rights on women when they need not have done so. Yes, suffragettes played their part. But had men not been willing to listen to reason, had they refused to be persuaded by appeals to their sense of justice, the struggle for the female vote might still be going on today.

Where men are concerned, feminism belabours the worst-case scenario while routinely ignoring not just typical, but best-case scenarios. A visitor from another planet whose information came solely from feminist sources would have no difficulty concluding that the average man is a rapist, child molester, and wife abuser. Yet the women's movement is silent about the hundreds of thousands of volunteer firemen who routinely put their brawn and their courage at the service of the community. It rarely mentions the men who go out of their way to mentor female colleagues. When such men are acknowledged by feminists, they get credit for being good human beings, not good men.

Males have traditionally been associated with aggression, but they've also been associated with honour. Among the many definitions my dictionary gives for honour is the one that reads: "a strong sense of what is right; keen moral judgment."

Honour is about doing the right thing, even when it may be to your own disadvantage. In 1987, speaking to more than 800 individuals at the New York University Law School, Catharine MacKinnon advocated for what she describes as an earlier, purer form of feminism that took "women's side in everything" and always asked: "'Is it good for women?'"[532]

Is it good for women? That is the standard influential feminists use to assess ideas. Not: *Is it just?* Not: *Does it treat some people inhumanely and spitefully?* Not: *Is it morally defensible?*

If men at the turn of the century had considered *Is it good for men?* the primary question, MacKinnon wouldn't be a lawyer today. She wouldn't be teaching and speaking at publicly funded institutions, publishing books, or influencing legal history.

A philosophy that consistently takes the side of one group at the expense of others is a philosophy that veers dangerously close to totalitarianism. Writes MacKinnon:

this movement believed in change. It intended to transform language, community, the life of the spirit and the
body and the mind, the definition of physicality and intelligence, the meaning of left and right, right and wrong,
and the shape and nature of power....it did mean to
change the face of the earth.[533]

There are frightening similarities between what is currently considered mainstream feminist thought and other
grandiose schemes that started out intending to build a
better world but ended up slaughtering millions of human
beings and confining others to death camps, prisons, and
insane asylums. MacKinnon's closing remarks on that occasion drew a deadly parallel: "there are more people at this
conference than it took Bolsheviks to topple the czar,"[534] she
declared.

In the dark days of Communism, Vaclav Havel, the renowned Czechoslovakian playwright, spent nearly five years
in prison for daring to say that the government-sanctioned
view of the world wasn't the only one. He has long warned
that high-sounding rhetoric can prevent us from seeing
life as it is.

In 1965, he began a speech titled *Evasive Thinking* by
talking about how parts of a decaying building in Prague
had come loose, fallen on a pedestrian, and killed her. In
the aftermath, an intellectual had attempted to deflect
public indignation by suggesting there were larger, more
important issues worthy of people's attention. Then a second incident occurred and another person was killed.
Havel commended the public's subsequent wage of outrage. In his words, ordinary people had understood better
than the intellectual that

the so-called prospects of mankind are nothing but an
empty platitude if they distract us from our particular
worry about who might be killed by a third window
ledge, and what will happen should it fall on a group of
nursery-school children out for a walk.[535]

We are presently at great risk of allowing terms such as 'sexism,' 'patriarchy,' 'male privilege,' 'misogyny,' and 'male supremacy,' to blind us to what's really going on in our communities. We need to see past language that disavows real people's lives, that reduces unique individuals to feminist caricatures.

Let us restore reason, compassion, and tolerance to gender relations.

About the Author

Donna Laframboise is a Canadian investigative journalist. She holds an undergraduate degree in Women's Studies from the University of Toronto. As a former vice president of the Canadian Civil Liberties Association, she is committed to free speech and to what librarians call intellectual freedom - the right of citizens to receive information from multiple points-of-view.

The Princess at the Window, Donna's first book, was published by Penguin in 1996. Between 1998 and 2001, she was a columnist, editorial board member, and feature writer for Canada's *National Post* newspaper. More recently, her work has appeared in venues as diverse as the *Wall Street Journal* and *VancouverDesi*.

Donna is the author of two books about the world's most important climate body, a UN organization called the Intergovernmental Panel on Climate Change (IPCC). In that context, she has been described by Germany's *Der Spiegel* as the IPCC's 'sharpest critic,' has testified before a committee of the British House of Commons, and has addressed audiences in Australia, Canada, France, Germany, Italy, Norway, Poland, and the UK.

Donna blogs at BigPicNews.com. She is the author of a 2016 report commissioned by the London-based Global Warming Policy Foundation. It explains that half of all published scientific literature may be wrong, including the climate research on which governments have been basing trillion-dollar decisions.

Acknowledgments (2016 edition)

Several people helped me bring this book back from the dead. Out-of-print for more than 15 years, and published before e-books existed, it was a big job that involved scanning, OCR correction, a fresh round of copyediting, and the design of a new cover.

I am especially grateful to Yvonne & John Cunnington for supplying a serene and spectacular writer's retreat. To Laura Wakeling, who was a second pair of eyes when they were most needed. To Donna Gollan & Kevin Speicher, who stuffed me with Thai food and lent me a comfy bed while I consulted the reference library. And to graphic design whiz Josh Gifford. As always, he was calm, talented, and good humoured.

I am blessed beyond reckoning to still be sharing the journey with my husband, Alan, to whom this book was and is dedicated. Louise, his glamorous mother, remains the most supportive mother-in-law a girl could ask for.

Acknowledgments (1996 edition)

My heartfelt thanks to all those who provided encouragement and assistance. To *Toronto Star* publisher John Honderich for taking a chance on a young, unknown writer four years ago. To Canadian Civil Liberties Association general counsel, Alan Borovoy, a hero from my teen years whom I never dreamed I'd get to have lunch with on a regular basis. To Robert Fulford for introducing me to my agent, Beverley Slopen, whose good cheer and firm manner keep me well grounded. To publisher Cynthia Good and all the other fabulous people at Penguin Canada, who've made my first book publishing experience a true delight.

Princess might not have been written if it were not for the generosity of my mother-in-law, Louise Jolley, who permitted me to escape to her hideaway and never let me know how worried she was that I was there alone. A big 'thank you,' also, to my parents, Euclide and Katherine; to Connie Cassis, Janice Dean, John Dunlop, Anne Francis, Amy Friedman, Donna Gollan, Peter Israel, Greg Laframboise, Catherine Marjoribanks, Marguerite Martindale, Irene Ogrizek, Lisa Pomerant, Marjaleena Repo, Kevin Speicher, John Sweet, Helen Takala, Stephen Trumper and Rebecca Walsh for all your help. Professionally and personally, I've been blessed.

Notes

It's never a good idea to take someone's word for it. Examining source material helps us gauge whether a writer is reporting matters accurately, or whether they're so thoroughly blinded by their own worldview that their account is suspect.

This book includes more than 500 footnotes. A hyperlinked version of these footnotes is available online at:

http://www.ivyavenue.com/princess_footnotes/index.html

Most documents cited in this book are over 20 years old. News clippings and photocopies have been converted into digital files so that readers may access them without spending hours or days in a library. They are part of the historical record, and are being made available in a fair use context for scholarly purposes.

Should the above page disappear from the Internet, copying-and-pasting its address into the WayBackMachine at Archive.org should retrieve it. Please regard that online page as the most complete version of these notes.

---

[1] Vaclav Havel, "Letter to Alexander Dubcek," *Open Letters: Selected prose 1965-1990* (London: Faber and Faber, 1991).

[2] Tatyana Mamonova, "A Discussion with the KGB," in *Women and Russia: Feminist Writings from the Soviet Union*, Tatyana Mamonova, ed. (Boston: Beacon Press, 1984), pp. 215-221. Profile of Tatyana Mamonova, website of the United Nations High Commissioner for Refugees.

[3] Michele Landsberg, "Backlash babes turn back clock on feminism," *Toronto Star*, 13 Sept. 1997, p. M1.

[4] Donna Laframboise, "Province funds studies of non-existent abuse," *Toronto Star*, 9 Jan. 1995, p. A15 and "Let public hear about conference," 16 Jan. 1995, p. A17.

[5] Judy Steed, "Ritual abuse does exist and must be combatted," *Toronto Star*, 18 Jan. 1995, p. A17.

[6] Donna Laframboise, "Battered shelters," *National Post*, 14 Nov. 1998, pp. B1 and B3.

" 'One-stop divorce shops,'" *National Post*, 21 Nov. 1998, p. A8.

"Sheltered from reality," *National Post*, 23 Nov. 1998, pp. D1 and D3.

See also Donna Laframboise, "Shelter in a storm," *National Post*, 16 Dec. 1999, p. E1

[7] Sally Armstrong, "Cheap shots," (editorial) *Homemaker's*, Jan-Feb. 1999, p. 4.

[8] According to the *Barrington Times* website, their circulation is 5,000. The New England newspaper directory pegs weekly circulation at 3,170. Barrington, Rhode Island Demographics Data. *TownCharts.com*.

[9] Alan Sorrentino, "Please, women, put away the yoga pants," *Barrington Times*, 19 Oct. 2016. Read the letter here.

[10] Jamie Burke, "Speaking out about 'body shaming,'" *Providence Journal*, 27 Oct. 2016.

[11] "Yoga Pants Critic: Please don't march on my house, I've received death threats," WPRO/John DePetro Show, 22 Oct. 2016.

[12] Barney Henderson, "Yoga pants protest after Rhode Island man states women of certain age or size should not wear them," *Telegraph*, 24 Oct. 2016.

[13] The op-ed gives her name as "Jamie Burke," and talks about the "response to a simple post I made on social media." The Facebook event page for the march identifies her as "Jamie Patrice."

[14] See her post here. The reference to Sorrentino was edited out later, but not before it had been reported by the UK's *Daily Mail* and a third party had taken a screen capture.

[15] Andree Massiah, "Yoga pants letter to editor prompts Rhode Island parade," *BBC.com*, 24 Oct. 2016.

[16] Jamie Burke, "Speaking out about 'body shaming,'" *Providence Journal*, 27 Oct. 2016.

[17] Jamie Burke, "Speaking out about 'body shaming,'" *Providence Journal*, 27 Oct. 2016.

[18] Yvonne Abraham, "In defense of the yoga pants guy," *Boston Globe*, 26 Oct. 2016.

[19] Rich Salit, "'It's not over,' says yoga pants critic," *Providence Journal*, 27 Oct. 2016.

[20] "Photos from the yoga pants parade in Rhode Island," *Boston Globe*, 23 Oct. 2015.

[21] Reid Mene, "Man Writes Public Letter Saying It's Disturbing for Grown Women to Wear Yoga Pants," *Independent Journal Review*, 24 Oct. 2016.

[22] "Yoga Pants Critic: Please don't march on my house, I've received death threats," WPRO/John DePetro Show, 22 Oct. 2016.

[23] Lucas Nolan, "Women take to the streets to protest right to wear yoga pants," *Breitbart*, 24 Oct. 2016.

[24] Bianca Buono, "Barrington man who wrote yoga pants letter now receiving death threats," ABC6.com, 22 Oct. 2016.

[25] Rich Salit, "'It's not over,' says yoga pants critic," *Providence Journal*, 27 Oct. 2016.

[26] Ally Hirschlag, "A man told women they shouldn't wear yoga pants. So they threw a yoga pants parade," *UpWorthy.com*, 25 Oct. 2016.

[27] Cuba 2015/2016. Amnesty International website.

[28] "Red Guards, Chinese Political Movement," Britannica.com.

[29] Brice Pedroletti, "China's former red guards turn their backs on Maoism: The footsoldiers of the Cultural Revolution are trying to make amends for the horrors of the past," *Guardian*, 5 May 2014.

[30] Nadine Strossen, *Defending Pornography: Free Speech, Sex, and the Fight for Women's Rights* (New York: Scribner, 1995), p.22.

[31] Daphne Patai and Noretta Koertge, *Professing Feminism: Cautionary tales from the strange world of women's studies* (New York: Basic Books, 1994).

David Sacks and Peter Thiel, *The Diversity Myth: Multiculturalism and the Politics of Intolerance at Stanford,* (Oakland: Independent Institute, 1996).

Katie Roiphe, *The Morning After: Sex, Fear, and Feminism* (Boston: Bay Back Books, 1993).

See also Greg Lukianoff, *Unlearning Liberty: Campus Censorship and the End of American Debate* (New York: Encounter Books, 2014).

[32] Table A-7. *Fatal occupational injuries by worker characteristics and event or exposure, all United States, 2013*. U.S. Bureau of Labour Statistics website. (US) National Institute for Occupational Safety and Health, *Fatal Injuries to Workers in the US 1980-1989: A decade of surveillance*, Aug. 1993, p. 4.

Statistics Canada, *Work Injuries: 1991-1993*, Dec. 1994, p. 13. Gender breakdown regarding 1993 fatalities secured through a private telephone conversation with Statistics Canada's Labour Division.

See also Katherine Marshall, "A job to die for," *Perspectives*, Summer 1996, p. 30.

[33] *Number of fatal work injuries, 1992-2014.* U.S. Bureau of Labour Statistics website. (In Canada, 96% of 2014 workplace fatalities involved men - see Table 23, Number of Fatalities, by Gender and Jurisdiction, 2012-2014. Association of Workers' Compensation Boards of Canada website.)

[34] Sally Curtin, et al., *Increase in Suicide in the United States, 1999-2014*. Centers for Disease Control and Prevention, NCHS Data Brief No. 241, April 2016, p.1.

[35] Sally Curtin and Margaret Warner, *Suicide Rates for Females and Males by Race and Ethnicity: United States, 1999 and 2014*, National Center for Health Statistics, April 2016, p. 6.

(In Canada, the news is more encouraging. Whereas five males aged 15 to 24 were committing suicide for every female in the early 1990s, by 2012 that ratio had dropped to three to one. The rate of female suicide has held steady, but the male rate has decreased. See *Suicides and suicide rate, by sex and by age group*, Statistics Canada website. Statistics Canada Table 102-0551.)

[36] Suicide in the world. *International Journal of Environmental Research and Public Health*, 2 Mar. 2012.

[37] Alexia Cooper and Erica Smith, "Homicide Trends in the United States, 1989-2008," U.S. Department of Justice, *Bureau of Justice Statistics*, Nov. 2011, p.9. For US males, the murder rate fell from 16.1 to 8.5 per 100,000 between 1980 and 2008—a spectacular improvement.

(In 1996, the year this book was first published, 68% of those murdered in Canada were male. Since then, that percentage has bobbed as low as 64% - in 2002 - and as high as 76% - in 2008. Statistics Canada Table 2253-0003.)

[38] Synopsis. *Daddy I Do* official website.

[39] "What to Expect With Purity Balls," *Purity Ball* website, 23 Dec. 2015.

[40] "The basics explained, and our direction for 2014," *Reddit.com/r/TheRedPill*, 1 Jan. 2014.

[41] "Rules for r/TheRedPill," *Reddit.com/r/TheRedPill*.

[42] "The basics explained, and our direction for 2014," *Reddit.com/r/TheRedPill*, 1 Jan. 2014.

[43] "100,000," *Reddit.com/r/TheRedPill*, 4 Mar. 2015.

[44] "NEWBIES READ THIS: A Comprehensive Guide to The Red Pill," *Reddit.com/r/TheRedPill*, 15 Dec. 2015.

[45] Cassie Jaye, "'The Red Pill' documentary extended sneak preview," *YouTube* video. Jaye utters that statement just after the 4-minute mark.

[46] Synopsis, (screen capture) The Red Pill movie website, 7 Nov. 2016.

[47] Cassie Jaye, *Reddit Ask Me Anything*, 23 Oct. 2015.

[48] Cassie Jaye, *Reddit Ask Me Anything*, 23 Oct. 2015.

[49] Milo Yiannopoulos, "'The Red Pill' filmmaker started to doubt her feminist beliefs...now her movie is at risk," *Breitbart.com*, 26 Oct. 2015.

Here Jaye says the *Breitbart* article "reported *exactly* what has been going on and never took me out of context." See also Jaye's answer to this question on *Reddit Ask Me Anything*, 23 Oct. 2015. [see online footnotes, as per top of Notes section, page 277]

[50] The Red Pill—a documentary film. *Kickstarter.com*, 12 Oct. 2015. See here for a breakdown of donors by country. [see online footnotes page, as per top of Notes section, p. 277 above]

[51] Cassie Jaye's Statement About the Smear Campaign, The Red Pill—a documentary film. *Kickstarter.com*, 3 Nov. 2015.

[52] See points #1 and #5 especially, "89th Academy Awards— Special Rules for the Documentary Awards," *Oscars.org*.

[53] World Premiere of Cassie Jaye's The Red Pill, (advertisement) *New York Times*, 7 Oct. 2016.

[54] See point #5, "89th Academy Awards—Special Rules for the Documentary Awards," *Oscars.org*. .

[55] Katie Walsh, "'The Red Pill' only makes worse the divide be- tween men's and women's rights activists," *Los Angeles Times*, 13 Oct. 2016.

[56] Palace Cinemas letter reproduced at "Stop Extremists Censoring What Australians Are Allowed To See. Save The Red Pill screen- ing," *Change.org*.

[57] "Stop Palace Cinemas screening 'The Red Pill' film," *Change.org*.

[58] Featuring Interviews with" (credits page), The Red Pill official website, *TheRedPillMovie.com*

[59] Rachel Woods, *Ban MRA Cassie Jaye from Australia*, Change.org, 31 Oct. 2016. In the comments that appear beneath this petition, the murder statistic cited in this petition is challenged. 56 people signed it.

[60] Cassie Jaye, "The secret inspiration for The Red Pill Part1," *YouTube* video. Hear that comment shortly after the 10-minute mark.

[61] Cassie Jaye, "The secret inspiration for The Red Pill Part1," *YouTube* video. These comments are uttered beginning at the 16:30 mark and end at the 18:52 mark.

[62] In "Backlash babes turn back clock on feminism," *Toronto Star*, 13 Sept. 1997, Michele Landsberg invoked Preston Manning, then the leader of the conservative Reform Party of Canada.

In "I'm Not a Feminist. But I Play One on TV," *Ms.*, Mar.-Apr. 1995, Susan Faludi mentions Republicans Dan Quayle, the first President George Bush, Norman Mailer, George Gilder, Dinesh D'Souza, Phyllis Schlafly, and Newt Gingrich.

On page 32 alone, she refers to "right-wing media," "conservative academic gatherings," "conservative Washington networking circuits," leadership that is "overwhelmingly rightward leaning," "conservative antifeminist journals," and "conservative luminaries."

In Donna Minkowitz, "The Newsroom Becomes a Battleground, *The Advocate*, 19 May 1992, Gloria Steinem dismissed Camille Paglia as: "Phyllis Schlafly with sex added" (p. 34).

[63] "Intellectual Freedom and Censorship Q&A," American Library Association website, *ALA.org*.

[64] Lines of defence: the martial art for women has arrived in high schools to show teen-agers they're far from helpless," *Globe and Mail*, 7 March 1992,p. D3.

"Female self-defence training in Canadian schools," *Canadian Woman Studies*, Spring 1992, pp. 103-105.

"Schools should teach girls to stop being passive," *Toronto Star*, 12 May 1992, p. A19.

"Best cure for violence could be self-defence," *Toronto Star*, 6 Dec. 1993, p. A17.

[65] Private telephone conversation with the Canadian Centre for Justice Statistics, Ottawa. Numbers from the Revised Uniform Crime Reporting Survey, based on 111 Canadian police forces in 1994 (representing one-third of the police caseload in the country).

Men under the age of 26 represent one-third of those accused of sexual assault, while those between the ages 26 and 40 account for approximately another third, for a total of about 70 percent. This pattern is even more pronounced with respect to violent crime in general. Males up to age 40 are accused in 80 percent of all violent crime.

[66] David W. Moore and Alec Gallup, "Are Women More Sexist Than Men?" *The Gallup Poll Monthly*, Sept. 1993, pp. 20-21.

[67] Lindsy Van Gelder, "The Truth About Bra-Burners," *Ms.*, Sept.-Oct. 1992, p. 81.

[68] Associated Press, "Prom 'queen' joke gets student arrested," *Toronto Star*, 3 May 1993, p. A2.

[69] D. Laframboise, "Real men don't have to wear a suit and tie," *Toronto Star*, 14 Nov. 1994, p. A21

Julie MacLellan, "Students don't skirt issue: offer support for beaten teen," *Barrie Examiner*, 4 Nov. 1994
"Two arrested after attack on teen taunted over kilt," *Toronto Star*, 25 Oct.1994, p. A24

John Ryan, "Beaten teen an innocent victim, friends say," *Barrie Examiner*, 25 Oct. 1994

John Ryan, "Youth beaten for wearing kilt," *Barrie Examiner*, 24 Oct. 1994.

[70] Doris Lessing, *Prisons We Choose to Live Inside* (Toronto: CBC Enterprises, 1986), p. 45.

[71] Ann Landers, appearing in *Toronto Star*: ST. LOUIS: 19 Jan. 1995, p. C8. SYD: 24 Dec. 1994, p. H9. CHINO: 5 Sept. 1994, p. E2. PEGGY and LOVE: 9 Sept. 1994.

[72] Ann Landers, appearing in *Toronto Star*: Alcoholic and philandering: 10 Nov. 1994, p. F2. Timid 39-year-old: 4 July 1994, p. C2. Wife batterers: 4 Sept. 1994, p. B3 and 16 Oct. 1994, p. F2. Acquaintance rape: 14 Aug. 1994, p. B3.

[73] Ann Landers, appearing in *Toronto Star*: Random kindness: 29 May 1995, p. D2. Teacher: 24 May 1995, p. E8. Loving mothers: 8 May 1994, p. B4.

Husband's ex-wife: 10 May 1995, p. C6. Manipulative grandmother: 16 Sept. 1994, p. C2. Soap operas: 15 Aug. 1994, p. E2. Credit cards: 13 Oct. 1994, p. C2. Snoops: 7 Apr. 1995, p. B2.

[74] Ann Landers, appearing in *Montreal Gazette*: Skinny dipping: 31 Aug. 1994, p. C6 and 1 Sept. 1994, p. C7.

Ann Landers, appearing in *Toronto Star*: GAINESVILLE: 24 Jan. 1995, p. C2. SEEN TOO MUCH: 20 May 1994, p. D3.

[75] Laura Hamilton, "Making feminism's message clear," *Globe and Mail*, 12 Feb. 1992, p. A14.

[76] Marilyn French, *The War Against Women* (New York: Ballantine Books, 1992), pp. 19 and 118.

[77] Ibid., pp. 21, 26 and 136.

[78] Marilyn French, *The War Against Women* (New York: Ballantine Books, 1992), p. 175.

[79] Ibid., pp. 14, 21-22, 105, 182-83.

[80] Ibid., p. 182.

[81] Ibid., pp. 35 and 75.

[82] Ibid., pp. 44, 181 and 199.

[83] Ibid., pp. 139-40 and 175-76.

[84] Ibid., pp. 113-14.

[85] Ibid., p. 197.

[86] "Bookwatch," *Ms.*, May-June 1992, p. 73 and "Where do we stand on pornography?" (cover story), *Ms.*, Jan.-Feb. 1994, pp. 32-45.

See also *Ms.*, Jan-Feb. 1993, p. 24 and Jan.-Feb. 1994, p. 73.

[87] Nancy Pollak, "Business as Usual," *Ms.*, May-June 1995, pp. 11 and 15.

[88] Nadine Strossen, *Defending Pornography: Free Speech, Sex, and the Fight for Women's Rights* (New York: Scribner, 1995), p. 77.

[89] Fred Strebeigh, "Defining Law on the Feminist Frontier," *New York Times Magazine* (cover story), 6 Oct. 1991.

[90] Rene Denfeld, *The New Victorians: A young woman's response to the old feminist order* (New York: Warner Books, 1995), pp. 8, 101 and 104.

Warren Farrell, *The Myth of Male Power: Why men are the disposable sex* (New York: Simon & Schuster, 1993), p. 316.

Harry Stein, Interview with Christina Hoff Sommers, *Penthouse*, Jan. 1995, p. 74.

[91] Rene Denfeld, *The New Victorians: A young woman's response to the old feminist order* (New York: Warner Books, 1995), pp. 12, 78, 100 and 238.

[92] Rene Denfeld, *The New Victorians: A young woman's response to the old feminist order* (New York: Warner Books, 1995), pp. 9-10.

Karen Lehrman, "Off Course" (cover story), *Mother Jones*, Sept.-Oct. 1993.

[93] For instance, see: *Ms.*, Sept-Oct. 1991, p. 76. Jan-Feb. 1992, pp. 70 and 86. July-Aug. 1992, pp. 29 and 64. May-June 1993, p. 10.

Jan-Feb. 1994, pp. 32-45 and Nov-Dec.1994, p. 75.

[94] Kathleen Barry, "Deconstructing Deconstructionism (or, Whatever Happened to Feminist Studies")," *Ms.*, Jan.-Feb. 1991, p. 84.

Ms. similarly promotes and publishes Dworkin. See Sept-Oct. 1990, p. 2. July-Aug. 1991, p. 82. July-Aug. 1992, pp. 29 and 64. Sept-Oct. 1991, p. 76. Sept-Oct. 1994, p. 75. Nov-Dec. 1994, pp. 52-58.

[95] Naomi Wolf, *The Beauty Myth: How images of beauty are used against women* (Toronto: Vintage Books, 1990), pp. 50, 57, 137 and 302.

[96] Rene Denfeld, *The New Victorians: A young woman's response to the old feminist order* (New York: Warner Books, 1995), p. 241. See also pp. 91, 97-98, 106-07, 110, 115 and 120-21.

[97] Catharine A. MacKinnon, *Toward a Feminist Theory of the State* (Cambridge, Massachusetts: Harvard University Press, 1989), p. 146.

[98] Catharine A. MacKinnon, "Feminism, Marxism, Method, and the State: Toward feminist jurisprudence," *Feminism and Methodology*, Sandra Harding, ed. (Bloomington, Indiana: Indiana University Press, 1987), p. 142.

[99] Catharine A. MacKinnon, "Liberalism and the Death of Feminism," *The Sexual Liberals and the Attack on Feminism*, Dorchen Leidholdt and Janice G. Raymond, eds. (New York: Pergamon Press, 1990), p. 4.

[100] Ibid., pp. 4, 9, 10 and 13.

[101] Ibid., p. 5.

[102] Catharine A. MacKinnon, "Standards of Sisterhood," *Broadside*, Dec. 1985-Jan. 1986, p. 6
and Fred Streheigh, "Defining Law on the Feminist Frontier," *New York Times Magazine*, 6 Oct. 1991, p. 56.

[103] Catharine A. MacKinnon, "Liberalism and the Death of Feminism," *The Sexual Liberals and the Attack on Feminism*, Dorchen Leidholdt and Janice G. Raymond, eds. (New York: Pergamon Press, 1990), p. 12.

[104] Catharine A. MacKinnon, "Turning Rape into Pornography: Postmodern Genocide," *Ms.*, July-Aug. 1993, pp. 24-26.

See also Vesna Kesic, "A Response to Catharine MacKinnon's Article 'Turning Rape into Pornography: Postmodern Genocide," *Hastings Women's Law Journal*, Vol. 5:2, 1994.

[105] Catharine A. MacKinnon, *Toward a Feminist Theory of the State* (Cambridge, Massachusetts: Harvard University Press, 1989), p. 138.

[106] James R. Petersen, "Catharine MacKinnon: Again," *Playboy*, Aug. 1992, p. 39.

[107] Catharine A. MacKinnon, "Liberalism and the Death of Feminism," *The Sexual Liberals and the Attack on Feminism*, Dorchen Leidholdt and Janice G. Raymond, eds. (New York: Pergamon Press, 1990), p. 11.

See also Nadine Strossen, *Defending Pornography: Free Speech, Sex, and the Fight for Women's Rights* (New York: Scribner, 1995), pp. 179-98.

[108] Wes Christensen, "*Ms.* is too good not to share..." (letter to the editor) *Ms.*, Jan.-Feb. 1992, p. 5.

[109] Kay Leigh Hagan, "Orchids in the Arctic: The predicament of women who love men," *Ms.*, Nov-Dec. 1991, pp. 31-33.

[110] *Ms.*, Jan-Feb. 1992. See cover here. [see online footnotes page, as per top of Notes section, page 277, above]

[111] Betty Friedan, "Why men die young...and why you'll live longer," *Playboy*, Apr. 1995. On p. 66, she writes: "Freud may have been wrong about women, but he wasn't wrong about everything."

[112] Robin Morgan, "Whose Free Press Is It, Anyway?" (editorial), *Ms.*, July-Aug. 1991, p. 1 and

Jane Caputi and Diana E.H. Russell, "'Femicide': Speaking the Unspeakable," *Ms.*, Sept.-Oct. 1990, p. 34.

[113] Marcia Ann Gillespie, "Delusions of Safety: a personal story," *Ms.*, Sept.-Oct. 1990, p. 51 and
"Where Do We Go From Here: An interview with Ann Jones," *Ms.*, Sept.-Oct. 1994, pp. 60-61.

[114] Robert L. Allen and Paul Kivel, "Men Changing Men," *Ms.*, Sept.-Oct. 1994, p. 50.

[115] Jane Caputi and Diana E.H. Russell, "'Femicide': Speaking the Unspeakable," *Ms.*, Sept.-Oct. 1990, pp. 36-37.

[116] Kathleen Hirsch, "Fraternities of Fear: Gang rape, male bonding, and the silencing of women," *Ms.*, Sept.-Oct. 1990, p. 53 and

Shere Hite, "Bringing Democracy Home: Shere Hite reports on the family" (cover story), *Ms.*, Mar.-Apr. 1995, pp. 57-58.

[117] Phyllis Chesler, "Mothers on Trial," *Ms.*, May-June 1991, p. 47.

[118] Lisa Maria Hogeland, "Fear of Feminism: Why young women get the willies," *Ms.*, Nov.-Dec. 1994, p. 20.

[119] Andrea Dworkin, "The Unremembered: Searching for Women at the Holocaust Memorial Museum," *Ms.*, Nov-Dec. 1994, p. 58.

[120] Jennifer Baumgardner, "Bold Type: Witchy Woman," *Ms.*, Mar.-Apr. 1995, p. 73.

[121] See Ann Landers, *Toronto Star*, 30 July 1993, p.E2 and 23 Sept. 1993, p. E5.

[122] "Majority oppose adult magazines Gallup poll shows," *Toronto Star*, 25 Apr. 1995, p. A13.

[123] Tony Wong, "Panel to make national study of violence against women," *Toronto Star*, 16 Aug. 1991, p. A5.

Sean Fine, "Panel takes aim at abuse of women," *Globe and Mail*, 17 Jan. 1992, p. A4.
David Vienneau, "Abuse of women at crisis level, panel says," *Toronto Star*, 30 July 1993, p. A22.

See also Canadian Panel on Violence Against Women, *Changing the Landscape: Ending violence - achieving equality*, Final Report, Minister of Supply and Services Canada, 1993, pp. v-vii.

[124] Barbara Aarsteinsen, "NAC's Rebick bows out, knocking 'Tory agenda,'" *Toronto Star*, 5 June 1993, p. A14.

Barbara Aarsteinsen, "New feminist leader attacks 'Tory agenda,'" *Toronto Star*, 7 June 1993, p. A2.

Kirk Makin, "NAC takes aim at the Tories," *Globe and Mail*, 11 Sept. 1993, p. A7.

[125] Status of Women Canada News Release No. 006, "Minister Collins Calls Panel's Report 'Historic,'" 29 July 1993.

[126] Canadian Panel on Violence Against Women, *Changing the Landscape: Ending violence - achieving equality*, Final Report, Minister of Supply and Services Canada, 1993, pp. 3, 4, 13, and so forth.

[127] Ibid., pp. 32 and 39.

[128] Ibid., p. 6.

[129] Ibid., p. 14.

[130] Canadian Panel on Violence Against Women, *Changing the Landscape: Ending violence - achieving equality*, Final Report, Minister of Supply and Services Canada, 1993, p. 19.

[131] Ibid., pp. 6-7.

[132] Ibid, pp. 4, 6, 10, 12, 14, and so forth.

[133] In fairness to *Ms.*, amid the scores of pages of coverage it has devoted to violence against women in recent years, it has also published two short pieces (half a page in length each) on the issue of lesbian battering. *Ms.*, Oct.-Nov. 1990, p. 48 and Sept.-Oct. 1994, p. 53.

[134] Theresa Boyle, "'House slave' suffered year of brutality, police say," *Toronto Star*, 27 July 1993, p. A6.

Wendy Darroch, "Woman guilty of enslaving roommate," *Toronto Star*, 12 Mar. 1994, p. A17.

Wendy Darroch, "Woman gets 18 months for abuse of roommate," *Toronto Star*, 15 Apr. 1994, p. A28.

[135] Roger Catlin, "Slain Selena's crossover dream comes true too late," *Toronto Star*, 22 July 1995, p. K12.

Associated Press, "Selena trial ends in conviction," *Globe and Mail*, 24 Oct. 1995, p. C2.

[136] Canadian Panel on Violence Against Women, *Changing the Landscape: Ending violence - achieving equality*, Final Report, Minister of Supply and Services Canada, 1993, p. 25.

[137] See Donna Laframboise, "Province funds studies of non-existent abuse," *Toronto Star*, 9 Jan. 1995, p. A15 and "Let public hear about conference," 16 Jan. 1995, p. A17.

Spokespersons from the Ontario Women's Directorate and the Ministry of Northern Development and Mines provided this justification in private telephone conversations.

[138] Status of Women Canada News Release No. 006, "Minister Collins Calls Panel's Report 'Historic,'" 29 July 1993.

[139] Janet Radcliffe Richards, *The Sceptical Feminist* (London: Penguin Books, 1980), 2nd edition, p. 48.

[140] Harold Mersky, "Multiple Personality Disorder and False Memory Syndrome" (editorial), *British Journal of Psychiatry* (1995), p. 281.

Debbie Nathan, "Dividing to Conquer? Women, Men, and the Making of Multiple Personality Disorder" *Social Text*, Fall 1994, pp. 79-82.

Mark Pendergrast, *Victims of Memory: Sex abuse accusations and shattered lives* (Hinesberg, Vermont: Upper Access, Inc., 1995), pp. 77 and 166-68.

[141] O.K. Ganaway, "Historical versus narrative truth: Clarifying the role of exogenous trauma in the etiology of MPD and its variants," *Dissociation* 2, No. 4, 1989, p. 209.

[142] Debbie Nathan, "Dividing to Conquer? Women, Men, and the Making of Multiple Personality Disorder" *Social Text*, Fall 1994, p. 79.

Harold Mersky, "Multiple Personality Disorder and False Memory Syndrome" (editorial), *British Journal of Psychiatry* (1995), p. 281.

Mark Pendergrast, *Victims of Memory: Sex abuse accusations and shattered lives* (Hinesberg, Vermont: Upper Access, Inc., 1995), pp. 76-77 and 157.

[143] Ibid., p. 157 note * and

Debbie Nathan, "Dividing to Conquer? Women, Men, and the Making of Multiple Personality Disorder" *Social Text*, Fall 1994, p. 101.

[144] August Piper, Jr., "'Truth Serum' and 'Recovered Memories' of Sexual Abuse: A review of the evidence," *Journal of Psychiatry and Law*, Winter 1993.

[145] Debbie Nathan, "Dividing to Conquer? Women, Men, and the Making of Multiple Personality Disorder" *Social Text*, Fall 1994, p. 79.

[146] Marilyn French, *The War Against Women* (New York: Ballantine Books, 1992), p. 196.

[147] Sylvia Fraser, "Freud's Final Seduction," *Saturday Night*, Mar. 1994, pp. 57 and 59.

[148] Canadian Panel on Violence Against Women, *Changing the Landscape: Ending violence - achieving equality*, Final Report, Minister of Supply and Services Canada, 1993, p. 18.

[149] Debbie Nathan, "Dividing to Conquer? Women, Men, and the Making of Multiple Personality Disorder" *Social Text*, Fall 1994, p. 100 refers to pediatrician Richard Kempe's "Battered Child Syndrome," in the *Journal of the American Medical Association*'s Vol. 181, 1962, as a 'landmark.'

[150] Canadian Panel on Violence Against Women, *Changing the Landscape: Ending violence - achieving equality*, Final Report, Minister of Supply and Services Canada, 1993, p. 14.

[151] Debbie Nathan, "Dividing to Conquer? Women, Men, and the Making of Multiple Personality Disorder" *Social Text*, Fall 1994, p. 79.

[152] In fairness, the new version of the Association's *Diagnostic and Statistical Manual*, DSM-IV, released in 1994, removed the word "full" from part B. Accordingly, John would now be considered a true MPD. However, this does not change the fact that, despite his failure to meet the then-official criteria, he was presented as a bone fide MPD sufferer. See Harold Mersky, "Multiple Personality Disorder and False Memory Syndrome" (editorial), *British Journal of Psychiatry* (1995), p. 281.

[153] Debbie Nathan, "Dividing to Conquer? Women, Men, and the Making of Multiple Personality Disorder" *Social Text*, Fall 1994, p. 79.

[154] August Piper, Jr., "'Truth Serum' and 'Recovered Memories' of Sexual Abuse: A review of the evidence," *Journal of Psychiatry and Law*, Winter 1993, p. 465.

[155] "The Search for Satan," Transcript #1402, *Frontline*, WOBH Educational Foundation, 1995.

[156] Private telephone conversation with Gretchen's mother, Nancy, in Nov. 1995. For the sake of her grandchildren, Nancy requested that her surname not be published.

[157] Elizabeth S. Rose, "Surviving the Unbelievable: A first-person account of cult ritual abuse," *Ms.*, Jan-Feb. 1993, pp. 40-41 and 43.

[158] Ibid., p. 44.

[159] Ibid., p. 42.

[160] Ibid., pp. 41 and 43.

[161] Ibid., pp. 41, 43 and 45.

[162] Elizabeth S. Rose, "Surviving the Unbelievable: A first-person account of cult ritual abuse," *Ms.*, Jan-Feb. 1993, p. 45.

[163] Kenneth V. Lanning, *Investigator's Guide to Allegations of "Ritual" Child Abuse*, Federal Bureau of Investigation, January 1992.

[164] Chi Chi Sileo, "Multiple Personalities: The Experts are Split," *Insight*, 25 Oct. 1993, p. 22.

[165] Kenneth V. Lanning, *Investigator's Guide to Allegations of "Ritual" Child Abuse*, Federal Bureau of Investigation, January 1992.

[166] National Center on Child Abuse and Neglect, *Ritual Abuse Allegations*, 1994. Report and/or Executive Summary available from the National Clearinghouse on Child Abuse and Neglect Information, Washington, D.C.

[167] Daniel Goleman, "Proof lacking for ritual abuse by Satanists," New York Times, 31 Oct. 1994.

[168] J.S. LaFontaine, *The Extent and Nature of Organized and Ritual Abuse*, (London: HMSO, 1994), p. 30.

[169] Randy Emon, "SRA and evidence." Posted to *witch-hunt@mit.edu*, 12 Jan. 1995. From sgtemon@aol.com.

[170] Kenneth V. Lanning, *Investigator's Guide to Allegations of "Ritual" Child Abuse*, Federal Bureau of Investigation, January 1992.

[171] Sherrill Mulhern, "Satanism, Ritual Abuse, and Multiple Personality Disorder: A sociohistorical perspective," *The International Journal of Clinical and Experimental Hypnosis*, Vol. XLII, No: 4, Oct. 1994, p. 280.

[172] Judy Steed, "Ritual abuse does exist and must be combatted," *Toronto Star*, 18 Jan. 1995, p. A17.

This piece was a rebuttal of two of my own columns: "Province funds studies of non-existent abuse," *Toronto Star*, 9 Jan. 1995, p. A15 and "Let public hear about conference," 16 Jan. 1995, p. A17.

[173] Connie M. Kristiansen, "FMS, PMS...they're all the same if you are a sexist," *Ottawa Citizen*, 25 Aug. 1994.
Michele Landsberg, "Let's clear up confusion over incest memories," *Toronto Star*, 6 May 1995, p. G16.

[174] *Herizons*, Fall 1992, p. 19. R.J., "R.J.'s Story: A Survivor's Account," p. 22. Amethya, "Amethya's Story: A Survivor's Account," p. 23.

[175] Marjaleena Repo, "'Ritual abuse,' my elbow!—a feminist critique of a hoax," *unpublished*, 1992.

[176] Penni Mitchell rejection letter to Majaleena Repo, 20 January 1993, *Herizons: Women's News & Feminist Views*, Winnipeg.

[177] Beckylane as told to Cathy Stonehouse, "Healing from Ritual Abuse: real memories, true courage," *Kinesis*, June 1995, p. 19.

[178]Canadian Panel on Violence Against Women, *Changing the Landscape: Ending violence - achieving equality*, Final Report, Minister of Supply and Services Canada, 1993, pp. 8, 27, 37, 45-56.

[179] *Ms.*, Jan-Feb. 1993, pp. 43-44.

[180] *Ms.*, Jan-Feb. 1993, p. 44 and Jan-Feb. 1995, p. 67. Other comments on recovered memories and/or ritual abuse can be found in *Ms.* at Nov.-Dec. 1993, p. 96, in an editorial May-June 1994, p. 1, July-Aug. 1994, p. 91 and Sept.-Oct. 1994, p. 78.

[181] Ellen Bass and Laura Davis; Ellen Bass and Laura Davis, *The Courage to Heal: A guide for women survivors of child sexual abuse* (New York: Harper & Row Publishers, 1988), p. 41.

[182] Ibid., p. 122. Subsequent page references appear in the text of the book you are reading, following each quote.

[183] Frederick Crews, "Thanks for the Memories," *New York Review of Books*, 16 Feb. 1995. See "Frederick Crew replies" halfway down.

[184] E. Sue Blume, *Secret Survivors: Uncovering incest and its after-effects in women* (New York: Ballantine Books, 1990). Steinem's quote on the front cover reads: "Explores the constellation of symptoms that result from a crime too cruel for mind and memory to face. This book, like the truth it helps uncover, can set millions free."

The first five pages are devoted to a 34-point checklist which purportedly identifies people who 'could be' survivors of incest. Among the conditions listed are: fear of the dark, gynecological disorders, wearing baggy clothing, depression, drug or alcohol abuse, compulsive behaviours, and so forth.

[185] Carol Tavris, "Beware the Incest-Survivor Machine," *New York Times Book Review*, 3 Jan. 1993.

[186] Beverly Engel, *The Right to Innocence: Healing the Trauma of Childhood Sexual Abuse* (New York: Ivy Books, 1989), p. 9.

[187] Carol Tavris, "Beware the Incest-Survivor Machine," *New York Times Book Review*, 3 Jan. 1993.

[188] Editors' Note, *Herizons*, Fall 1992, p. 19.

[189] Peter Hellman, "Crying Rape: The politics of date rape on campus," *New York*, 8 Mar. 1993, pp. 32, 34 and 36.

[190] Some of the relevant articles appearing in the *Hamilton Spectator* are as follows: 3 Feb. 1993, p. B1 - 4. Feb. 1993, p. D3. 12 Feb. 1993, p. B2. 16 June 1993, p. Al. 21 June 1993, p. B1.

The report, by Avebury Research & Consulting Ltd., is titled *Independent Client Service Review of the Sexual Assault Centre* (Hamilton and Area), 17 June 1993.

[191] Avebury Research & Consulting Ltd., *Independent Client Service Review of the Sexual Assault Centre* (Hamilton and Area), 17 June 1993, pp. ii, 7 and 9-10.

[192] Avebury Research & Consulting Ltd., *Independent Client Service Review of the Sexual Assault Centre* (Hamilton and Area), 17 June 1993, pp. 12-13, 26, 32 and 46.

[193] Ann Landers, appearing in *Toronto Star*, 17 Sept. 1993, p. D4.

[194] Ann Landers, appearing in *Toronto Star*, 12 Dec. 1993, p. F3 and 18 Nov. 1993, p. D2.

[195] Laura Pasley, "Misplaced Trust: A first-person account of how my therapist created false memories," *Skeptic*, Vol. 2, No. 3, 1994, pp. 62-67.

[196] Gail Fisher-Taylor, "Ritual Abuse: Towards a feminist understanding," *Herizons*, Fall 1992, p. 21.

[197] Christie Blatchford, "Innocence lost," *Toronto Sun*, 7 Apr. 1994, pp. 16-18. Philip Mascoll, "Café killers linked to another robbery," *Toronto Star*, 8 Apr. 1994, p. Al.

[198] "What's your reaction to these faces?" (editorial), *Toronto Star*, 9 Apr. 1994, p. B2.

Julie Smyth, "Search for shooting suspects widens," *Globe and Mail*, 11 Apr. 1994, p. A6.

Kirk Makin, "Young blacks brace for crime's aftermath," *Globe and Mail*, 9 Apr. 1994, p. A6.

Rosie DiManno, "Sharing guilt 'appalling,' blacks told," *Toronto Star*, 18 Apr. 1994, p. A6.

[199] John Barber, "Assertions on racism unfounded, outrageous," *Globe and Mail*, 14 June 1994, p. A7.

[200] Amy Friedman, *Nothing Sacred: A conversation with feminism* (Ottawa: Oberon Press, 1992), p. 74.

[201] "'Abducted' boys died strapped to car seats," *Toronto Star*, 5 Nov. 1994, p. A3. Associated Press, "Jury gives Susan Smith life in prison," *Toronto Star*, 29 July 1995, p. A2.

[202] Henry Gale, "Not collective guilt, but collective responsibility," *Globe and Mail*, 23 Nov. 1994, p. A24.

[203] Canadian Panel on Violence Against Women, *Changing the Landscape: Ending violence - achieving equality*, Final Report, Minister of Supply and Services Canada, 1993, p. 6.

[204] Canadian Panel on Violence Against Women, *Changing the Landscape: Ending violence - achieving equality*, Final Report, Minister of Supply and Services Canada, 1993, p. 274.

[205] Canadian Panel on Violence Against Women, *Changing the Landscape: Ending violence - achieving equality*, Final Report, Minister of Supply and Services Canada, 1993, p. 4.

[206] Camille Paglia, *Sex, Art, and American Culture: Essays*, (New York: Vintage Books, 1992), pp. 56-57.

[207] Canadian Panel on Violence Against Women, *Changing the Landscape: Ending violence - achieving equality*, Final Report, Minister of Supply and Services Canada, 1993, p. 6.

[208] Canadian Panel on Violence Against Women, *Changing the Landscape: Ending violence - achieving equality*, Final Report, Minister of Supply and Services Canada, 1993, p. 74.

[209] Claire M. Renzetti, *Violent Betrayal: Partner Abuse in Lesbian Relationships* (Newbury Park, California: Sage Publications, 1992), pp. 17-24.

See also "Lesbian Battery," *Ms.*, Sept.-Oct. 1990, p. 48 and Achy Ohejas, "Women Who Batter Women," *Ms.*, Sept.-Oct. 1994, p. 53.

[210] Canadian Panel on Violence Against Women, *Changing the Landscape: Ending violence - achieving equality*, Final Report, Minister of Supply and Services Canada, 1993, p. 161.

[211] Canadian Panel on Violence Against Women, *Changing the Landscape: Ending violence - achieving equality*, Final Report, Minister of Supply and Services Canada, 1993, p. 169.

[212] John Fekete, *Moral Panic: Biopolitics rising* (Montreal: Robert Davies Publishing, 1994), p. 224.

[213] Marilyn French, *The War Against Women* (New York: Ballantine Books, 1992), pp. 114, 146-47 and 175-76.

[214] Wendy Dennis, *Hot and Bothered: Sex and Love in the Nineties* (Toronto: Seal Books, 1992), pp. 59-60.

[215] Canadian Panel on Violence Against Women, *Changing the Landscape: Ending violence - achieving equality*, Final Report, Minister of Supply and Services Canada, 1993, Part 5, p. 70.

[216] Naomi Wolf, *The Beauty Myth: How images of beauty are used against women* (Toronto: Vintage Books, 1990), p. 47.

[217] Naomi Wolf, *The Beauty Myth: How images of beauty are used against women* (Toronto: Vintage Books, 1990), pp. 47-48.

[218] Alice Walker, "How Long Shall They Torture Our Mothers? The Trials of Winnie Mandela," *Ms.*, May-June 1991, pp. 22-25.

Philip Van Niekerk, in *Globe and Mail*, "Winnie Mandela convicted of kidnapping," 14 May 1991, p. Al and "Women's group bounces Mandela," 26 May 1992, p. A16.

Bill Schiller in *Toronto Star*, "Mandela's marriage over paper reports," 5 Apr. 1992, p. A3 and "Is ANC making another mistake?" 16 Apr. 1992, p. A31.

See also Jonathan Manthorpe, "Getting the story on Winnie Mandela," *Toronto Star*, 14 Apr. 1992, p. A17

and Ellen Bartlett, "Mandela divorce turns messy," *Globe and Mail*, 19 Sept. 1995, pp. Al and A13.

[219] *Ms.*, Jan.-Feb. 1992, p. 12 and Sept.-Oct. 1990, p. 6.

[220] See Christina Hoff Sommers, *Who Stole Feminism? How Women Have Betrayed Women* (New York: Simon & Schuster, 1994), p. 161.

[221] (US) National Center for Health Statistics, *Monthly Vital Statistics Report*, Vol. 43, No. 6, 22 Mar. 1995, pp. 24-25.
Statistics Canada, *Causes of Death 1993*, 1995.

[222] Warren Farrell, *The Myth of Male Power: Why men are the disposable sex* (New York: Simon & Schuster, 1993), p. 100.

[223] Canadian Centre for Justice Statistics, *Homicide Survey*, Policing Services Program, 1995 and Statistics Canada, *Causes of Death 1993*, 1995.

[224] Betty Friedan, "Why men die young...and why you'll live longer," *Playboy*, Apr. 1995. p. 65.

Statistics Canada, *Life Expectancy at birth, by sex, by province.* For those born between 1990-1992, male life expectancy is 75 years. Female life expectancy is 81.

[225] Marilyn French, *The War Against Women* (New York: Ballantine Books, 1992, p. 20.

[226] (US) National Center for Health Statistics, *Monthly Vital Statistics Report*, Vol. 43, No. 6, 22 Mar. 1995, p. 8.

[227] (US) National Center for Health Statistics, *Monthly Vital Statistics Report*, Vol. 43, No. 6, 22 Mar. 1995, p. 45.
Canadian Centre for Justice Statistics, *Homicide Survey*, Policing Services Program, 1995.

Canadian Centre for Justice Statistics, *Juristat*, Vol. 15, No. 2, Jan. 1995, p. 8.

[228] John Fekete, *Moral Panic: Biopolitics rising* (Montreal: Robert Davies Publishing, 1994), p. 68.

[229] Canadian Centre for Justice Statistics, *Juristat*, Vol. 15, No. 2, Jan. 1995, p. 1.

[230] See See Christina Hoff Sommers, *Who Stole Feminism? How Women Have Betrayed Women* (New York: Simon & Schuster, 1994), pp. 137-87.

Donna Laframboise, "Do we care if boys fall back?" *Toronto Star*, 27 Feb. 1995, p. A17. Charles Hymas and Julie Cohen,

"The trouble with boys," *London Sunday Times*, 19 June 1994, p. 14.

[231] Andrew Duffy, "School system fails blacks, Portuguese," *Toronto Star*, 11 Feb. 1995, p. A1.

Margaret Philp, "Dropout rate high for Portuguese, black students," *Globe and Mail*, 14 Feb. 1995, p. A6.

[232] (US) National Institute for Occupational Safety and Health, *Fatal Injuries to Workers in the US 1980-1989: A decade of surveillance*, Aug. 1993, p. 4.

Statistics Canada, *Work Injuries: 1991-1993*, Dec. 1994, p. 13. Gender breakdown regarding 1993 fatalities secured through a private telephone conversation with Statistics Canada's Labour Division.

See also Katherine Marshall, "A job to die for," *Perspectives*, Summer 1996, p. 30.

[233] Warren Farrell, *The Myth of Male Power: Why men are the disposable sex* (New York: Simon & Schuster, 1993), pp. 110 and 118.

[234] Warren Farrell, *The Myth of Male Power: Why men are the disposable sex* (New York: Simon & Schuster, 1993), p. 105.

[235] David Vienneau, "3 women reluctant to join top court PM told," *Toronto Star*, 20 Aug. 1992, p. A3, and Canadian Press,

"Few women willing to join top court, Campbell says," *Globe and Mail*, 17 Nov. 1992, p. A6.

[236] Letty Cottin Pogrebin, "The Stolen Spotlight Syndrome," *Ms.*, Nov.-Dec. 1993, p. 96.

[237] Marilyn French, *The War Against Women* (New York: Ballantine Books, 1992), pp. 19, 69-72, 75, 84 and 99.

[238] Leslie Scrivener, "Bare-breasts debate simmers in wake of topless protests," *Toronto Star*, 26 July 1992, pp. Al and A6.
Susan Allan, "Women protest indecency laws," *Globe and Mail*, 20 July 1992, pp. Al and A8.

[239] Margo Roston, "MPs seeing lots of red in the House of Commons," *Toronto Star*, 8 Dec. 1994, p. G5.

[240] Nicholas Van Rijn, "Postal supervisor fights to keep long hair, beard," *Toronto Star*, 14 Dec. 1994, p. A3

Alan Barnes, "Bearded mail worker to keep job - for now," *Toronto Star*, 15 Dec. 1994, p. A5.

[241] Warren Farrell, *The Myth of Male Power: Why men are the disposable sex* (New York: Simon & Schuster, 1993), p. 135.

[242] In a 1992 *Ms.* article, for example, a bestselling feminist author suggests that expecting men to "get out of a warm bed to fix the snow on the TV screen" is "the very least owed to me *personally* in compensation for centuries of virtual enslavement" (italics in the original).

Anything, no matter how petty, can be justified by those who believe their gender has been subjected to "centuries of virtual enslavement." Naomi Wolf, "Radical Heterosexuality...or how to love a man and save your feminist soul," *Ms.*, July-Aug. 1992, p. 30.

[243] Warren Farrell, *The Myth of Male Power: Why men are the disposable sex* (New York: Simon & Schuster, 1993), p. 130.

[244] Naomi Wolf, *The Beauty Myth: How images of beauty are used against women* (Toronto: Vintage Books, 1990), pp. 181-82.

[245] Ibid., pp. 207-08 and 194-95.

[246] See Christina Hoff Sommers, *Who Stole Feminism? How Women Have Betrayed Women* (New York: Simon & Schuster, 1994), pp. 11-12.

[247] Ibid., p. 12 and Ann Landers, appearing in *Toronto Star*, 29 Apr. 1992, p. D12.

[248] See Christina Hoff Sommers, *Who Stole Feminism? How Women Have Betrayed Women* (New York: Simon & Schuster, 1994), pp. 13-15.

[249] Sarah Crichton, "Sexual correctness: has it gone too far?" *Newsweek*, 25 Oct. 1993, pp. 55-56.

See also "US study says 1 in 8 women is raped," *Toronto Star*, 24 Apr. 1992, p. A3.

[250] Ann Landers, appearing in *Toronto Star*: 4 Sept. 1994, p. B3. 14 Aug. 1994, p. B3. 16 Oct. 1994, p. F2. 3 Dec. 1994, p. L14.

[251] Alanna Mitchell, "50% of women report assaults," *Globe and Mail*, 19 Nov. 1993, pp. Al and A4.

[252] Theresa Boyle, "98% of Metro women suffer sexual violation, panel says," *Toronto Star*, 30 July 1993, p. A23.

[253] Ontario Women's Directorate, *Sexual Assault: Dispelling the myths*, Apr. 1994.

[254] See John Fekete, *Moral Panic: Biopolitics rising* (Montreal: Robert Davies Publishing, 1994), pp. 134-45, esp. p. 144.

David Lees, "The War Against Men," *Toronto Life*, Dec. 1992, pp. 98-99.

[255] David Lees, "The War Against Men," *Toronto Life*, Dec. 1992, pp. 47, 99-100.

See also Eugene Lupri, "Male Violence in the Home," *Canadian Social Trends*, Statistics Canada 1989, pp. 19-21.

[256] David Lees, "The War Against Men," *Toronto Life*, Dec. 1992, pp. 47, 99-100.

[257] Michele Landsherg, "The male myth of 'battered husbands,'" *Toronto Star*, 18 Dec. 1993, p. J1.

[258] Reena Sommer, Gordon F. Barnes and Robert P. Murray, "Alcohol Consumption; Alcohol Abuse, Personality and Female Perpetrated Spouse Abuse," *Personality and Individual Differences*, Vol. 13, No. 12, 1992, pp. 1315-23.

Reena Sommer, "Male and Female Perpetrated Partner Abuse: Testing a Diathesis-Stress Model," University of Manitoba Ph.D. Thesis, unpublished, 1994.

See also John Fekete, *Moral Panic: Biopolitics rising* (Montreal: Robert Davies Publishing, 1994), pp. 89-90.

[259] Larry Saidman, "Some people still just don't get it," (letter to the editor) *Toronto Star*, 31 Oct. 1992, p. D3.

[260] David Lees, "The War Against Men," *Toronto Life*, Dec. 1992, p. 100.

[261] Canadian Panel on Violence Against Women, *Changing the Landscape: Ending violence - achieving equality*, Final Report, Minister of Supply and Services Canada, 1993, p. 7.

See also "Where Do We Go From Here: An interview with Ann Jones," *Ms.*, Sept.-Oct. 1994, p. 56.

[262] Maria Augimer, "Abuse study is a perversion of years of analysis and action," (letter to the editor), *Toronto Star*, 31 Oct. 1992, p. D3.

David Greenberg, "The myth of abusive wives is laughable...almost," *Globe and Mail*, 16 Nov. 1993, p. A28.

Michele Landsberg, "The male myth of 'battered husbands," *Toronto Star*, 18 Dec. 1993, p. J1.

263 Ron Csillag, "When the wife is the primary breadwinner," *Globe and Mail*, 12 Apr. 1995, p. A26.

264 Warren Farrell, *The Myth of Male Power: Why men are the disposable sex* (New York: Simon & Schuster, 1993), p. 19.

265 Ann Landers, appearing in *Toronto Star*: MICHIGAN: 9 Nov. 1993, p. B2. ST. LOUIS: 3 June 1994, p. D3.

266 Dear Abby, appearing in *Ottawa Citizen*, 5 Dec. 1994, p. B4.

267 "Suicides of family of 3 tied to Lepine massacre," *Toronto Star*, 17 July 1991, p. A3.

268 Janet Radcliffe Richards, *The Sceptical Feminist* (London: Penguin Books, 1980), 2nd edition, p. 112.

269 Susan Faludi, "I'm Not a Feminist. But I Play One on TV," *Ms.*, Mar.-Apr. 1995, pp. 30-39.

270 Robin Morgan, "Bearing Witness" (editorial), *Ms.*, Jan.-Feb. 1992, p. 1.

271 Doris Lessing, *Prisons We Choose to Live Inside* (Toronto: CBC Enterprises, 1986), pp. 46 and 69.

272 John Allemang, "Why Isaiah Berlin Matters," *Globe and Mail*, 25 1994, p. A18. See also partial transcript of Berlin's speech, "Beware the one true answer," same page. Full transcript here. [see online footnotes page, as per top of Notes section, page 277 above]

273 Camille Paglia, *Sex, Art, and American Culture: Essays*, (New York: Vintage Books, 1992), p. 47.

274 Katie Roiphe, *The Morning After: Sex, Fear and Feminism* (Boston: Bay Back Books, 1993), pp. 19-21.

[275] Rene Denfeld, *The New Victorians: A young woman's response to the old feminist order* (New York: Warner Books, 1995), p. 133.

[276] See Christina Hoff Sommers, *Who Stole Feminism? How Women Have Betrayed Women* (New York: Simon & Schuster, 1994), pp. 220-21.

[277] *Ms.*, Jan-Feb., 1992. See pages 10-11, 50-51, 58-60, 86-87, 95-96. See cover here.

[278] Robin Morgan, *Going Too Far: The Personal Chronicle of a Feminist* (New York: Random House, 1977), p. 169.

[279] Some other *Ms.* references to porn in recent years:
May-June 1991 (editorial), p. 1. On p. 32, surrogate motherhood is negatively linked to pornography and prostitution.

In May-June 1992, on p. 14, Canadian feminist Michele Landsberg says that Canada's Supreme Court has "acknowledged the large body of scholarship documenting pornography's harms to the self-respect and safety of women."

Sept.-Oct. 1992 (editorial), p. 1,
Nov.-Dec. 1994, pp. 19, 52 and 54.

[280] Catharine A. MacKinnon, "Liberalism and the Death of Feminism," *The Sexual Liberals and the Attack on Feminism*, Dorchen Leidholdt and Janice G. Raymond, eds. (New York: Pergamon Press, 1990), p. 12.

Pete Hamill, "Woman on the Verge of a Legal Breakdown," *Playboy*, Jan. 1993, p. 186.

Wendy Kaminer, "Exposing the new authoritarians," *San Francisco Examiner*, 29 Nov. 1992.

[281] Robin Morgan, "On the Road" (editorial), *Ms.*, May-June 1993, p.1.

[282] Rene Denfeld, *The New Victorians: A young woman's response to the old feminist order* (New York: Warner Books, 1995), p. 260.

[283] Donna Minkowitz, "The Newsroom Becomes a Battleground: Is the media siege on lesbians in the women's movement a desperate attempt to undermine feminism?" (cover story), *The Advocate*, 19 May 1992, p. 34.

[284] Camille Paglia, *Sex, Art, and American Culture: Essays*, (New York: Vintage Books, 1992), pp. xii and 120.
Playboy Interview: Camille Paglia, *Playboy*, May 1995, p. 64.

[285] Harry Stein, interview with Christina Hoff Sommers, *Penthouse*, Jan. 1995, p. 70.

Camille Paglia, *Sex, Art, and American Culture: Essays*, (New York: Vintage Books, 1992), p.56.

[286] Camille Paglia, *Sex, Art, and American Culture: Essays*, (New York: Vintage Books, 1992), pp. 49-50. See also p. 67.

[287] Ibid., pp. 57 and 74.

[288] Katie Roiphe, *The Morning After: Sex, Fear and Feminism* (Boston: Bay Back Books, 1993), p. xix.

See also *Ms.*, May-June 1991, p. 61 and Nov-Dec. 1994, p. 75.

[289] Headline on front cover of the Sept.-Oct. 1993 issue of *Ms.*: "No, Feminists Don't All Think Alike (Who Says We Have To?)." Inside, Steinem admits to the name-calling, p. 41, but doesn't apologize and

Rene Denfeld, *The New Victorians: A young woman's response to the old feminist order* (New York: Warner Books, 1995), pp. 198-99.

[290] Sally Quinn, "Who killed feminism?" *Washington Post*, 19 Jan. 1992, p. Cl.

Donna Minkowitz, "The Newsroom Becomes a Battleground: Is the media siege on lesbians in the women's movement a desperate attempt to undermine feminism?" (cover story), *The Advocate*, 19 May 1992, p. 35.

[291] Harry Stein, interview with Christina Hoff Sommers, *Penthouse*, Jan. 1995, p. 67. See also the reference to "feminist-basher Christina Hoff Sommers," in *Ms.*, July-Aug. 1995, p. 92.

[292] Betty Friedan, "Why men die young...and why you'll live longer," *Playboy*, Apr. 1995, p. 152.

[293] Sarah Crichton, "Sexual correctness: has it gone too far?" *Newsweek*, 25 Oct. 1993.

See also *Ms.* editorial, May-June 1994, p. 1 and Jan.-Feb. 1994, p. 47.

[294] Katie Roiphe, *The Morning After: Sex, Fear and Feminism* (Boston: Bay Back Books, 1993), pp. 5-6.

[295] Amy Friedman, *Nothing Sacred: A conversation with feminism* (Ottawa: Oberon Press, 1992), pp. 41, 45-46, 59 and 86.

[296] Danielle Crittenden, "New stereotypes replace the old," *Globe and Mail*, 27 Dec. 1990, p. A20.

[297] Margaret Atwood, "If You Can't Say Something Nice, Don't Say Anything At All," *Language in Her Eye: Writing and Gender*, Libby Sheier, Sarah Sheard and Eleanor Wachtel, eds. (Toronto: Coach House Press, 1990), p. 24.

[298] Rene Denfeld, *The New Victorians: A young woman's response to the old feminist order* (New York: Warner Books, 1995), p. 43.

[299] Donna Laframboise, "Women's Day doesn't have much to do with women," *Globe and Mail*, 8 Mar. 1991, p. A13

Carmencita R. Hernandez and Jane Walsh, "Moving toward a new emancipation," *Globe and Mail*, 19 Mar. 1991, p. A21.

[300] Salome Lucas, *et. al.*, "Gender isn't everything - all issues are women's issues," *Globe and Mail*, 14 May 1991, p. A17. See also Catharine A. MacKinnon, "Liberalism and the Death of Feminism," *The Sexual Liberals and the Attack on Feminism*, Dorchen Leidholdt and Janice G. Raymond, eds. (New York: Pergamon Press, 1990), p. 4.

[301] Dianne Allen, "The end of NAC," (letter to the editor), *Globe and Mail*, 9 Feb. 1995, p. A22.

[302] Michelle Shephard and Vicki White, "Gay Pride draws 500,000 people," *Toronto Star*, 3 July 1995, pp. Al and A3.

[303] Mark Zwolinski, "Women mark 'historic year,'" *Toronto Star*, 6 Mar. 1994, p. A4.

[304] Ingrid MacDonald, "Conditions of Coalition," *Broadside*, Apr. 1986, p.6.

[305] Isabella Bardoel, "Women's rally stresses day care, deportations," *Globe and Mail*, 13 Mar. 1978, p. 29.

[306] Dave Norris, "'Sisters' on parade," *Toronto Star*, 11 Mar. 1979, p. A6.

[307] Faith Nolan, "Angela Davis: Making Connections," *Broadside*, Apr. 1985, p. 6.

[308] Alfred Holden, "Cheers great Sophia Cook's speech at rally denouncing racism, violence," *Toronto Star*, 4 Mar. 1990, p. Al.

Eric Skelton, "Attempted murder charge sought in Cook shooting," *Globe and Mail*, 18 Dec. 1989, p. Al2.

Bonnie M. Meyer, "Women's Day divisive," (letter to the editor) *NOW*, 15-21 Mar. 1990, p. 9.

[309] Naomi Klein, "Politics of booze dampens annual Women's Day dance," *NOW*, 12-18 Mar. 1992, p. 17.

[310] Sunera Thobani, "Why I am a feminist," *Toronto Star*, 3 June 1993, p. A21.

See also Salome Lucas, et. al., "Gender isn't everything - all issues are women's issues," *Globe and Mail*, 14 May 1991, p. A17.

[311] "Women threaten to boycott violence hearings," *Toronto Star*, 8 June 1992, p. Al and "Feuding in the family," (editorial), *Toronto Star*, 8 Aug. 1992, p. C2.

[312] David Vienneau, "Feminists boycotting panel on violence," *Toronto Star*, 1 Aug. 1992, p. A10.

See also "$10 million study a 'cheap' ploy critics charge," *Toronto Star*, 30 July 1993, p. A23 and Geoffrey York, "$10-million inquiry fuelled bitter fight," *Globe and Mail*, 30 July 1993, p. A4.

[313] Margaret Wente, "Success stories: Which ones really count?" *Globe and Mail*, 23 July 1994, p. A2.

[314] Michelle Shephard, "Callwood tribute helps homes," *Toronto Star*, 28 Sept. 1995, p. A28.

315 Adele Freedman, "White Woman's Burden," *Saturday Night*, Apr. 1993, p. 74.

316 Elaine Dewar, "Wrongful Dismissal," *Toronto Life*, Mar. 1993, p. 37.

317 June Callwood, "The Nellie's furor: June Callwood tells her side", *Toronto Star*, 23 July 1992, p. Fl.

318 I was hand-delivering a story proposal to *Toronto Life* the day of the protest and was given a photocopied flyer which had this message superimposed over the magazine's cover: "Toronto Life Magazine's: racist attacks against women of colour." [sic]

319 Jean Kavanagh, "Racism charge 'the worst thing ever in my life,'" *Toronto Star*, 15 June 1992, p. Al.

320 Rene Denfeld, *The New Victorians: A young woman's response to the old feminist order* (New York: Warner Books, 1995), pp. 40 and 264.

321 Tiya Miles, "On the Rag," *Ms.*, May-June 1995, pp. 35-36.

322 See Christina Hoff Sommers, *Who Stole Feminism? How Women Have Betrayed Women* (New York: Simon & Schuster, 1994), pp. 29-31.

323 Rene Denfeld, *The New Victorians: A young woman's response to the old feminist order* (New York: Warner Books, 1995), p. 203

and Camille Paglia, *Sex, Art, and American Culture: Essays*, (New York: Vintage Books, 1992), p. 90.

324 Daphne Patai and Noretta Koertge, *Professing Feminism: Cautionary tales from the strange world of women's studies* (New York: Basic Books, 1994), pp. xvi-xvii.

[325] Ibid., pp. 67 and 204.

[326] Karen Lehrman, "Off Course" (cover story), *Mother Jones*, Sept.-Oct. 1993, p. 64.

[327] Daphne Patai and Noretta Koertge, *Professing Feminism: Cautionary tales from the strange world of women's studies* (New York: Basic Books, 1994), pp. 101-102 and 195.

[328] Karen Lehrman, "Off Course" (cover story), *Mother Jones*, Sept.-Oct. 1993, pp. 48, 66 and 68.

[329] Ibid., pp. 47, 51 and 64.

[330] Backtalk, *Mother Jones*, Nov.-Dec. 1993, pp. 4-5 and 7. See also *Ms.*, Jan.-Feb. 1994, p. 47.

[331] Daphne Patai and Noretta Koertge, *Professing Feminism: Cautionary tales from the strange world of women's studies* (New York: Basic Books, 1994), p. 176.

[332] Janet Radcliffe Richards, *The Sceptical Feminist* (London: Penguin Books, 1980), 2nd edition, p. 31.

[333] Donna Minkowitz, "The Newsroom Becomes a Battleground: Is the media siege on lesbians in the women's movement a desperate attempt to undermine feminism?" (cover story), *The Advocate*, 19 May 1992, p. 34.

[334] bell hooks, "Men in Feminist Struggle - The Necessary Movement," *Women Respond to the Men's Movement*, Kay Leigh Hagan, ed. (San Francisco: Pandora, 1992), pp. 113 and 117.

[335] Gloria Steinem, "Foreword," *Women Respond to the Men's Movement*, Kay Leigh Hagan, ed. (San Francisco: Pandora, 1992), pp. v-ix.

[336] Kay Leigh Hagan, "Introduction," *Women Respond to the Men's Movement*, Kay Leigh Hagan, ed. (San Francisco: Pandora, 1992), p. viii.

[337] Starhawk, 'A Men's Movement I Can Trust," *Women Respond to the Men's Movement*, Kay Leigh Hagan, ed. (San Francisco: Pandora, 1992), p. 29.

[338] Rosemary Radford Ruether, "Patriarchy and the Men's Movement," p. 16, Jane Caputi and Gordene O. MacKenzie, "Pumping Iron John," p. 71 and Elizabeth Dodson Gray, "Beauty and the Beast: A Parable for Our Time," p. 166 in *Women Respond to the Men's Movement*, Kay Leigh Hagan, ed. (San Francisco: Pandora, 1992).

[339] Gloria Steinem, "Foreword," *Women Respond to the Men's Movement*, Kay Leigh Hagan, ed. (San Francisco: Pandora, 1992), p. ix.

[340] Kay Leigh Hagan, "Introduction," *Women Respond to the Men's Movement*, Kay Leigh Hagan, ed. (San Francisco: Pandora, 1992), p. xii.

[341] hattie gossett, "mins movement??? a page drama," *Women Respond to the Men's Movement*, Kay Leigh Hagan, ed. (San Francisco: Pandora, 1992), pp. 19-21.

[342] Starhawk, "A Men's Movement I Can Trust," *Women Respond to the Men's Movement*, Kay Leigh Hagan, ed. (San Francisco: Pandora, 1992), p. 27.

[343] Judy Steed, "Breaking the cycle of violence against women," *Toronto Star*, 4 Dec. 1994, pp. Al and A18.

[344] John Gray, "Which men are in trouble?" (letter to the editor) and Richard H. Velvart, "Violent beasts are unfamiliar," (letter to the editor) *Toronto Star*, 11 Jan. 1995, p. E2.

Wayne Jones, "Men and housework," (letter to the editor) *Globe and Mail*, 23 Sept. 1992, p. A25.

[345] Cyra McFadden & Isabelle de Courtivron, "Women Have Always Hated Men...And With Good Reason," *New York Times Review of Books*, 5 July 1992, p. 8.

[346] Gloria Steinem, "Foreword," p. v, Kathleen Carlin, "The Men's Movement of Choice," p. 120, Phyllis Chesler, "The Men's Auxiliary: Protecting the Rule of the Fathers," p. 139 in *Women Respond to the Men's Movement*, Kay Leigh Hagan, ed. (San Francisco: Pandora, 1992).

[347] Laura S. Brown, "Essential Lies: A Dystopian Vision of the Mythopoetic Men's Movement," *Women Respond to the Men's Movement*, Kay Leigh Hagan, ed. (San Francisco: Pandora, 1992), pp. 93-94 and 98.

[348] Vicki Noble, "A Helping Hand from the Guys," *Women Respond to the Men's Movement*, Kay Leigh Hagan, ed. (San Francisco: Pandora, 1992), pp. 104-105.

[349] Starhawk, "A Men's Movement I Can Trust," *Women Respond to the Men's Movement*, Kay Leigh Hagan, ed. (San Francisco: Pandora, 1992), p. 34.

[350] See "Return of the Gender Gap - Just in Time for November," *Ms.*, Jan.-Feb. 1992, p. 88.

[351] bell hooks, "Men in Feminist Struggle—The Necessary Movement," p. 114

and Elizabeth Dodson Gray, "Beauty and the Beast: A Parable for Our Time," p. 167 in *Women Respond to the Men's Movement*, Kay Leigh Hagan, ed. (San Francisco: Pandora, 1992).

[352] Margo Adair, "Will the Real Men's Movement Please Stand. Up?" p. 55 and Margaret Randall, "'And So She Walked Over and Kissed Him...' Robert Bly's Men's Movement," p. 143 in *Women Respond to the Men's Movement*, Kay Leigh Hagan, ed. (San Francisco: Pandora, 1992).

[353] Jane Caputi and Gordene O. MacKenzie, "Pumping Iron John," *Women Respond to the Men's Movement*, Kay Leigh Hagan, ed. (San Francisco: Pandora, 1992), p. 75.

See also Robert Bly, *Iron John: A book about men* (New York: Vintage Books, 1990), pp. 93-94.

[354] Starhawk, "A Men's Movement I Can Trust," p. 31 and Laura S. Brown, "Essential Lies: A Dystopian Vision of the Mythopoetic Men's Movement," p. 98 in *Women Respond to the Men's Movement*, Kay Leigh Hagan, ed. (San Francisco: Pandora, 1992).

[355] Lindsy Van Gelder, "The Truth About Bra-Burners," *Ms.*, Sept.-Oct. 1992, p. 80.

[356] Wendy Dennis, *Hot and Bothered: Sex and Love in the Nineties* (Toronto: Seal Books, 1992), p. 62.

[357] Riane Eisler, "What Do Men Really Want? The Men's Movement, Partnership, and Domination," *Women Respond to the Men's Movement*, Kay Leigh Hagan, ed. (San Francisco: Pandora, 1992), pp. 50 and 52.

[358] "Like a Hole in the Head," *Ms.*, Jan.-Feb. 1995, p. 94 and "Worldwide," *Ms.*, May-June 1995, p. 17.

See also Sharon Donbiago, "'Enemy of the mother': A feminist response to the men's movement," *Ms.*, Mar.-Apr. 1992, pp. 82-85.

[359] Warren Farrell, *The Myth of Male Power: Why men are the disposable sex* (New York: Simon & Schuster, 1993), pp. 12-13.

[360] Warren Farrell, *The Myth of Male Power: Why men are the disposable sex* (New York: Simon & Schuster, 1993), p. 174.

[361] Ibid., pp. 164, 172-74, 210, and 259-60.

[362] Ibid., pp. 15 and 42.

[363] Ibid., p. 46 and

Wendy Dennis, *Hot and Bothered: Sex and Love in the Nineties* (Toronto: Seal Books, 1992), pp. 22-23.

[364] Warren Farrell, *The Myth of Male Power: Why men are the disposable sex* (New York: Simon & Schuster, 1993), pp. 14-15.

[365] *Sexual Assault: Dispelling the Myths*, Ontario Women's Directorate, Apr. 1994, p. 2 and

Iris S. Gorfinkel, Letter to the editor, *Globe and Mail*, 20 June 1995, p. A14.

[366] Warren Farrell, *The Myth of Male Power: Why men are the disposable sex* (New York: Simon & Schuster, 1993), p. 310.

[367] Camille Paglia, "Challenging the Masculine Mystique," *Washington Post Book World*, 25 July 1993, pp. 1 and 8.

[368] Susan Faludi, *Backlash: The undeclared war against women* (New York: Anchor Books, 1991), pp. 300-304.

[369] Jane Caputi and Diana E.H. Russell, "'Femicide': Speaking the Unspeakable," *Ms.*, Sept.-Oct. 1990, pp. 36-37.

[370] Judy Steed, "Ritual abuse does exist and must be combatted," *Toronto Star*, 18 Jan. 1995, p. A17.

[371] Donna Minkowitz, "The Newsroom Becomes a Battleground: Is

the media siege on lesbians in the women's movement a desperate attempt to undermine feminism?" (cover story), *The Advocate*, 19 May 1992, p. 34.

[372] Naomi Wolf, *The Beauty Myth: How images of beauty are used against women* (Toronto: Vintage Books, 1990), p. 208.

[373] Vicki Noble, "A Helping Hand from the Guys," *Women Respond to the Men's Movement*, Kay Leigh Hagan, ed. (San Francisco: Pandora, 1992), pp. 104-105.

[374] Liane Faulder, "Male power is no myth, but pain is real," *Toronto Star*, 22 Feb. 1994, p. Cl and

Tom Wayman, "Who suffers more?" *Toronto Star*, 13 Nov. 1993, p. J15.

[375] David Thomas, *Not Guilty: In defence of the modern man* (London: Weidenfeld & Nicolson, 1993), pp. 11-12.

[376] Ibid., pp. 1-3, 7 and 9.

[377] Ibid., pp. 54-55.

[378] Ibid., pp. 57-58.

[379] Ibid., pp. 58 and 60.

[380] Ann Landers, appearing in *Toronto Star*, 19 July 1994, p. C2.

[381] David Thomas, *Not Guilty: In defence of the modern man* (London: Weidenfeld & Nicolson, 1993), pp. 75-78.

[382] Ibid., pp. 79-80.

[383] Ibid., pp. 75-78.

[384] Statistics Canada, *Juristat*, Vol. 15, No. 11, Aug. 1995, p. 14.

[385] Police Response to Wife Assault, *Policing Standards Manual* 0217.00, 13 Jan. 1994, pp. 3 and 7.

[386] David Thomas, *Not Guilty: In defence of the modern man* (London: Weidenfeld & Nicolson, 1993), p. 145.

[387] David Thomas, *Not Guilty: In defence of the modern man* (London: Weidenfeld & Nicolson, 1993), p. 147.

[388] Ibid., p. 13.

[389] Wendy Dennis, *Hot and Bothered: Sex and Love in the Nineties* (Toronto: Seal Books, 1992), pp. 10 and 271.

[390] Tom Harpur, "Beginning again this new year with the courage to forgive others," *Toronto Star*, 1 Jan. 1995, p. A16.

[391] Michele Barrett, ed., *Virginia Woolf: Women and Writing* (Dunvegan, Ontario: Quadrant Editions, 1984), p. 152. Woolf's article on George Eliot originally appeared in *The Times Literary Supplement*, 20 Nov. 1919.

[392] George Eliot, *Middlemarch*. No particular edition or page numbers are cited here. Many digital editions of this book are available (some free). These may be searched quickly for all quotations appearing here.

[393] hattie gossett, "mins movement??? a page drama," *Women Respond to the Men's Movement*, Kay Leigh Hagan, ed. (San Francisco: Pandora, 1992), pp. 21 and 24.

[394] Margaret Atwood, "If You Can't Say Something Nice, Don't Say Anything At All," *Language in Her Eye: Writing and Gender*, Libby Sheier, Sarah Sheard and Eleanor Wachtel, eds. (Toronto: Coach House Press, 1990), p. 15.

[395] Susan Faludi, *Backlash: The undeclared war against women* (New York: Anchor Books, 1991), p. 65.

See also David Thomas, *Not Guilty: In defence of the Modern Man* (London: Weidenfeld & Nicolson, 1993), pp. 63-64.

[396] Stephen Hawking, ed., *Stephen Hawking's A Brief History of Time: A Reader's Companion* (New York: Bantam Books, 1992), pp. 53-54.

[397] Kurt Vonnegut, *Fates Worse Than Death: An autobiographical collage of the 1980s* (New York: G.P. Putnam's Sons, 1991), pp. 22-23.

[398] Ibid., p. 28.

[399] Warren Farrell, *The Myth of Male Power: Why men are the disposable sex* (New York: Simon & Schuster, 1993), p. 52.

[400] Ann Landers, appearing in *The Toronto Star*. UNEASY: 10 Mar. 1994, p. E7 and 23 May 1994, p. D3.

[401] Ann Landers, appearing in *The Toronto Star*. 1 Mar. 1995, p. C7; 19 May 1995, p. 62; and 31 May 1995, p. C6. See also 8 Aug. 1993, p. D6.

[402] Marilyn French, *The War Against Women* (New York: Ballantine Books, 1992), pp. 139-40.

[403] Letty Cottin Pogrebin, "The Stolen Spotlight Syndrome," *Ms.*, Nov.-Dec. 1993, p. 96.

[404] Phyllis Chesler, "The Men's Auxiliary: Protecting the Rule of the Fathers," *Women Respond to the Men's Movement*, Kay Leigh Hagan, ed. (San Francisco: Pandora,. 1992), pp. 137-38.

[405] Betty Friedan, "Why men die young...and why you'll live longer," *Playboy*, Apr. 1995, p. 151.

[406] Warren Farrell, *The Myth of Male Power: Why men are the disposable sex* (New York: Simon & Schuster, 1993), pp. 35-36.

[407] David Thomas, *Not Guilty: In defence of the Modern Man* (London: Weidenfeld & Nicolson, 1993), pp. 80-84.

Warren Farrell, *The Myth of Male Power: Why men are the disposable sex* (New York: Simon & Schuster, 1993), pp. 33 and 374.

[408] Anastasia Higginbotham, "Chicks going at it," *Ms.*, May-June 1995, p. 30.

[409] Erica Jong, "Is Sex Sexy Without Power?" *Penthouse*, Apr. 1995, p. 56. Italics in the original.

[410] Johanna Lindsey, *Prisoner of My Desire* (New York: Avon Books, 1991), p. 136.

[411] Ibid., p. 141.

[412] Ibid., pp. 151 and 174.

[413] Ibid., pp. 182 and 185.

[414] Ibid., p. 243.

[415] Johanna Lindsey, *Surrender My Love* (New York: Avon Books, 1994).

[416] Johanna Lindsey, *Captive Bride* (New York: Avon Books, 1977), p. 46.

[417] Ibid., p. 62.

[418] Johanna Lindsey, *Captive Bride* (New York: Avon Books, 1977), p. 69.

[419] Ibid., p. 87.

[420] Ibid., pp. 124-25.

[421] Johanna Lindsey, *Secret Fire* (New York: Avon Books, 1987), pp. 67 and 71.

[422] Johanna Lindsey, *Secret Fire* (New York: Avon Books, 1987), p. 248.

[423] Amanda Quick, *Mistress* (New York: Bantam Books, 1994).

[424] Mary Lou Rich, *Bandit's Kiss* (New York: Diamond Books, 1993).

[425] Karen Robards, *To Love a Man* (New York: Warner Books, 1985).

"Portrait: Karen Robards," *Romantic Times Magazine*, Oct. 1995, p. 76.

[426] Heather Graham, *A Pirate's Pleasure* (New York: Dell, 1989) Ann Lynn, *Slave of My Heart* (New York: Zebra Books, 1990).

[427] Catherine Hart, *Silken Savage* (New York: Leisure Books, 1993), p. 53.

[428] Ibid., *Silken Savage* (New York: Leisure Books, 1993), p. 113.

[429] Caroline Bourne, *Allegheny Captive* (New York: Zebra Books, 1990), p. 245.

[430] Ann Lynn, *Slave of My Heart* (New York: Zebra Books, 1990), p. 245.

[431] Susan Johnson, *Pure Sin* (New York: Bantam Books, 1994), pp. 155-56.

[432] Ibid., *Pure Sin* (New York: Bantam Books, 1994), p. 162.

[433] Ibid., pp. 162 and 170.

[434] Katie Roiphe, "Date rape hysteria," *New York Times*, Nov. 20, 1991.

[435] Canadian Panel on Violence Against Women, *Changing the Landscape: Ending violence - achieving equality*, Final Report, Minister of Supply and Services Canada, 1993, p. 50.

[436] Ibid., pp. 45 and 49.

The writings of many women who consider themselves feminists and yet oppose censorship can be found in:

Ann Snitow, Christine Stansell and Sharon Thompson, eds., *Powers of Desire: The Politics of Sexuality* (New York: Monthly Review Press, 1983)

Carole S. Vance, ed., *Pleasure and Danger: Exploring Female Sexuality* (Boston: Routledge & Kegan Paul, 1984)

Varda Burstyn, ed., *Women Against Censorship* (Vancouver: Douglas & McIntyre, 1985).

See also Sallie Tisdale, *Talk Dirty to Me* (New York: Doubleday, 1994).

[437] Rene Denfeld, *The New Victorians: A young woman's response to the old feminist order* (New York: Warner Books, 1995), pp. 105-106.

See also Marcia Pally, *Sex and Sensibility: Reflections on Forbidden Mirrors and the Will to Censor* (Hopewell, N.J.: Ecco Press, 1994)

and Nadine Strossen, *Defending Pornography: Free Speech, Sex, and the Fight for Women's Rights* (New York: Scribner, 1995), especially pp. 247-64.

[438] Rene Denfeld, *The New Victorians: A young woman's response to the old feminist order* (New York: Warner Books, 1995), p. 108.

Marcia Pally, *Sex and Sensibility: Reflections on Forbidden Mirrors and the Will to Censor* (Hopewell, N.J.: Ecco Press, 1994), pp. 99-108.

Nadine Strossen, *Defending Pornography: Free Speech, Sex, and the Fight for Women's Rights* (New York: Scribner, 1995), pp. 258-59.

Michael S. Kimmel, "Does Pornography Cause Rape?" *Violence Update*, Vol. 3, No. 10, June 1993.

[439] Canadian Panel on Violence Against Women, *Changing the Landscape: Ending Violence—Achieving Equality*, Final Report, Minister of Supply and Services Canada, 1993, pp. 45 and 49.

[440] Catharine A. MacKinnon, *Only Words* (Cambridge, Massachusetts: Harvard University Press, 1993), p. 12.

[441] *R. v. Butler*, Canada Supreme Court Reports, 1992, Vol. 1 (Ottawa: Queen's Printer for Canada, 1992), p. 479.

[442] Michele Landsberg, "Canada: Antipornography Breakthrough in the Law," *Ms.*, May-June 1992, p. 14.

"Porn mutilates women's fight for equality," *Toronto Star*, 11 June 1991, p. Fl.

Jeff Sallot, "Legal victory bittersweet," *Globe and Mail*, 29 Feb. 1992, p. A6.

In "Supreme Court porn ruling is ignored," *Toronto Star*, 14 Dec. 1993, p. Dl, Michele Landsberg writes that "MacKinnon triumphed by having her views embedded in the language of the Butler decision."

[443] John Duffy, "Masturbation and Clitoridectomy: A Nineteenth Century View," *Journal of the American Medical Association*, 19 Oct. 1963, pp. 166-68

Alex Comfort, *The Anxiety Makers: Some Curious Preoccupations of the Medical Profession* (London: Thomas Nelson and Sons Ltd., 1967), pp. 98-104.

[444] *Time* article reported in Wendy Dennis, *Hot and Bothered: Sex and Love in the Nineties* (Toronto: Seal Books, 1992), p. 227.

[445] Mark Edwards, "Sex in the 90s," *Arena*, Spring 1993, p. 64. (Survey was conducted jointly with *New Woman*).

Details/Mademoiselle survey reported in Rene Denfeld, *The New Victorians: A young woman's response to the old feminist order* (New York: Warner Books, 1995), pp. 258-59.

[446] Val Ross, "Labours of love," *Globe and Mail*, 11 Feb. 1995, p. Cl.

[447] Gloria Steinem, "Women in the Dark: of Sex Goddesses, Abuse, and Dreams," *Ms.*, Jan.-Feb. 1991, p.35.

[448] Ibid., p.35.

[449] Kathleen Morgan, *Heart's Surrender* (New York: Pinnacle Books, 1994), p. 94.

[450] Heather Graham, *A Pirate's Pleasure* (New York: Dell, 1989), pp. 20 and 22.

[451] Katharine Kincaid, *Beloved Bondage* (New York: Zebra Books, 1993), pp. 5, 28, 63 and 129.

[452] Susan Johnson, *Pure Sin* (New York: Bantam Books, 1994), p. 233.

[453] See Ann Landers, *Toronto Star*, 7 Sept. 1995, p. C2.

Michelle Shephard, "30% of Canadians tell poll chocolate better than sex," *Toronto Star*, 30 Sept. 1995, p. L3.

[454] Canadian Panel on Violence Against Women, *Changing the Landscape: Ending Violence—Achieving Equality*, Final Report, Minister of Supply and Services Canada, 1993, p. 51.

See also Catharine A. MacKinnon, *Toward a Feminist Theory of the State* (Cambridge, Massachusetts: Harvard University Press, 1989), p. 13 and *Ms.*, Jan.-Feb. 1994, pp. 37 and 42.

[455] John de St. Jorre, "The unmasking of O," *New Yorker*, 1 Aug. 1994, pp. 42-50.

[456] Carole S. Vance, "Epilogue," *Pleasure and Danger: Exploring Female Sexuality* (Boston: Routledge & Kegan Paul, 1984), p. 433.

[457] Wendy Dennis, *Hot and Bothered: Sex and Love in the Nineties* (Toronto: Seal Books, 1992), p. 187.

[458] Ibid., pp. 15-16 and 225.

[459] Ibid., p. 190.

[460] William French, "Penthouse's black dots a black mark for censor," *Globe and Mail*, 3 May 1983, p. 15. [continues on next page]

Canadian government-mandated censorship extends well beyond black dots. In this six-page comic strip, most of pages 5 and 6 were blacked out in order to get the US-published magazine into Canada (*Penthouse*, Nov. 1996, pp. 128-33). [see online footnotes, as per top of Notes section, page 277 above]

Not a single page in this illustrated story made it into Canada unscathed. Graphics were censored on eight pages, text on seven pages (*Penthouse*, July 1995, pp. 141-49).

In this instance, a limerick was partially censored. See the following page for the non-censored, US edition (*Penthouse*, Oct. 1997, p. 49). In the April 1997 issue of *Penthouse*, a limerick, a letter to the editor, a comic strip, an illustration, and paid advertisements were all censored (pp. 49, 131-38, 169).

This is what government censorship in the name of protecting women looks like. This is Canada's Supreme Court 'Butler decision' in action, the one that incorporated Catharine MacKinnon's radical feminist perspective.

[461] Diana E.H. Russell, *Rape in Marriage* (New York: Macmillan Publishing Co, 1982), pp. 156-66.

See also Robin Warshaw, *I Never Called It Rape* (New York: Harper & Row, 1988), p. 44.

[462] Sarah Crichton, "Sexual correctness: has it gone too far?" *Newsweek*, 25 Oct. 1993, p. 54.

[463] Catharine A. MacKinnon, "Liberalism and the Death of Feminism," *The Sexual Liberals and the Attack on Feminism*, Dorchen Leidholdt and Janice G. Raymond, eds. (New York: Pergamon Press, 1990), p. 9.

[464] Catharine A. MacKinnon, *Toward a Feminist Theory of the State* (Cambridge, Massachusetts: Harvard University Press, 1989), p.

202 and "Where Do We Stand on Pornography?" *Ms.*, Jan.-Feb. 1994, p. 34.

[465] Nadine Strossen, *Defending Pornography: Free Speech, Sex, and the Fight for Women's Rights* (New York: Scribner, 1995), pp. 149-51 and 168.

[466] Nadine Strossen, *Defending Pornography: Free Speech, Sex, and the Fight for Women's Rights* (New York: Scribner, 1995), p. 104.

[467] See Donna Laframboise, "Another look at Playboy," *Toronto Star*, 27 Mar. 1995, p. A19.

[468] "The Perils of Touching" (editorial), *Globe and Mail*, 18 Aug. 1995, p. A14.

[469] Ontario Human Rights Complaints 60-926M, 60-9267M, 60-028M.

See also Donna Laframboise, "Anti-porn crusade victimizes 3 stores," *Toronto Star*, 5 July 1993, p. A17 and

James Wallace, Christie Blatchford and Tracy Nesdoly, "Skin Deep: Human Rights porno fiasco," *Toronto Sun*, 18 Apr. 1993, pp. 7, 46-47.

[470] Lynda Ackroyd, "Case Summary" (first), Human Rights Commission, undated, p. 4.

[471] Ontario Human Rights Complaints 60-926M, 60-9267M, 60-028M.

[472] James Wallace, Christie Blatchford and Tracy Nesdoly, "Skin Deep: Human Rights porno fiasco," *Toronto Sun*, 18 Apr. 1993, pp. 7 and 47.

[473] Lynda Ackroyd, "Case Summary" (first), Human Rights Commission, undated and Owen Mahoney, Case Analysis, 15 Aug. 1995.

[474] Letter to Four Star Variety, from Daniel B. Pascoe, Registrar, Ontario Human Rights Commission, 12 Jan. 1993, p. 1.

[475] "In the matter of the Complaints of P. Findlay dated April 15, 1988 and M. McKay dated April 13, 1988, alleging discrimination against women against Mike's Smoke and Gifts and Mr. Soon Hwan Kim, Jug Mart and Four Star Variety," (official transcript), Vol. 3, p. 24.

[476] James Wallace, Christie Blatchford and Tracy Nesdoly, "Skin Deep: Human Rights porno fiasco," *Toronto Sun*, 18 Apr. 1993, p. 7.

[477] "Board dismisses magazine complaint," *Toronto Star*, 26 Oct. 1993, p. C1 and "Inquiry halts probe of explicit magazines," *Toronto Star*, 24 Oct. 1993, p. A16.

[478] Written decision by Loretta Mikus, 22 Oct. 1993, pp. 16 and 25.

[479] See Howard Levitt, "Human Rights Commission failing to attack workplace discrimination," *Toronto Star*, 6 Nov. 1995, p. C3.

[480] Lynda Ackroyd, "Case Summary" (first), Human Rights Commission, undated, p. 2 and
James Wallace, Christie Blatchford and Tracy Nesdoly, "Skin Deep: Human Rights porno fiasco," *Toronto Sun*, 18 Apr. 1993, p. 46.

[481] Letter to Peter Israel, legal representative of Four Star Variety, from Fern Gaspar, Ontario Human Rights Commission, 20 Mar. 1995.

Letter to Ontario Human Rights Commission from Peter Israel, 17 Feb. 1995.

Owen Mahoney, Case Analysis, 15 Aug. 1995, p. 1.
Letter to Peter Israel, from the Ontario Human Rights Commission, 16 Aug. 1995.

[482] Ontario Human Rights Commission Respondent Questionnaire, completed by Peter Kwon, 28 July 1988.

[483] Human Rights Code, Revised Statutes of Ontario, 1990, Chapter H. 19, Section 41, article 1(b).

[484] "In the matter of the Complaints of P. Findlay dated April 15, 1988 and M. McKay dated April 13, 1988, alleging discrimination against women against Mike's Smoke and Gifts and Mr. Soon Hwan Kim, Jug Mart and Four Star Variety" (official transcript), Vol. 3, pp. 27 and 59.

On p. 22, Geri Sanson, representing the Human Rights Commission, says: "The Commission requests that both complainants' names not be published, nor any other identifying circumstances which would enable a member of the public to identify the claimants."

[485] Lynda Ackroyd, "Case Summary" (first), Human Rights Commission, undated, p. 4. Reva Landau, "Bread, milk and pornography," *Toronto Star*, 22 Feb. 1994, p. A21.

[486] Owen Mahoney, *Case Analysis*, 15 Aug. 1995, p. 6.

[487] Peter Hamill, "Woman on the Verge of a Legal Breakdown," *Playboy*, Jan. 1993, p. 187.

[488] Andrea Dworkin, *Pornography: Men Possessing Women* (New York: Pedigree Books, 1981), p. 222-223.

[489] Michele Landsberg, "Real story behind call by feminist to 'kill men,'" *Toronto Star*, 21 May 1991, p. Cl. Canadian Press, "Activist wants wife-beaters jailed—or killed," *Toronto Star*, 13 May 1991, p. Al.   See also footnote #94 regarding *Ms.* magazine's record of promoting Dworkin's ideas.

[490] Susan Brownmiller and Dolores Alexander, "From Carmita

Wood to Anita Hill," *Ms.*, Jan-Feb. 1992, p. 70.

See also *Ms.*, May-June 1992, p. 96, which explains: "In 1986, the U.S. Supreme Court first recognized sexual harassment as a form of sex discrimination in the case of Mechelle Vinson, who was represented from the beginning by her lawyer, Patricia Barry, and by Professor MacKinnon, who wrote the brief."

[491] Nadine Strossen, *Defending Pornography: Free Speech, Sex, and the Fight for Women's Rights* (New York: Scribner, 1995), p. 127.

[492] Ibid., pp. 26-27.

[493] Ibid., p. 28.

[494] Ruth Shalil, "Sexual harassment hits the sandbox," *Globe and Mail*, 10 Apr. 1993, p. Dl. (Reprinted from *The New Republic*.)

[495] Nadine Strossen, *Defending Pornography: Free Speech, Sex, and the Fight for Women's Rights* (New York: Scribner, 1995), p.22.

[496] Ibid., p. 134.

[497] See Christina Hoff Sommers, *Who Stole Feminism? How Women Have Betrayed Women* (New York: Simon & Schuster, 1994), p. 186.

[498] Quoted in Nadine Strossen, *Defending Pornography: Free Speech, Sex, and the Fight for Women's Rights* (New York: Scribner, 1995), p. 122.

[499] Camille Paglia, *Sex, Art, and American Culture: Essays*, (New York: Vintage Books, 1992), p. 47.

[500] Katie Roiphe, *The Morning After: Sex, Fear and Feminism* (Boston: Bay Back Books, 1993), p. 162.

See also *Ms.*, Jan-Feb. 1993, p. 89.

[501] Canadian Panel on Violence Against Women, *Changing the Landscape: Ending violence - achieving equality*, Final Report, Minister of Supply and Services Canada, 1993, p. 3.

See also *Ms.*, Sept.-Oct. 1990, p. 34 and July-Aug. 1991, p. 1 (editorial).

[502] John Fekete, *Moral Panic: Biopolitics rising* (Montreal: Robert Davies Publishing, 1994), p. 323.

[503] Canadian Panel on Violence Against Women, *Changing the Landscape: Ending violence - achieving equality*, Final Report, Minister of Supply and Services Canada, 1993, pp. xiii-xiv and so forth.

[504] Eric Schlosser, "Marijuana and the Law," *The Atlantic Monthly*, Sept. 1994, p.90.

[505] See Editorial, *New York Times*, 11 Oct. 1993, p. A16,

George F. Will, "Sex Amidst Semicolons," *Newsweek*, 4 Oct. 1993, p. 92.

Jeff Giles, "There's a Time for Talk, and a Time for Action," *Newsweek*, 7 Mar. 1994, p. 54.

[506] Tracey Tyler, "US feminist applauds Canada's rape-law plan," *Toronto Star*, 17 Feb. 1992, p. A3.

[507] Marlys Edwardh, quoted in Geoffrey York, "Lawyers oppose proposed rape law," *Globe and Mail*, 15 May 1992, p. A3.

[508] Sean Fine, "No-means-no law still misunderstood," *Globe and Mail*, 31 May 1995, p. A1.

[509] *Some important things for men to know about sex and dating.*

Funded by "the Ministry of Colleges and Universities as part of the Government of Ontario interministerial initiative on sexual assault."

[510] Robin Warshaw, *I Never Called It Rape* (New York: Harper & Row, 1988), p. 2.

[511] Mary Koss, "Rape, the ultimate humiliation," (letter to the editor), *Wall Street Journal*, 25 July 1991, p. A9.

[512] Dale Brazao, "Lap dancing crosses line from striptease to sleaze," *Toronto Star*, 5 Aug. 1995, p. A16.

Layton's wife and fellow Metro councillor, Olivia Chow, said of lap dancing a few days earlier, "I would call it rape; you can't call it anything else." Quoted in Gail Swinson, "Metro may ban lap dancing," *Toronto Star*, 1 Aug. 1995, first and last page of A section.

[513] Camille Paglia, *Sex, Art, and American Culture: Essays*, (New York: Vintage Books, 1992), p. 5.

See also *Ms.*, May-June 1991, p. 61.

[514] Deborah Wilson, "Judge's remarks raise storm," *Toronto Star*, 27 Apr. 1991, p. A4.

[515] Robin Warshaw, *I Never Called It Rape* (New York: Harper & Row, 1988), p. 63.

[516] Ibid., p. 154. See also p. 42.

[517] *Some important things for men to know about sex and dating* and *Some important things for women to know about sex and dating*. Funded by "the Ministry of Colleges and Universities as part of the Government of Ontario interministerial initiative on sexual assault."

[518] Robin Warshaw, *I Never Called It Rape* (New York: Harper & Row, 1988), p. 140.

[519] Michele Landsberg, "Rape shield law offered protection," *Toronto Star*, 10 Sept. 1991, p. Dl.

[520] Jack Kammer, "The Other Kind of Rape: An interview with rape-trial lawyer Rikki Klieman," *Balance*, Fall 1994, pp. 18-21.

[521] Canadian Centre for Justice Statistics, *Juristat*, Vol. 14, No. 7, March 1994, p. 10.

[522] Eugene J. Kanin, "False Rape Allegations," *Archives of Sexual Behaviour*, Vol. 23, No. 1, 1994, p. 88.

[523] Ibid., pp. 85-87.

[524] Donna Laframboise, "Schools should teach girls to stop being passive," *Toronto Star*, 12 May 1992, p. A19 and

Mary Lui, "Women tired of taking the blame," (letter to the editor) *Toronto Star*, 20 May 1992, p. A18.

[525] Katie Roiphe, *The Morning After: Sex, Fear and Feminism* (Boston: Bay Back Books, 1993), p. 101.

[526] Camille Paglia, *Sex, Art, and American Culture: Essays*, (New York: Vintage Books, 1992), p. 53.

[527] Louis Menand, "The war of all against all," *New Yorker*, 14 Mar. 1994, p. 85.

[528] Doris Lessing, *Prisons We Choose to Live Inside* (Toronto: CBC Enterprises, 1986), p. 34.

[529] Susan Crean, "Writing along Gender Lines," *Language in Her Eye: Writing and Gender*, Libby Sheier, Sarah Sheard and Eleanor Wachtel, eds. (Toronto: Coach House Press, 1990), p. 83.

[530] Dates from "A Selected Chronology of Women and Work in Canada," *Women's History Month*, Canadian Committee on Women's History, Government of Canada, Oct. 1993, pp. 8-12

and *Towards Equality for Women*, Status of Women Canada, 1983.

[531] Nadine Crenshaw, *Edin's Embrace* (New York: Zebra Books, 1989), p. 221.

[532] Catharine A. MacKinnon, "Liberalism and the Death of Feminism," *The Sexual Liberals and the Attack on Feminism*, Dorchen Leidholdt and Janice G. Raymond, eds. (New York: Pergamon Press, 1990), p. 5.

[533] Ibid., 5-6.

[534] Ibid., p. 13.

[535] Vaclav Havel, *On Evasive Thinking*: Speech at Union of Writers, 1965.

72688647R00207

Made in the USA
Columbia, SC
31 August 2019